1700s to 1800s

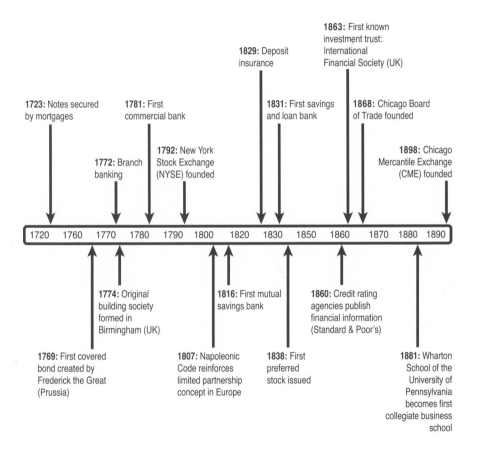

1863: First known investment trust: International Financial Society (UK)

1829: Deposit insurance

1723: Notes secured by mortgages

1781: First commercial bank

1831: First savings and loan bank

1868: Chicago Board of Trade founded

1772: Branch banking

1792: New York Stock Exchange (NYSE) founded

1898: Chicago Mercantile Exchange (CME) founded

| 1720 | 1760 | 1770 | 1780 | 1790 | 1800 | 1820 | 1830 | 1850 | 1860 | 1870 | 1880 | 1890 |

1774: Original building society formed in Birmingham (UK)

1816: First mutual savings bank

1860: Credit rating agencies publish financial information (Standard & Poor's)

1769: First covered bond created by Frederick the Great (Prussia)

1807: Napoleonic Code reinforces limited partnership concept in Europe

1838: First preferred stock issued

1881: Wharton School of the University of Pennsylvania becomes first collegiate business school

1900 to 1949

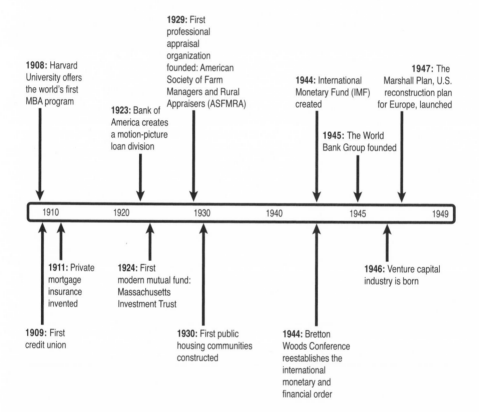

1929: First professional appraisal organization founded: American Society of Farm Managers and Rural Appraisers (ASFMRA)

1908: Harvard University offers the world's first MBA program

1944: International Monetary Fund (IMF) created

1947: The Marshall Plan, U.S. reconstruction plan for Europe, launched

1923: Bank of America creates a motion-picture loan division

1945: The World Bank Group founded

| 1910 | 1920 | 1930 | 1940 | 1945 | 1949 |

1911: Private mortgage insurance invented

1924: First modern mutual fund: Massachusetts Investment Trust

1946: Venture capital industry is born

1909: First credit union

1930: First public housing communities constructed

1944: Bretton Woods Conference reestablishes the international monetary and financial order

1950 to 1969

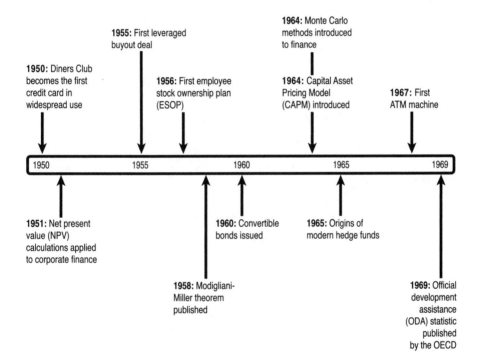

1964: Monte Carlo methods introduced to finance

1955: First leveraged buyout deal

1950: Diners Club becomes the first credit card in widespread use

1956: First employee stock ownership plan (ESOP)

1964: Capital Asset Pricing Model (CAPM) introduced

1967: First ATM machine

1950   1955   1960   1965   1969

1951: Net present value (NPV) calculations applied to corporate finance

1960: Convertible bonds issued

1965: Origins of modern hedge funds

1958: Modigliani-Miller theorem published

1969: Official development assistance (ODA) statistic published by the OECD

Financing the Future

Market-Based Innovations for Growth

Franklin Allen
Glenn Yago

Vice President, Publisher: Tim Moore
Associate Publisher and Director of Marketing: Amy Neidlinger
Wharton Editor: Steve Kobrin
Executive Editor: Jim Boyd
Editorial Assistant: Pamela Bolan
Operations Manager: Gina Kanouse
Senior Marketing Manager: Julie Phifer
Publicity Manager: Laura Czaja
Assistant Marketing Manager: Megan Colvin
Cover Designer: Chuti Prasertsith
Managing Editor: Kristy Hart
Senior Project Editor: Lori Lyons
Copy Editor: Hansing Editorial Services
Proofreader: Sheri Cain
Senior Indexer: Cheryl Lenser
Senior Compositor: Gloria Schurick
Manufacturing Buyer: Dan Uhrig

© 2010 Milken Institute
Pearson Education, Inc.
Publishing as Wharton School Publishing
Upper Saddle River, New Jersey 07458

Printed in the United States of America

First Printing March 2010

ISBN-10: 0-13-701127-X
ISBN-13: 978-0-13-701127-8

Pearson Education LTD.
Pearson Education Australia PTY, Limited.
Pearson Education Singapore, Pte. Ltd.
Pearson Education North Asia, Ltd.
Pearson Education Canada, Ltd.
Pearson Educación de Mexico, S.A. de C.V.
Pearson Education—Japan
Pearson Education Malaysia, Pte. Ltd.

Library of Congress Cataloging-in-Publication Data

Allen, Franklin, 1956-
  Financing the future : market-based innovations for growth / Franklin Allen, Glenn Yago.
    p. cm.
  ISBN 978-0-13-701127-8 (hbk. : alk. paper) 1. Finance. 2. Capital market. I. Yago, Glenn.
II. Title.
  HG173.A4334 2010
  332'.041—dc22
                                    2009053172

Contents

Acknowledgments

If our efforts to illuminate the applications of financial innovation to long-standing social, economic, and environmental problems meet with any success, it is due to the extraordinary assistance of our colleagues. We are indebted to many individuals who made this book possible.

First and foremost, we'd like to thank Lisa Renaud, our editor at the Milken Institute, for her unflagging assistance on this project. Lisa moved us closer to achieving our goals for this volume, and we are deeply grateful for her significant contribution to this book. Without her, it would never have come together.

Much gratitude also goes to Professors Jerry Wind and Steve Kobrin of the Wharton School of the University of Pennsylvania and of Wharton School Publishing, who encouraged this project and an ongoing collaboration with the Milken Institute. We'd also like to thank Tina Horowitz at the Wharton School for her many efforts. Jim Boyd at Pearson has been very encouraging of this process; we thank him for his patience and the opportunity to launch a new series.

The Milken Institute supported all of the incredibly hard work that went into this volume. Mike Klowden, the Institute's president and CEO, and Skip Rimer, its director of communications, advanced this project from its inception. We are grateful for the resources they allocated toward the labor-intensive process of editing, researching, and writing. Karen Giles was also encouraging, but took no prisoners in rallying us to create order out of chaos, carving out time for writing and research amid our demanding schedules. She is a generous and patient colleague. Patricia Reiter was the lead research analyst, providing bibliographic and research assistance. Her efforts have been considerable and are much appreciated. Lisa Montessi has been an extraordinary source of knowledge about financial innovations and markets. Her commitment to documenting and creating an ongoing record and legacy of financial innovation at the Milken Institute has made our research possible. Jorge Velasco also provided timely research assistance. Special thanks go to Caitlin Maclean, manager of our Financial Innovations Labs, for all her work on the many Lab reports that served as important sources for this book.

We'd also like to thank other Milken Institute colleagues and researchers who have been involved in our work on global capital markets and financial innovations: Martha Amram, Penny Angkinand, James Barth, Komal Sri-Kumar, Joel Kurtzman, Tong Li, Wenling Lu, Peter Passell, Jill Scherer, and especially Betsy Zeidman. Through their interest, insights, and intelligence, they have been major contributors to this volume.

We have learned much from the leading minds who have advanced this field, including the late Merton Miller, Douglas Gale, Michael Jensen, Stewart Myers, Robert Merton, Robert J. Shiller, Michael Spence, Elena Carletti, Eugene Kandel, Naomi Lamoreaux, Ross Levine, Bradford Cornell, Myron Scholes, Steven Kaplan, Peter Tufano, Josh Lerner, Stuart Gilson, Jun Qian, and Lawrence White.

A number of pioneers in financial innovation have passed away in recent years, but their legacies continue to shape our world and our thinking about the uses of capital. Current and future financial innovators stand on the shoulders of giants like Georges Doriot, who invented venture capital; Louis Kelso, who advocated worker capitalism; Martin Dubilier, who went from crisis management to restructuring troubled companies through leveraged buyouts; George E. Stoddard, who devised real estate transactions known as sale-leasebacks to provide financing to companies that had trouble gaining access to traditional sources of capital; Walter J. Lopp II, who created municipal bond insurance and the concept of tax-exempt financing for pollution-control projects; Walter Wriston, whose innovations extended from negotiable certificates of deposits to ATM networks; Richard A. Musgrave, whose work in public finance enabled us to allocate financial resources for social needs; and many others.

Discussions and debates with many current practitioners have informed this book project. At the Milken Institute, we've made a habit of assembling leading financial innovators so that we can learn from their experiences and insights. They include Lewis Ranieri, Richard Sandor, Muhammad Yunus, Alan Patricof, Sir Ronald Cohen, Jacqueline Novogratz, Mary Houghton, Leo Melamed,

Wayne Silby, Shari Berenbach, Sucharita Mukherjee, Chris Larsen, and Bert van der Vaart.

Finally, we'd like to thank Michael Milken for his vision as a financial and social innovator in many fields, especially our own. Without his inspiration, interest, and support, the publication of this book would not have been possible. He's always wisely said that the best investor is a good social scientist—that investors need to understand how to enable people to realize their hopes and dreams, a process that ultimately creates economic growth and prosperity. But, since not all social scientists are good investors, we are grateful for his ongoing support of critical and independent research in this field. His work has inspired us not only to popularize financial innovations and explore the questions that surround them, but also to find practical uses for them.

We are grateful to the organizations that have supported research on financial innovations at the Milken Institute, including the Ford Foundation, the Bill & Melinda Gates Foundation, Google.org, the German Marshall Fund, the Packard Foundation, the F. B. Heron Foundation, the Koret Foundation, the U.S. Department of Commerce, the U.S. Department of Agriculture, the Minority Business Development Agency, and others.

With all this assistance, however, none of this would have been accomplished without the trust, equity, and bonds in our families, to whom we are indebted.

Franklin Allen, The Wharton School
of the University of Pennsylvania

Glenn Yago, Milken Institute

About the Authors

Franklin Allen is the Nippon Life Professor of Finance and Professor of Economics at the Wharton School of the University of Pennsylvania, where he has been on the faculty since 1980. A current codirector of the Wharton Financial Institutions Center, he was formerly vice dean and director of Wharton Doctoral Programs, as well as executive editor of the *Review of Financial Studies*, one of the nation's leading academic finance journals. Allen is a past president of the American Finance Association, the Western Finance Association, the Society for Financial Studies, and the Financial Intermediation Research Society. His main areas of interest are corporate finance, asset pricing, financial innovation, comparative financial systems, and financial crises. He is a coauthor, with Richard Brealey and Stewart Myers, of the eighth and ninth editions of the textbook *Principles of Corporate Finance*. Allen received his doctorate from Oxford University.

Glenn Yago is director of Capital Studies at the Milken Institute. He is also a visiting professor at Hebrew University of Jerusalem and directs the Koret–Milken Institute Fellows program. Yago's work focuses on the innovative use of financial instruments to solve long-standing economic development, social, and environmental challenges. His research and projects have contributed to policy innovations fostering the democratization of capital to traditionally underserved markets and entrepreneurs in the United States and around the world. Yago is the coauthor of several books, including *The Rise and Fall of the U.S. Mortgage and Credit Markets*, *Global Edge*, *Restructuring Regulation and Financial Institutions*, and *Beyond Junk Bonds*. He was a professor at the State University of New York at Stony Brook and at the City University of New York Graduate Center. Yago earned his Ph.D. at the University of Wisconsin, Madison.

About the Milken Institute

The Milken Institute is an independent economic think tank whose mission is to improve the lives and economic conditions of diverse populations in the United States and around the world by helping business and public policy leaders identify and implement innovative ideas for creating broad-based prosperity. We put research to work with the goal of revitalizing regions and finding new ways to generate capital for people with original ideas.

We focus on:

- **Human capital:** The talent, knowledge, and experience of people, and their value to organizations, economies, and society
- **Financial capital:** Innovations that allocate financial resources efficiently, especially to those who ordinarily would not have access to them, but who can best use them to build companies, create jobs, accelerate life-saving medical research, and solve long-standing social and economic problems
- **Social capital:** The bonds of society that underlie economic advancement, including schools, health care, cultural institutions, and government services

By creating ways to spread the benefits of human, financial, and social capital to as many people as possible—by *democratizing* capital—we hope to contribute to prosperity and freedom in all corners of the globe.

We are nonprofit, nonpartisan, and publicly supported.

1

The Evolution of Finance

It was a perfect storm. Beginning in 2007, a cascade of extreme events rocked the global financial system, outstripping the risks imagined by central bankers, financial professionals, and policymakers. Within a year's time, international stock market declines had destroyed trillions of dollars in wealth. In the wake of the housing meltdown and the ensuing "Great Recession," pension systems remain fragile and household balance sheets are a wreck.

A confusing alphabet soup of acronyms (think CDOs squared, then cubed, and stuffed with SIVs, CMOs, CLOs, and CDSs) dominated the headlines. With their leverage levels on steroids, many financial institutions and firms had gorged on these overly complex products. The press was aghast to learn that some CEOs didn't have a grasp on the convoluted products on which their traders had placed staggering bets.

The financial crisis of 2007–2009 brought many chickens home to roost in global capital markets. Some $9 trillion of assets in the United States alone had been securitized. By fall 2008, lower-grade securities had been reworked into roughly a half-trillion dollars' worth of long-term capital instruments (through collateralized debt obligations) and $1.2 trillion of short-term money market instruments (through asset-backed commercial paper and structured investment vehicles). These were underwritten by almost $800 billion of private mortgage insurance, issued by bond insurers that ultimately backed a total of more than $2 trillion of debt. The whole conflict-ridden system was hedged in a murky $45 trillion credit default swap market—a fine mess, indeed. When the underlying asset bubbles began to implode, liquidity froze and markets cratered.[1]

Fear and loathing of Wall Street is once again loose in the land, but precious little analysis has been offered to distinguish genuine innovation from the churning out of copycat devices designed to conceal the shakiness of the underlying assets, and far too prone to exacerbating systemic risk. The long and storied tradition of *real* financial innovation—the drive to build new tools that increase clarity in valuation and promote capital formation for productive enterprises—was co-opted during the bubble years, perverted into schemes meant to obfuscate and create opacity in asset pricing.

The purpose of this book is to move beyond the noise and reclaim the concept of financial innovation. Throughout history, advances in financing have expanded opportunities and democratized societies—and their potential is still ready to be grasped today. If the right tools are deployed responsibly, financial innovations have the capacity to help us shape a more sustainable and prosperous future.

Finance, at its core, is the catalyst for launching productive ventures and the most effective tool for managing economic risks. Today that process takes place with split-second global transactions and cutting-edge software, but the essential concepts of finance are timeless and rooted in antiquity.

To fully grasp the underpinnings of modern finance, it is useful to note the seminal—and ever more sophisticated—innovations that have marked its evolution, whether it was the first use of credit in Assyria, Babylon, and Egypt more than 3,000 years ago, or the introduction of the bill of exchange in the fourteenth century.[2] Many of these advances democratized economic participation, such as when consumer credit took hold in the 1700s. (By the early part of the twentieth century, tallymen were hawking clothes in return for small weekly payments.[3]) Home mortgages, the founding of stock markets and exchanges, and the wider availability of farm and small-business credit and investment followed in turn.

Financial innovation not only threw open the door to a vast expansion of land, home, and business ownership—broadening prosperity in ways that were unimaginable in earlier centuries—but it also eventually devised ways to value intellectual property. That ability to transform ideas into new industries dramatically quickened the pace of change. By the mid-1980s, Nobel laureate Merton Miller correctly noted, "The word *revolution* is entirely appropriate for describing the changes in financial institutions and instruments that have occurred in the past 20 years."[4]

Multiple studies have documented the positive and profound effects of consumer and business finance on economic growth. Any country that forgoes the building of deep, broad financial institutions and markets is also likely to forgo growth. Cross-country comparisons show that nations with higher levels of market development experience faster aggregate growth and smaller income gaps with the wealthiest nations. Recent empirical estimates suggest that if emerging nations doubled bank credit to the private sector as a percent of gross domestic product (GDP), they could increase annual GDP growth by almost 3%. Doubling the trading volume in their securities markets would increase GDP growth by 2%.[5]

At its best, finance can be used to balance the interests of producers, consumers, owners, managers, employees, investors, and creditors. At the risk of stating the obvious, these disparate actors on the economic stage often fail to get along, for a whole host of reasons. When they don't, economic value is destroyed, business plans are laid to waste, new technologies and ideas wither on the vine, and scarcity— the ultimate bane that economics seeks to overcome—prevails.

The purpose of finance, carried out with technology and sometimes a dash of art, is to create a capital structure that aligns the cooperating and sometimes conflicting interests within an enterprise—whether private, public, government, or nonprofit— toward a common objective. Finance mediates among these interests, addressing the frictions and risks inherent in transactions.

It is through the design and construction of a capital structure that a public or private enterprise finances its assets and leverages them into a greater flow of productivity, innovation, and enterprise. Capital structure is the way a firm, household, enterprise, or project (even those involving partnerships of public and private actors) allocates its liabilities through debt, equity, and hybrid instruments. These operating and investment decisions affect the value of any good or service that is produced.

The cash flow through an enterprise is as vital to its survival as oxygen. It must be distributed based on various claims from creditors, owners, employees, and so forth. Capital structure allocates shares of that cash flow pie and seeks to grow it. Finance seeks to optimize the sustainability of cash flow, creating positive feedback loops among all the relevant players. Financial frameworks can serve as both carrot and stick, creating incentive structures that maintain an enterprise and enable it to grow.

As Bradford Cornell and Alan Shapiro have demonstrated, financial innovations and business policies can increase the value of an individual firm through the complex web of contracts that binds investors, management, employees, customers, suppliers, and distributors. Strengthening relations with noninvestor stakeholders through management and employee incentives, increasing the confidence of suppliers and customers, and linking public and private interests can increase the value of an enterprise.[6]

Innovation can also be used to resolve information asymmetries— that is, the situation in which some market participants have information that others do not, thereby making markets inefficient and costly to all. Information asymmetries are a core challenge in finance, increasing the risk of unknowns and uncertainties in any transaction, especially those concerning interest rates. Finance assigns costs to the risks of undisclosed information that might eventually emerge. In bridging these gaps between parties, their claims on the cash flows from any enterprise can be assigned, priced, packaged into a financial product, and exchanged.

Finance is more than simply a method of allocating capital. When harnessed correctly, it has the capacity to drive social, economic, and environmental change, transforming ideas into new technologies, industries, and jobs.

Overcoming the remaining gaps in capital access and sound market structure represents the challenge and opportunity of our age. We can understand and resolve an array of urgent global problems— financial crises, environmental degradation, world hunger, post-conflict reconstruction, housing, and disease—if we carefully analyze them through the lens of finance.

The Language of Finance

Finance emerged as a social construct from the way people gave voice to their day-to-day economic interests, defined them, and sought to measure and manage them in real markets. In many cases, the words they devised live on in common usage today, underlining the fact that, despite its sophisticated high-tech profile, the fundamental role of finance remains much the same as it ever was.

One way to understand finance at its most elemental level is to walk through an example of how a social unit becomes sustainable, a process Figure 1.1 illustrates. Imagine any basic unit of social organization: a family, a household, a community, a business, a nonprofit, or a project. Common to all is the necessity of enterprise—that is, undertaking activities that will define, build, and strengthen the unit as it seeks to transform and survive from one set of circumstances to another, whether it be a growing season, a market cycle, a time of life, or a natural disaster. Finance provides the means to bridge uncertain circumstances, such as the costs of discovery, retirement, illness, new technologies, family additions, or a future college education. Innovations that can lower the cost of these objectives are the subject of financial history.

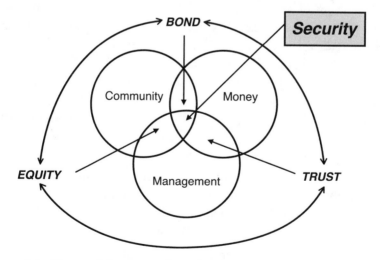

Figure 1.1   The social construction of capital

Common to all social units is the need to form a community of interests that can be managed and financed. All households have a division of labor and tasks, management of resources, and a need to sustain itself with cash flow. The same is true for any social enterprise—a company, church, state, railroad, or war. Since Adam Smith's *Theory of Moral Sentiments* appeared in 1759, those attempting to understand finance have dealt with the human interactions that underpin economic outcomes.

For a community, household, family, or enterprise to balance competing and conflicting claims, it must establish *trust* to sustain and continue transactions to build toward any common objective. As a moral sentiment and social link, trust embodies and secures a claim. We can trace the genesis of trust as a legal concept to late in the Roman Empire. It was through trusts that ownership and management of property first became possible beyond those lands granted, restricted, or seized by a monarch. In medieval England, when knights set off to do battle or join the Crusades, they entrusted their rights to land and property to the church or bishop, who managed them in their absence. From these arrangements sprouted sophisticated legal measures to preserve family estates and keep them out of the hands of the king. England's trust laws became key instruments of finance, contributing moral, legal, and, ultimately, financial underpinnings that democratized markets.

The point of social interaction, in which monetary resources are allocated to pay for community needs (homes, machinery and equipment, and infrastructure), requires some **bond** that will hold together and steward the economic resources necessary for the community or enterprise's survival. We can trace references to bonds as covenants that obligate as far back as the early fourteenth century. As codified under English law in the sixteenth century, a bond came to be understood as a deed that binds someone to pay a certain sum of money; the *Oxford English Dictionary (OED)* cites its early use in 1592 as "a contract whereby any man confesseth himselfe by his writing orderly made, sealed, and delivered to owe anything unto him with whom he contracteth." "Go with me to a notary," says Shakespeare's *Merchant of Venice*, "seal me there your single bond."

Already by the seventeenth century, bonds had become synonymous with debentures (notes backed by credit). Companies and governments issued them to finance everything from building infrastructure to waging war.

When capital resources are deployed to fund an enterprise's ongoing operations, ownership **equity** is created. In accounting terms, equity is what remains as the interest in assets after all liabilities or other claims are paid. The underlying premise of equity in this sense implies evenhanded dealing. Colloquially and quite literally, it became something you could count on—a piece of the action, some skin in the game. By the nineteenth century, the notion of equity encompassed a recognizable right or claim, such as a wife's equity to a suitable provision to maintain herself and her children, or the right to redeem an equity claim from a trust for a home or property. Finally, as stock markets became more ubiquitous, equity came to be understood as the stock (or residue) of a company's assets after creditors were paid. The building of equity in a home, business, or any aspect of productive society is the underlying factor driving real growth; this process embodies the value created by social collaboration in a household, company, or industry.

If all these values can be realized through social constructs and codified in binding legal arrangements, **security** is the ultimate result. When social relationships reinforce bonds, create trust, and build equity in the household, enterprise, or community, the result is greater overall security.

According to the *OED*, the first appearance of the term *security* suggesting property deposited or value derived as a legal obligation to secure fulfillment of a financial claim turns up in the sixteenth-century register of the Scottish Privy Council. Shakespeare's *Henry IV* expressed the vagaries of valuation: "He said sir, you should procure him better Assurance ... he would not take his Bond and yours, he lik'd not the security." By the seventeenth century, land registries mention securities held by creditors as guarantees for right of payment, as well as stocks, shares, or other form of investment guaranteed by security documents. When this system of exchange functions smoothly, the byproduct is the nonfinancial sense of security—that condition of being protected and safe or enjoying freedom from doubt and want.

This brief tour through the pages of the dictionary reflects not only the origins of the words we use in finance: It also illuminates the foundational concepts that inspired early markets and enabled them to work—concepts that are very much alive and at work today.

What Is Financial Innovation?

Financial innovation is the creation of new financial instruments, technologies, institutions, and markets. As in other technologies, innovation in finance includes research and development functions as well as the demonstration, diffusion, and adoption of these new products or services.[7]

In finance, particularly, innovation involves adapting and improvising on existing products and concepts. Advances emerge initially as either products (such as derivatives, high-yield corporate bonds, and mortgage-backed securities) or processes (such as pricing mechanisms, trading platforms, and means and methods for distributing securities). By moving funds or enabling investors to pool funds, these tools increase liquidity to facilitate the sale and purchase of goods or the management of risks in markets and enterprises.

Exchange-traded derivatives, credit derivatives, equity swaps, weather derivatives, new insurance contracts, and new investment-management products such as exchange-traded funds can all be classified as innovations. But the field also encompasses developments that make the allocation of capital more efficient and operational methods that reduce transaction costs, whether in primary markets where equity and debt originate or in the secondary market where those products are traded.

The process of financial innovation, as Nobel laureate Robert Merton has explained, is similar to high-speed rail technology: The velocity the train can achieve depends on the state of the roadbed and the physical infrastructure along which the train travels.[8] Similarly, White House National Economic Committee Chairman Larry Summers observed, "Global capital markets pose the same kinds of problems that jet planes do. They are faster, more comfortable, and they get you where you are going better. But the crashes are much more spectacular."[9] In finance, we have rapidly developed the ability to absorb and process information about risk management, to create products and services that seize on new technologies, to restructure companies and industries, and to build completely new markets. But the regulatory and market infrastructure to monitor the trading and pricing of risk has not always kept pace with the lightning-fast speed of information transmission, product trading, and pricing that streams through today's market. From that point emerges many problems we will explore in the process of innovation.

Our discussion of financial innovations focuses on the following:

- New products and services (such as bank deposits, warrants, futures, options, high-yield securities, venture capital, and securitization)

- New processes and operations (such as net present value, Black–Scholes estimation, and asset pricing)

- New organizational forms (such as types of banks, exchanges, special-purpose vehicles, limited liability corporations, private equity, and leveraged buyout firms)

Innovations have given rise to new financial intermediaries (such as venture capitalists and private equity firms), new types of instruments (collateralized loan obligations and credit derivatives, for example), and new services or techniques (such as e-trading). At their best, these creations can overcome a variety of risks in a global economy.

The traditional function of finance is to transfer money from areas of surplus to areas with a demand and need for it. Financial innovation accomplishes this, becoming the central input for virtually all productive activity. Better finance encourages more saving and investment while improving productivity and investment decisions.

Finance is simply an intermediary that catalyzes other aspects of capital inputs to production. Its multiplying power derives from financial technologies that mobilize all the dimensions of capital: real capital (inputs of natural resources, land, buildings, machinery and equipment, cash, and the like), human capital (knowledge, intellect, skills, talents, and all qualities of human resources), and social capital (the social networks of people, institutions, and traditions).

Each section of this book addresses common questions about the means, methods, and processes of financial innovation:

- What triggers financial innovation, and why?
- What challenge is the innovation trying to address?
- Which form (product, service, organizational form) does a financial innovation take?
- What changes are created in the market as a result?

Invariably, some historical shift that generates an increased demand for capital sparks financial innovation. Some structural break occurs, requiring new vehicles that can move the markets forward.

Centuries ago, population growth and increased trade provided those triggers as the need arose for a system that would enable merchants to store commodities for future use. In the ancient societies of Mesopotamia, Egypt, and Rome, new advances emerged to finance the future production of precious goods such as olive oil, wine, and date sugar. In eighteenth-century Japan, warehouse owners sold receipts against stored rice, which eventually became a commercial currency that could be traded, standardized, and exchanged more broadly as future contracts. By the nineteenth century, this kind of trading in wheat, corn, and livestock was formalized as commodities markets were established in the United States and Europe. Tracing these developments reveals the historical dynamics at work in the evolution of finance.

The First Financial Innovations: From Capital to Credit

Before there could be access to capital, which would be used to create wealth, someone had to come up with the *idea* of capital as a factor of production. In ancient times, goods were traded through barter or, in rare cases, paid for with bars of gold, silver, bronze, copper, or other metals. In these cases, buyers and sellers had to confirm the weight and quality of the metal, a practice that existed in Mesopotamia and Egypt at the beginning of the first millennium B.C.

Access to capital in these ancient societies was limited to rulers, priests, craftsmen, and merchants. The first three groups were admired (and feared), but the merchants were considered a disreputable lot (after all, they didn't actually *create* anything—they just moved goods from point A to point B). The vast majority of people were peasants who tilled plots of land owned by the monarchs in Egypt and Mesopotamia. Wealth to them meant land, not metal bars. The thought of ever accumulating wealth was beyond their imagining. They caught glimpses of wealth in temples and palaces, and nowhere else.

However, a would-be merchant knew he could turn a profit by taking goods from areas where they were cheap to areas where they were expensive. He might have started out as a pottery maker, a fabricator of armor, a weaver of cloth, or a breeder of cattle, and then, by selling his products, emerge with those bars of metal and, later, the coins. For the most part, he had to rely upon his own capital. He might be able to obtain credit, but interest rates were sky-high because of the scarcity of capital and the risks associated with ventures. During the first half of the first millennium B.C., interest rates in Mesopotamia, Egypt, and southern Europe were rarely less than 30%. Transaction costs were oppressive, so simply moving up to the status of merchant was a major accomplishment.

The arrival of coinage, which was introduced in Lydia in Asia Minor sometime around 650 B.C., began to simplify and standardize transactions. The issuer guaranteed the weight and purity of the coins—but even so, they were eyed with a fair degree of suspicion, since shady types engaged in counterfeiting and shaving coins. The Athenians had an elaborate system of coinage, though they did not use the paper money, credit, securities, or joint-stock companies seen in Mesopotamia.

In Athens and other Greek cities, money changers eventually came on the scene to make small loans and act as middlemen. These "trapezites" would borrow then loan these borrowed funds to others who were willing to pay higher rates. Trapezites were not exactly bankers, but rather loan brokers. Merchants borrowed money from these individuals to purchase goods in distant lands, using their reputations and the cargos as security. They could also sell a contract to deliver the cargo at a specified price, receiving payment in advance. When the merchant returned with his cargo, he would sell it in the marketplace. If the price was higher than that of the futures contract, he would pocket the difference. If not, he would have to make up the loss.

The next great change came courtesy of Alexander the Great, who took control of Macedonia in northern Greece at the age of 20. In 334 B.C., he crossed into Asia with 40,000 troops and swept through Persia, seizing the vast wealth he found there. As a result of the Persian victories alone, he captured 180,000 talents of gold and silver (the modern-day equivalent of approximately $500 million). He immediately poured a good deal of this money into construction projects, especially temple reconstruction and road building. Irrigation canals were dredged, and sailing fleets were built. But perhaps most important, a great store of capital that previously had been unproductive entered the monetary stream, promoting further trade and industry (call it the ancient world's version of a stimulus package). This had the initial effect of lowering interest rates, which further sparked economic activity. Business loans at 6% became fairly common, although loans to cities were somewhat higher (presumably because the lender wielded more muscle over private citizens than municipalities). This was the economic underpinning inherited by Rome, the first great universal empire, one in which the merchant and the banker were honored and achieved power.[10]

The moral of this story? When transaction costs are lowered and capital can be obtained more easily, economic activity quickens and prosperity widens. Without these elements, economies languish and the standard of living declines.[11]

Financial Innovations in the Age of Discovery

The Spanish, Portuguese, and French voyages of exploration were sponsored by ambitious rulers and financed through taxes, plunder, mining, and loans. The expeditions were purely commercial in nature, with hoped-for profits fueling expectations.

England, Europe's relatively poor cousin during this period, was ruled by monarchs whose taxation powers were limited by the Magna Carta and common law. The nobles, some of whom were wealthy, were not interested in such crass matters as commerce. England did have a large and growing merchant class, with a centuries-old interest in commerce and a willingness to invest in ventures. But if England's monarchs were to enter the colonial race on a large scale, they would have to find some other means of obtaining capital.

One method was outright theft. Queen Elizabeth unleashed the "sea dogs," who robbed Spanish vessels laden with wealth from South and Central America. The other strategy was an alliance of monarch and merchant in joint stock companies that received charters in the New World.

The Crown chartered several trading companies in the sixteenth century. They were open to all who had money to purchase shares in one venture or another. At first, they sponsored single voyages or enterprises and were dissolved on completion of the mission. But as the century wore on, they became permanent. The first of these, the Muscovy Company, held a monopoly on trade with Russia for hundreds of years. Decades later, the Levant Company was founded to trade with Turkey, and the Barbary Company was created to trade with North Africa.[12]

The East India Company, destined to be the most important of all the joint stock companies, obtained its charter in 1600. It was granted a 15-year monopoly for English trade between the Cape of Good Hope and the Straits of Magellan. By 1610, the company had 19 facilities and was sending shipments of spices and fabrics from the Orient to England. The merchants pocketed handsome profits, and the Crown taxed that wealth, ending its sole dependence on Parliament for funding. Later, joint stock companies would enter the history books by settling several of the English colonies in North America and elsewhere.

The joint stock idea continued throughout the seventeenth, eighteenth, and nineteenth centuries. Its popularity was due in large part to the voluntary nature of the enterprises, the hopes of great profit, and the sharing of risks.

The Rise of Financial Capitalism

New financial innovations emerged with the explosion of global trade in the seventeenth century. When the Treaty of Westphalia (1648) ended the bloody and protracted Thirty Years' War, the Holy Roman Empire broke apart into 300 sovereign political entities, creating a structural need to finance these nation-states and territories, along with the enterprises that fueled their economies.

Amid the turmoil of the Thirty Years' War, the Dutch managed to establish and defend a thriving merchant fleet, financing their commercial supremacy through long-distance trade through the Baltic, Russia, and the East and West Indies. These wealthy merchants minimized the need for cash by issuing liquid trade receipts backed by a unified system of payments. Amsterdam reigned as Europe's center of commercial credit, extending credit on the basis of bills of exchange payable in Holland. This was the dawn of modern public finance, with the introduction of debt instruments backed by taxes dedicated to a specific purpose, such as erecting levees to hold back the sea or building great sailing ships for trade. As in England, the demand for capital gave rise to joint stock companies—and to the world's first organized securities markets.[13]

The Dutch, British, and French created alternative structures of finance—merchant banks, money markets, and information networks for private credit and public finance. Each nation developed new capacities for transportation, communications, and storage, and financial innovations were necessary to fund long-distance trade, industry, and military expansion.

The British, however, eventually reshaped the rules of the game. By the beginning of the eighteenth century, they were relying not just on financial institutions alone, but on a combination of institutions and financial markets. The British were embroiled in a succession of wars during the eighteenth and early nineteenth centuries, and the need to fund these campaigns led to a financial revolution. Peter Dickson has argued that the ability of the British to fund their government debt so effectively was an important factor that enabled them to regularly defeat the French for more than a century, despite the fact that their population was roughly one-third that of France.[14] This sturdy British architecture proved flexible to shocks and changes, while elsewhere in Europe, the reliance upon financiers and credit institutions stunted the development of financial markets. Without capital markets at work, excessive volatility distorted the prices of assets. Capital was priced to protect entrenched interests instead of financing new and more efficient producers. Payment systems and monetary regimes in much of Europe were subject to the vagaries of politics, but the British capital markets promoted efficiency and productivity.

Rail, steel, and coal emerged as the backbones of a new industrial economy by the 1800s. The resulting economic and geographic integration of markets created vast new demands for capital. Significant external financing was especially needed for rail systems, which required mighty infusions of investment and labor. New forms of equity and debt securities appeared at this time, from the use of common and preferred stock to various income-related debt instruments and equipment trust certificates.

In more recent times, the dramatic expansion of public equities and the initial public offering market after World War II led to the ability to finance large-scale manufacturing and new mass-consumer markets, from aviation and automobiles to entertainment. The automobile–rubber–oil industrial cluster that drove U.S. economic growth in the twentieth century demanded huge capital investment.

The 1970s brought soaring inflation to the United States, and against this backdrop, interest rate derivatives appeared. These instruments (based on the right to exchange a given amount of money at a set interest rate) now enable 80% of the world's top companies to control cash flow.[15] By the beginning of the 1980s, businesses were struggling with unimagined challenges in dealing with interest rate and current exchange rate risks. Industrial manufacturers found that exchange rate shifts could wipe out price advantages because of the absence of hedging mechanisms. This situation could and did drive corporate bankruptcies and sovereign debt insolvency in the developing world. The "new" asset of interest rate derivates provided the ability to pay or receive an amount of money at a given interest rate. That interest rate derivative market is now the largest in the world, estimated at more than $60 trillion.

High-yield corporate bonds were also devised around this time as an attempt to create longer-term, fixed-rate financing for growth companies and even emerging industries that could not get financing elsewhere. These new bonds were especially useful to companies that had been shocked by the interest rate spikes of bank lending in the 1970s or stymied by banks' reluctance to lend to the high-potential businesses of the future based on their prospective cash flows instead of their existing book assets. Iconic names such as News Corporation, Barnes & Noble, Turner Broadcasting, Time Warner, McCaw Cellular (later AT&T Wireless), and Cablevision turned to the high-yield market to finance growth.

Mortgage-backed securities also emerged in the 1970s as the demand for housing spiked, far outstripping the ability of government agencies to provide sufficient liquidity for home lending. Yes, overcomplexity and leverage were layered onto the backs of these instruments during the bubble years, but mortgage-backed securities worked smoothly for decades. Securitization contributed in a monumental way to the development of the mortgage market by tapping into a broader base for funding and providing vital liquidity.

Market innovators have never stopped searching for new strategies that can address price instability and risk. Later chapters of this book detail the most visionary financing concepts currently being deployed to reboot the housing market, protect the environment, promote faster medical cures, and tackle a host of other social problems.

Landmarks in Financial Innovation

Multiple factors must be in place for new financial structures to work, including transparency, standardization, a system of exchange, and price discovery. These are necessary ingredients for overcoming information asymmetries and helping all parties to price and manage risk. Just as physical infrastructure is required for transportation and communications, an adequate information infrastructure must be in place for financial innovations to take hold and succeed.[16]

Uniform Commodity and Security Standards

Transaction costs are reduced and markets are made more reliable when uniform commodity and security standards are defined. The ability to measure, monitor, and manage data about any security underlies the ability to price or trade it. Standardization is key to ensuring that accurate valuation can occur. The underlying asset must be specified, whether it is a bushel of corn or an interest rate. Benchmarking, auditing, and information management allow transparent transactions to take place. Standardization delineates the type of settlement (cash or physical), the number of units of the underlying asset per contract, the currency or unit of exchange, the grade (type of commodity or grade of security), and the timing of the trade (delivery, trading date, and maturation). The process of standardization is carried out by establishing broadly accepted principles for determining accounting values, while still allowing some degree of methodological flexibility. Competing interests must be overcome to harmonize measurements so that accurate valuations can be made.

Legal Instruments Providing Evidence of Ownership

Property rights constitute one of the fundamental building blocks that make financial innovations and markets possible. Ownership grows as cash flows from operations, trading, and commerce. The registration and protection of property rights—whether involving a parcel of land or intellectual property—is necessary for the mobilization of all forms of capital for productive use. The ability to establish proprietary interests in economic activity underlies what Hernando de Soto has appropriately called "the mystery of capital."[17] Claims that can leverage other means of finance toward creative goals of economic activity must be established and protected. Tangible ownership stakes provide the physical means and incentives for individuals to take transformative action.

Exchanges

Exchanges grew out of the need to provide channels for the flow of savings to investment. The prospects of long-term capital gains for investors emerged systematically as firms that had growing demands for capital reinvested earnings to attract investors seeking higher returns. The earliest exchanges grew out of the need to finance trades and fairs through bills of exchange, drafts, notes, and instruments. From exchanges for bills and notes, the movement toward more complex securities came swiftly as the structural needs for external financing grew to accommodate new markets, technologies, and challenges. Exchange-traded financial innovations are standardized and can be margined and financed.

Futures, Options, and Forward Markets

Futures are standardized contracts committing parties to buy or sell goods at a specific quality and price for delivery at a specific point in the future. Traders on a mercantile exchange can use them to swap pork belly futures, or airlines can use them to hedge oil prices. They have been at work for centuries—in fact, they surface as Aristotle relates the story of Thales of Miletus in the sixth century B.C.[18] Thales overcame his legendary poverty by developing forecasting and estimation skills relative to weather and geography: He predicted a bumper crop of olives and raised money to deposit for olive presses, which he then claimed and traded at profit.

Futures exchanges act as clearinghouses between buyers and sellers, guaranteeing their contracts. They monitor the credit of buyers and sellers, process new information about supply and demand, and generally provide stability in an unstable environment by ensuring future prices and availability.

Futures are standardized and exchange-traded, while forwards and options are customized for a counterparty and therefore not frequently traded on exchanges. (The "forward market" is a general term used to refer to the informal market in which these contracts are entered and exited.) Informal spot markets form when economic actors make only limited contractual obligations to the future by negotiating a cash price for a good, service, or commodity on the spot at current market prices. Later, the ability to commit to forward prices occurs.

In all cases of the evolution of these markets, standardization of the underlying good or asset is required to measure price variability, arrive at competitive prices, ensure that viable cash markets exist, and determine patterns of forward contracting. Patterns of contract design emerge that are consistent with legal and tax restrictions, enabling trade.

Over-the-Counter (OTC) Markets

The need for customized solutions to control financial risk gave rise to OTC markets. If a standardized exchange-based option is inadequate, a corporation can write a more tailored contract that is designed and priced to provide greater stability. For example, a corporation needing to plan production might need to hedge a stream of foreign currency revenue for a longer period than what is available via an exchange-traded instrument. In a bilateral over-the-counter contract (such as a corporate bond), two parties agree on how a particular trade or transaction is to be settled in the future. While exchange-traded instruments are standardized contracts, OTC options are tailored to particular risks. Price discovery on exchange-traded options is important for determining prices of OTC options. Banks, investment banks, insurance companies, large corporations, and other

parties participate in OTC markets. Forwards and swaps are prime
examples of OTC contracts; without futures, insurance and risk management for these more customized instruments can be extreme.

Did Financial Innovation Cause the Crisis?

As we discuss further in Chapter 4, "Innovations in Housing
Finance," the housing sector has seen a considerable amount of financial innovation in recent years—and a number of commentators have
argued that this played an important role in causing the crisis.[19]
Although new mortgage products and the predatory practices of many
lenders in persuading people to take on mortgages they could not afford
exacerbated the impact of the meltdown, we believe they were not its
fundamental cause. There are clearly many factors that drove the crisis
and a wide divergence of opinion about their relative importance. For
example, a number of people argue that moral hazard caused by the
government safety net and the prospect of bailouts for banks and entities like Fannie Mae and Freddie Mac led to excessive risk-taking by
financial institutions. While we believe this was an important factor—
and an area in which financial innovation needs to focus in the future in
order to better align incentives—we argue that the primary problem
was a loose monetary policy that led to a massive run-up in home prices.

Carmen Reinhart and Kenneth Rogoff have also pointed to the
outsized bubble in house prices as the primary culprit.[20] They tracked
real housing prices in the United States from 1891 until 2008, showing that prices remained remarkably stable until the early 2000s,
when they spiked dramatically before starting to fall precipitously in
2006. In the decade between 1996 and 2006, real housing prices in
the United States grew about 92%—three times more than the total
increase (27%) they had posted from 1891 until 1996. When this bubble burst, it first hit subprime mortgages before spilling over to the
rest of the financial system.

The United States was hardly the only place that produced a housing bubble. Spain and Ireland, to name just two examples, were also
hard hit—and, interestingly, in neither of these countries was financial
innovation a major factor. Securitized mortgages in Spain were
required to have loan-to-value ratios of 80% or less (meaning borrowers had to contribute at least 20% down payments).[21] In Ireland, the

main financial innovation introduced during the bubble years was simply the lengthening of mortgage terms.[22] Yet both of these countries have felt even more severe consequences than the United States. In Spain, the impacts have been serious, even though the major commercial banks (such as Santander and BBVA) came through the crisis much better than most of their international counterparts.

John Taylor has made a direct connection between lax monetary policy and the bubble in home prices in the United States, Spain, and Ireland.[23] He considered what would have happened in the United States if the Federal Reserve had maintained the same approach that had prevailed since the 1980s, during the period known as the Great Moderation. His simulations suggest that under that scenario, the housing price boom would have been much smaller. Although Spanish interest rates never approached lows like the 1% rate set by the Federal Reserve from 2003–2004, monetary policy was nevertheless very loose, taking into account the high rate of inflation in Spain at the time and other economic factors. In fact, Spain had the loosest monetary policy and the largest housing boom in the Eurozone. The story in Ireland was similar.

The growing issuance of subprime mortgages in the United States, particularly as home prices moved toward their peak, meant that the bursting of the bubble caused immediate damage. Because many subprime borrowers had little to no cushion, their default rates went up soon after home prices began to fall, sparking problems in the money market. Given what happened in other countries with less financial innovation, a major crisis would have occurred even without subprime mortgages. Reinhart and Rogoff cite real estate bubbles as the causes behind banking crises in Spain in 1977, Norway in 1987, Finland and Sweden in 1991, Japan in 1992, and many Asian countries in 1997. In all these cases, a collapse in housing prices caused banking crises.[24]

Many of the recent financial innovations in the mortgage market were aimed at expanding homeownership to people with low incomes and few assets—and this policy is in fact desirable in many ways. However, these new products relied heavily on the assumption that home prices would continue to rise. As long as this was the case, an individual's mortgage could be refinanced or the house could simply be sold to pay off the mortgage if problems occurred. Although it seems obvious in retrospect that there was a bubble in housing prices, it was not so clear at the time. Some observers, such as economist Nouriel Roubini, did sound warnings. *The Economist* even ran an analysis in mid-2005 cautioning that "it looks like the biggest bubble in history."[25] But nevertheless, the Federal Reserve, the other bank regulators, and many market participants missed (or chose to ignore) the signs. The rewards to anybody who realized the existence of the bubble and invested appropriately were staggering. For example, hedge fund manager John Paulson made $3.7 billion in 2007 by taking positions to exploit the fall in house prices.[26]

There is no sugarcoating the fact that some of the complex mortgage products developed during this period were explicitly designed to mislead people. But making things complicated to fool people is a practice that is hardly restricted to financial innovation. In the markets for many products, from car rentals to mobile phones, vendors take advantage of the unwitting. Xavier Gabaix and David Laibson have shown how this can happen even in competitive markets.[27]

This book is about the many benefits that financial innovation can create. This is not to say that financial innovation is universally beneficial. Some "innovations," particularly those that are complex for complexity's sake, with the aim of fooling consumers, are not desirable. However, these aberrations should not obscure the past accomplishments and future potential of financial innovation. They should instead motivate the financial community to find new ways to safely test new products, manage risk, and increase transparency.

The major lessons from the crisis can be boiled down to this: Complexity does not equal innovation, and *leverage* is not a synonym for *credit*. Everything new under the sun is not automatically an innovation. As noted in our discussion of the vocabulary of finance, equity emerges from the variety of interactions that build real value in an enterprise, be it a household, business, government, or community. Credit, as its root, implies the reliance on the truth or reality of something—its ability to be valued in a manner that becomes an accounting entry, representing the balance of cash in one's favor. True innovation in capital markets and finance has made access to credit and the ability to build equity more flexible and less costly.

But in recent years, as new products became increasingly Byzantine and financial institutions became dangerously leveraged, credit was often used for speculation, not necessarily to enhance value or productivity. A host of Rube Goldberg financial products were introduced simply for the sake of product differentiation and marketing; many were embedded with high leverage or disguised with intentionally opaque structures. The recent financial crisis illustrated vividly that excessive complexity is the enemy of transparency, ultimately hampering the market efficiency that financial systems need to operate.

With the advent of banking, insurance, securities, futures, and other derivative markets, the strengths and imperfections of finance have remained. As in any area, innovation in finance is dynamic, disruptive, and nonlinear. Financial growth, despite its newly broad reach and seemingly boundless potential, is still inadequate and unequally shared. Until the evolution of finance and the markets serving it are fully complete, the risk of crisis remains present—and that risk has even intensified over time as an intricate web of global connections has formed.

But risk management is a fundamental component of financial innovation, and new breakthroughs will be the key to controlling the potential for outsized global shocks. The overall objective is to reduce the cost of capital while mitigating systemic risk—the cascading failures of businesses, financial institutions, and intermediaries that sometimes arise when economic actors trade without possessing adequate information.[28]

It is crucial to look beyond the hype and hysteria that surfaced during the most recent financial crisis. We believe that financial innovations are the cure for instability, not the cause.

Using Finance to Manage Risk and Democratize Access to Capital

All types of enterprises involve risks, many of which are difficult to quantify. The role of finance is to understand those risks and provide the institutional framework to resolve them and build linkages to the capital markets.

As Robert Shiller has noted, numerous financial innovations arose from attempts to insure risk. Coincident with the growth of global trade in the seventeenth century came an increased under-standing of probability theory—and, with it, the creation of actuarial tables for various risks. Initially, Shiller explains, only narrow risks were insured, such as death, the sinking of ships, or destruction by fire. Gradually, insurance extended to disability, floods, and accidents. Today he sees financial innovation broadening the use of risk man-agement, extending it to new classes of risks that limit global growth, such as income inequality.[29]

Increasingly, managing complex risks within a firm requires the integration of finance into all aspects of accounting, corporate strat-egy, and industrial organization. Capital structure comes to reflect and enable those strategies. The ability to measure and monitor risk has taken a leap forward with information technology, and major innovations have arisen to manage newly conceptualized factors. The underlying technologies of telecommunications and data processing have had a transformational effect on this field.

Financial innovation and information technology intersect most profoundly around the issues of overcoming information asymme-tries and improving the ability to price risk. Lenders that faced diffi-culties in determining who was creditworthy or monitoring performance after a loan or investment was made paved the way to new advances in fundamental credit analysis and scoring geared toward overcoming problems of adverse selection and moral hazard. New credit and investment products that can build on valuation methodologies derived from larger relational database management have the capacity to overcome problems of asset pricing models. Breakthroughs in financial IT have improved methods of assessing market risk and the fragility or strength of portfolio mixes.

Fundamental analysis is based on an honest evaluation of the financial conditions, management, and competitive advantages of a business or project; this process necessarily includes scrutiny of pro-duction, distribution, earnings, interest rates, and management. The ability to conduct such analysis underlies all valuations of firms and projects, encompassing projections of their performance and calcula-tion of the credit risk involved in extending them financing.

The financial instruments introduced over time are built on this essential ability to ascribe, measure, and monitor value. Improving the

means and methods of valuation is central to overcoming the information barriers of price discovery—a major goal of financial innovation.
The components subject to valuation can be translated into equity,
debt, and combination (hybrid) structures, running the spectrum of
external and internal financing methods available. The linkage of savings into investment is the key process at the heart of finance, and
these tools make the translation between the two possible.

The proposition inherent in financial innovation is that the
expansion of finance can improve productivity in a way that will
solve economic, social, and environmental problems, thereby leading to job creation and better standards of living. Financial innovations can align interests to achieve poverty reduction (through
microfinance and impact investing), entrepreneurial growth
(through small business financing), the mitigation of environmental
problems (through markets for emissions permits and transferable
fishing quotas), and medical cures (through new financing strategies
to support the R&D process). The objective of finance, as with economics in general, is to overcome problems of scarcity by increasing
prosperity.

The recent meltdown did not halt the evolution of financial
innovation. On the contrary, the need for fresh solutions has never
been greater. Innovations can lay the groundwork for reconstruct-
ing a more robust set of institutions and instruments, ultimately
building a new global economy based upon sustainability and wider
participation.

By examining both history and contemporary case studies, this
book explores how innovations can deliver the benefits of finance to
increasingly broader segments of the population, expanding access to
capital and opportunity.

Endnotes

[1] Joseph R. Mason, "The Summer of '07 and the Shortcomings of Financial Innovation," *Journal of Applied Finance* 18, no. 1 (2008): 8–15; Markus K. Brunnermeier,
"Deciphering the Liquidity and Credit Crunch 2007–8," *Journal of Economic Perspectives*" 23, no. 1 (Winter 2009): 77–100.

[2] William N. Goetzman and K. Geert Rouwenhorst, *The Origins of Value: The Financial Innovations That Created Modern Capital Markets* (New York: Oxford University Press, 2005).

[3]These merchants were called tallymen because they kept a record, or tally, of what people had bought on a wooden stick. One side of the stick was marked with notches to represent the amount of debt, and the other side was a record of payments.

[4]Merton H. Miller, "Financial Innovation: The Last Twenty Years and the Next," *Journal of Financial and Quantitative Analysis* 21, no. 4 (December 1986): 437.

[5]Ross Levine, "Finance and Growth: Theory and Evidence" (working paper no. 10766, National Bureau of Economic Research, September 2004).

[6]Bradford Cornell and Alan C. Shapiro, "Financing Corporate Growth," *The Revolution in Corporate Finance*, 4th ed. (London: Blackwell, 2003).

[7]Robert Merton, "Financial Innovation and Economic Performance," *Journal of Applied Corporate Finance* 4, no. 4 (1992): 12–22.

[8]*Ibid.*

[9]Joshua Cooper Ramo, "The Three Marketeers," *Time* (15 February 1999).

[10]Paul Millet, *Lending and Borrowing in Ancient Athens* (New York: Cambridge University Press, 2002). For further background on origins, see Peter Bernstein, *Against the Gods: The Remarkable Story of Risk* (New York: Wiley, 1998); and Michael Hudson and Marc Van de Mieroop (eds.), *Debt and Economic Renewal in the Ancient Near East* (Potomac, MD: CDL Press, 2002).

[11]Franceso Boldizzoni, *Means and Ends: The Idea of Capital in the West, 1500–1970* (London: Palgrave Macmillan, 2008).

[12]Karl Polanyi, Conrad Arensberg, and Harry Pearson, eds., *Trade and Market in the Early Empires* (New York: The Free Press, 1957).

[13]Larry Neal, *The Rise of Financial Capitalism: International Capital in the Age of Reason* (New York: Cambridge University Press, 2002); and Walter Russell Meade, *God and Gold: Britain, America, and the Making of the Modern World* (New York: Knopf, 2008).

[14]Peter G. M. Dickson, *The Financial Revolution in England, A Study in the Development of Public Credit, 1688–1756* (New York: St. Martin's Press, 1967).

[15]Richard L. Sandor and Howard Sosin, "Inventive Activity in Futures Markets: A Case Study of the Development of the First Interest Rate Futures Market," *Futures Markets: Modeling, Managing, and Monitoring Futures Trading* (Oxford: Basil Blackwell, 1983).

[16]Thanks to our colleague Richard Sandor for his work in identifying the stages of financial innovation.

[17]Hernando de Soto, *The Mystery of Capital: Why Capitalism Triumphs in the West and Fails Everywhere Else* (New York: Basic Books, 2000).

[18]Aristotle, 1259 a 6-23; Plutarch *Vit. Sol.* II.4.

[19]Simon Johnson and James Kwak, "Finance: Before the Next Meltdown," *Democracy,* issue 13 (Summer 2009); www.democracyjournal.org/article2.php?ID=6701&limit=0&limit2=1000&page=1.

[20]Carmen S. Reinhart and Kenneth S. Rogoff, *This Time Is Different: Eight Centuries of Financial Folly* (Princeton and Oxford: Princeton University Press: 2009).

[21]Gregario Mayayo, President of the Spanish Mortgage Association, "The Spanish Mortgage Market and the American Subprime Crisis," Asociación Hipotecaria Española, December 2007.

[22]David Miles and Vladimir Pillonca, "Financial Innovation and European Housing and Mortgage Markets," *Oxford Review of Economic Policy* 24 (2008): 145–175.

[23]John Taylor, "The Financial Crisis and Policy Responses: An Empirical Analysis of What Went Wrong" (working paper, Stanford University, November 2008).

[24]Reinhart and Rogoff, Table 10.8, p. 160.

[25]Stephen Mihm, "Dr. Doom," *New York Times Magazine* (15 August 2008). See also "In Come the Waves," *The Economist* (16 June 2005).

[26]James Mackintosh, "Record Profits for Fund Shorting Subprime," *Financial Times* (15 January 2008); and Henny Sender, "Hedge Fund Chief Pessimistic About UK Property," *Financial Times* (18 June 2008).

[27]Xavier Gabaix and David Laibson, "Shrouded Attributes and Information Suppression in Competitive Markets," *Quarterly Journal of Economics* 121, no. 206 (May 2004): 505–540.

[28]Michael Magill and Martine Quinzi, *Theory of Incomplete Markets* (Cambridge: MIT Press, 1996).

[29]Robert Shiller, *The New Financial Order: Risk in the 21st Century* (Princeton: Princeton University Press, 2003).

2

A Framework for Financial Innovation: Managing Capital Structure

While this volume is not designed to be a technical guide or a textbook, this chapter offers a basic grounding in the foundational theories that have shaped modern finance. It is a good starting place for readers who want a formal introduction to the science behind the numbers. More casual readers, however, may want to skip ahead to subsequent chapters, which focus on real-world applications of financial technologies.

In 1958, Franco Modigliani and Merton Miller published their famous paper on the irrelevance of capital structure for total firm value—and in the process, they ignited a revolution in corporate finance.[1] Their great contribution was to provide a clear conceptual framework for thinking about a firm's choice among debt and equity and other types of securities. In an ideal world, with perfect and complete capital markets and no taxes, they declared, this choice does not matter.

Although this "irrelevance proposition" is the most-often-quoted result from Modigliani and Miller's paper, the underlying point is a little more subtle. Since we *don't* operate in an ideal world, capital market imperfections and taxes become crucial in determining firms' actual choices of capital structure. The "M&M theorem"—and other important breakthroughs in financial theory—illuminated when, why, and how capital structure matters. Modigliani and Miller's abstract markets contained no incentive to innovate. Everything could be done with the securities at hand. It is the imperfections in practice— the rough edges of real markets—that lead to financial innovation.

To lay the groundwork for understanding the practical applications of financial innovation described later in this book, we start with an overview of the Modigliani and Miller result. Then we will run down several other basic tools that make innovation possible, including the Capital Asset Pricing Model (CAPM), the Black–Scholes option pricing formula, and Monte Carlo simulation techniques. Together they form a toolkit that has been used in various forms in the innovations described later in the book. These advances in financial theory have found their way into practice, creating new flexibility in the capital structures available to finance firms and projects. At their most powerful, these tools can reinvent, restructure, and relaunch whole economic sectors.

The ability of these models to factor in uncertainty has increased their relevance in a knowledge-based economy.[2] Whether dealing with intellectual property in entertainment, biodiversity, or pharmaceuticals, the models outlined in this chapter can account for uncertainty in the cost of completing projects, uncertainty of cash flows, and output impacts of financial innovations on firms and the real economy. Advances in financial technology have intersected with new efficiencies in information processing, resulting in a declining cost of external funds. These lower costs of capital—made possible by financial innovations to overcome frictions, imperfect markets, and sometimes market failures—have fueled growth in the real economy and moderated the business cycle, despite increasing volatility in financial markets.[3]

All of these models demand an extensive understanding of the relationship between a firm or project and the markets in which it operates. They assume and require data derived from fundamental analyses of financial statements and the cash-flow conditions of a firm or project, of markets, competitive advantages, management, and productivity. The linkages between financial capital and human capital embedded in the corporate leadership, strategy, and structure of a firm are key. As high-profile financial product failures and financial crises continuously remind us, even good models can fail with bad data inputs (as the saying goes in data processing, "Garbage in equals garbage out"). Information asymmetries, agency costs, moral hazard, adverse selection, and other underlying concepts in financial economics help us understand how and why crises can emerge at a firm or in the macroeconomy.

The breakthrough insights described in this chapter garnered Nobel prizes for many of the pioneering thinkers involved in their formulation and application (including Modigliani, Miller, Markowitz, Sharpe, Merton, Scholes, and others). Together they created a body of work that drove financial innovation by an entire generation of practitioners who linked theory to new corporate policy, strategy, and capital structure.[4]

The Modigliani–Miller Capital Structure Propositions

Historically, corporations have financed their activities with two major types of securities: equity and debt. The owners of the equity (the shareholders) have responsibility for the operation of the firm through the election of the board of directors. The dividends they receive in return for their subscription of capital are not guaranteed and are paid at the discretion of the board of directors. In contrast, the owners of debt (the bondholders) are promised a particular rate of return. They have no rights of control unless payments by the firm do not materialize, in which case they can force the firm into bankruptcy.

The traditional question about firms' choice of capital structure has been "What is the optimal debt-equity ratio?" This was the focus of Modigliani and Miller's paper. To understand their basic ideas, let's consider the case of the hypothetical FI Company, which is reviewing its capital structure.[5] It pays no taxes and has access to *perfect capital markets*. Among other things, this means that the markets are frictionless—there are no transaction costs, and everybody can borrow and lend at the same rate.

FI's current position is as follows:

Number of shares	100
Price per share	$20
Market value of shares	$2,000
Market value of debt	$0

The company currently has no debt, and all the operating income is paid out as dividends to the owners of the equity.

The company's ultimate result depends on the performance of its business. The operating income generated by the firm can take on a whole range of values. For simplicity, we focus on three outcomes: poor, average, and good.

	Scenario 1 (Poor)	Scenario 2 (Average)	Scenario 3 (Good)
Operating income	$100	$250	$300
Earnings per share	$1	$2.50	$3
Return on equity	5%	12.5%	15%

When the operating income is $100, the earnings per share (EPS) are $100 / 100 = $1 (since there are 100 shares). Given that the stock price is $20, the return on equity (ROE) is $1 / $20 = 5%. The EPS and ROE for the other levels of operating income are calculated in the same way.

To keep everything as simple as possible, we assume that the possible scenarios for operating income are expected to be the same every year for the foreseeable future.

By chance, the firm's president and chief executive officer is Mr. Modigliani. He has considered the situation and come to the conclusion that shareholders would be better off if the company issued some debt. His reasoning goes like this: Suppose the firm issues $1,000 of debt at the risk-free lending and borrowing rate of 10% and uses the proceeds to repurchase 50 shares (leaving 50 shares outstanding). The debt will be rolled over every year, so there is no need to repay it out of earnings. The payoffs to the owners of equity in the three different scenarios are as follows:

	Scenario 1 (Poor)	Scenario 2 (Average)	Scenario 3 (Good)
Operating income	$100	$250	$300
Interest	$100	$100	$100
Equity earnings	$0	$150	$200
Earnings per share	$0	$3	$4
Return on equity	0%	15%	20%
Return on debt	10%	10%	10%

The difference from the situation with no debt is that now the firm must pay 10% interest on the $1,000 the firm has borrowed (or $100). This must be subtracted from the operating income when calculating equity earnings. For example, equity earnings in Scenario 2 are $250 - $100 = $150. Since there are now 50 shares outstanding, the earnings per share are $150 / 50 = $3 per share. The return on equity is $3 / $20 = 15%. Because the company pays the interest in full, the return on the debt is 10%. The calculations are similar for the other scenarios.

We can compare the current situation (with all equity and no debt) to Mr. Modigliani's proposal to have $1,000 of debt.

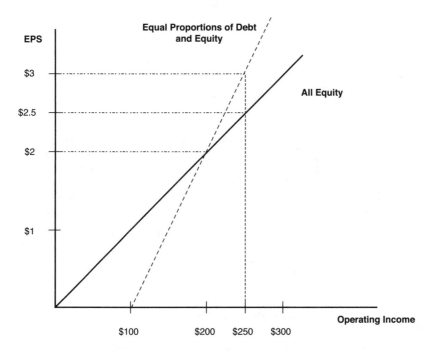

Figure 2.1   Varying the proportion of debt and equity

Mr. Modigliani argues that the effect of leverage depends on the company's operating income. If operating income is greater than $200, leverage increases the EPS and the shareholders are better off. If operating income is less than $200, leverage reduces the EPS. The capital structure decision, therefore, depends on the level of operating income. The average operating income is $250. Because this amount is above the critical level of $200, Mr. Modigliani argues that the shareholders will be better off with the capital structure with debt.

The company has just hired a young executive on the fast track. Her name, by chance, is Ms. Miller. She points out that Mr. Modigliani's analysis ignores the fact that shareholders have the alternative of borrowing on their own account. For example, suppose that a person borrows $20 and then invests a total of $40 in two all-equity FI shares. This person has to put up only $20 of his own money. The payoff on the investment is as follows:

	Scenario 1 (Good)	Scenario 2 (Average)	Scenario 3 (Poor)
Earnings on the two all-equity shares	$2	$5	$6
Less interest at 10% on $20	$2	$2	$2
Net earnings on investment	$0	$3	$4
Return on $20 investment	0%	15%	20%

By buying two shares in the all-equity company and borrowing $20, the returns are exactly the same as buying one share of the firm with the $1,000 of debt. Therefore, a share in the company with debt must sell for (2 × 20 - 20) = $20. If the company goes ahead and borrows, it will not enable its investors to do anything that they could not already do; therefore, the action will not increase value.

This is the idea behind Modigliani and Miller Proposition 1.

Modigliani and Miller Proposition 1

With perfect capital markets and no taxes, the total value (meaning the sum of the debt and the equity) of any firm is independent of its capital structure.

Therefore, Modigliani and Miller argue that, with perfect capital markets and no taxes, capital structure is irrelevant. You can't create value by borrowing or lending. Any combination of securities is as good as another; the value of the firm is unaffected by its choice of capital structure. Why? Because individuals can essentially do or undo anything the firm can do on its own. This is an extremely powerful argument. We illustrated it in the FI Company example, but it works in many others. As Miller once explained, "The firm is like some gigantic pizza, represented by its underlying earning power. You can't increase the value of that pizza by cutting it up into different slices—in this case, of debt and equity securities."[6]

The assumptions of no taxes and perfect capital markets are crucial for the result. If individuals are taxed differently than firms (say, if interest is deductible for corporations but not for individuals), then the result will not hold. The assumption of perfect capital markets ensures that individuals can borrow at the same 10% rate as the firm. If this rate were different, the result would not hold.

For a firm with any proportion of risk-free debt in its capital structure, investors can create the equivalent payoffs from any other proportion by borrowing or lending on their own account. Investors will always hold the level of debt that is optimal for them. If the firm changes its capital structure, investors will simply take offsetting positions to undo what the firm has done so they can go back to their optimal level. Therefore, a firm cannot create value by changing its capital structure—provided there are perfect capital markets and no taxes.

Before considering what happens with taxes and capital market imperfections, and how these introduce possibilities for financial innovation, let's continue a little further with our example of the FI Company.

The Relationship between Return and Debt

Consider the expected returns on FI stock in the two cases we examined:

	All Equity	**50% Debt + 50% Equity**
Expected EPS	$2.5	$3
Price per share	$20	$20
Expected return per share	12.5%	15%

Intuitively, what is happening here? Why is the expected return on the firm with debt higher? The firm can borrow at 10% and the return on its assets is 12.5%. It therefore makes 12.5% - 10% = 2.5% from borrowing against its assets. If it borrows half its value, it makes

2.5% on the half it borrows plus 12.5% on the half it still owns. This gives a total return of 2.5% + 12.5% = 15%.

This example illustrates that borrowing leads to a higher return on equity because the firm can borrow at a rate that is lower than the return on its assets. The more the firm borrows, the higher the return on the equity; the spread between the return on assets and debt is earned on a larger amount of debt. This idea underlies Modigliani and Miller's second result.

Modigliani and Miller Proposition 2

The expected rate of return on the equity of a firm increases in proportion to the firm's debt-to-equity ratio, expressed in market values. The rate of increase depends on the spread between the return on assets and the return on debt.

Modigliani and Miller's second proposition has the important implication that it is possible to raise the expected return on equity by borrowing. However, their first proposition shows that this does not create value for shareholders. How can the expected return go up while value stays the same?

The Relationship between Risk and Debt

Total value remains the same, even though expected return is going up as debt is increased, because the risk of the equity is also increasing—which exactly offsets the increase in expected return. To see this intuitively, consider our example. Look at what happens to the risk of FI's equity if it moves from all equity to 50% debt and 50% equity.

	Operating Income	
	$100	**$300**
All equity:		
EPS	$1	$3
Return on shares	5%	15%
50% debt + 50% equity:		
EPS	$0	$4
Return on shares	0%	20%

The difference in operating income between Scenarios 1 and 3 is $300 - $100 = $200, regardless of whether the firm is all equity or has $1,000 debt. With all-equity financing, this $200 change is spread over 100 shares, so the variation in EPS is $2 per share. With 50% debt and 50% equity, the same change in operating income is spread over 50 shares, so the variation in earnings is $4 per share. The spread of percentage returns is also amplified: The percentage spread with debt is 20%, as opposed to 10% with all equity. Therefore, the risk is doubled.

The Modigliani and Miller propositions revolutionized corporate finance because they provided a clear framework for thinking about the effects of debt. It is possible to obtain a higher expected return by borrowing. But this does not create value because risk is going up in a manner that exactly offsets the increase in expected return. This leads to one of the most basic insights in finance: When comparing expected returns in different investments, be sure to adjust for risk. In many parts of the financial services industry, such as private equity, returns are not adjusted for the amount of debt used in the financing. This makes them *seem* more attractive than they are in reality.

The Modigliani–Miller Propositions and Optimal Capital Structure

The Modigliani–Miller propositions were initially used as a starting point in analyzing how firms should choose their optimal capital structure. They indicate what we should look for to answer this question. Earnings per share and return on equity are not important in determining optimal capital structure—firms can always increase these ratios by borrowing more. Shareholders are not any better off, however, and risk has gone up, offsetting any increase in expected return. The factors that are important in determining optimal capital structure are taxes and market imperfections.

In the United States and many other countries, interest on debt is deductible from taxable corporate income, but dividends on equity are not. This creates a clear bias in favor of debt.[7] If a payment to owners of securities is labeled as interest, the firm pays less in taxes to the government. On the other hand, if it is labeled dividends, no reduction in taxes occurs. If the tax deductibility of interest is the only factor in play, then firms will have an incentive to use large amounts of debt to shield their income from corporate taxes. But in practice, firms do not use such large amounts of debt, and most of them do in fact pay corporate income taxes. Why?

If a corporation has a large amount of debt, its chances of going bankrupt are high. An important implication of the perfect capital markets assumption in the Modigliani–Miller framework is that bankruptcy is not costly. The firm can quickly be refinanced without interfering with its operations. However, this is not the case in practice. Bankruptcy is an expensive process. A number of authors have suggested that firms trade off the benefits of reduced taxes with the increased expected costs of bankruptcy when debt is increased.[8] This became the textbook theory of capital structure. Many other models have been suggested, but none has fully replaced the "trade-off" theory.

Our interest in the Modigliani–Miller propositions is somewhat different. In their ideal world, with no taxes and perfect capital markets, there would be no benefit from financial innovation. There are no problems preventing the smooth allocation of resources, and thus no problems for financial innovation to solve. In the next section, we turn to the world of capital market imperfections and taxes to understand the role that financial innovation has to play.

Innovations in an Imperfect World

Modigliani and Miller posed the question, how should a firm choose the optimal amount of debt and equity as well as other securities? With financial innovation, the relevant question is, how can we change securities, markets, or processes to improve the situation? In this section, we consider imperfections in the context of the Modigliani–Miller framework that provide a role for financial innovation.[9]

Incomplete Markets

In the simple example of the FI Company, the debt the company issued was risk free and shareholders borrowing on their own account was also risk free. If FI were to borrow more than $1,000, it would not be able to pay the interest in Scenario 1 and would go bankrupt. Even when bankruptcy is cost free, the Modigliani–Miller results would not hold unless the individual shareholders could borrow on exactly the same terms as the company. This is the case in which markets are *complete,* meaning it is possible to trade a security where the payoff is contingent on any conceivable event. (In this case, the event would be the bankruptcy of FI.)[10] In a complete market, the individual shareholder could borrow on exactly the same terms as the firm, and the logic of the proof for Modigliani and Miller's Proposition 1 would be valid. However, if markets are *incomplete* such that individual shareholders cannot borrow on the same terms as the FI Company, then the firm's capital structure matters.

Suppose the firm can borrow on better terms than individual stockholders (since banks incur large costs when making and servicing small loans to consumers). In this case, a firm might be able to increase its value by borrowing and issuing debt that allows the individual shareholders to reduce their more costly personal borrowing. The problem a financial innovator would face in this circumstance how to design debt contracts so they are attractive to small investors. Small denominations and ease of trading such debt would certainly be important factors. By designing and issuing such debt, a firm might be able to obtain a premium and increase its value.

This simple example provides one illustration of how an incomplete market might enable a financial innovator to profit. However, the principle is much more general. Whenever markets are incomplete and do not provide full opportunities to trade state-contingent securities, potential exists for financial innovation to improve the allocation of resources.

One of the most important roles of the financial markets is to allow risks to be fully shared, and many innovations are designed to improve risk sharing. Investors are prepared to pay a premium for securities with risk characteristics they prefer. One simple example is a situation in which the equity of a company is split into two components: prime and score. The prime component receives the dividends and capital gains up to a prespecified price, while the score component receives the capital appreciation above this price. A careful study by Robert A. Jarrow and Maureen O'Hara found that the sum of the values of the prime and score components exceeded the value of the equity.[11] In other words, splitting the equity into two parts created value for shareholders.

In the 1970s, many new specialized financial markets were introduced to make the overall markets more complete and improve risk sharing. These included markets for financial futures, which allowed investors to buy a security on a future date at a price that is fixed today. Futures on government securities that enable financial institutions to hedge the risks on their substantial holdings of these instruments were particularly successful. The greater the improvement in risk sharing that a contract created, the more likely it was to be viable.[12]

Another significant market introduced during this period traded options on stocks. The Chicago Board Options Exchange (CBOE) was introduced in 1973 to enable trading of standardized options (which give investors the option to buy or sell stocks at a prespecified price on or before the maturity date of the instrument). The CBOE was instantly successful, and by 1984, it had become the second-largest securities market in the world (trailing only the New York Stock Exchange). Theoretical work suggests that introducing an option on a stock can enable better sharing of the risk associated with the stock. As a result, demand for the stock increases, raising its price.[13] Empirical studies support this finding. During the 1970s and early 1980s, when an option was introduced, the price of the stock that the option was written on increased by approximately 2%–3%, and the volatility of the stock was reduced. When an option was delisted, the opposite effects occurred (that is, the stock price fell and the volatility increased).[14]

James Van Horne has argued that the incompleteness of markets provides a large part of the rationale for financial innovation, accounting in particular for the rapid growth in futures and options and other derivative markets that occurred around the world in the 1970s.[15] It can also explain the introduction new securities, such as prime and scores, by corporations. Market incompleteness has been the basic driver of financial innovation in many other situations.[16]

Agency Concerns, Information Asymmetries, and Transaction Costs

In a seminal paper, Michael Jensen and William Meckling pointed to the importance of agency problems (or misaligned incentives for different parties) in the determination of capital structure. Agency problems occur when conflicts of interests arise between creditors, shareholders, and management because of differing goals.[17] Jensen and Meckling argued that a firm could be thought of as a set of contracts between different parties with different interests. According to this view, the form of securities issued is crucial in regulating the relationships between different groups. If a firm has a large amount of debt outstanding, the equity holders earn a return only if there is a high payoff. They (or the managers acting on their behalf) have an incentive to undertake risky projects even if the projects are not profitable.

Consider the following simple example. The interest rate is 10%. Suppose there is a safe project in which, for every unit of funds invested, there is a return of 1.25 one period later. A risky project also arises in which, for every unit invested, the probability is 0.5 of a 0 payoff and the same for a 1.8 payoff. The next table summarizes these payoffs.

Project	Investment	Payoff	Expected Payoff
Safe project	1	1.25	1.25
Risky project	1	0 with probability 0.5	$0.5 \times 0 + 0.5 \times 1.8$
	1.8	0 with probability 0.5	= 0.9

Clearly, the risky project should not be undertaken, since it cannot recover its investment on average. However, a firm with sufficient debt outstanding would choose the risky project instead of the safe one.

Suppose the firm starts with 0.7 in debt. Because the interest rate is 10%, the firm would owe $1.1 \times 0.7 = 0.77$ at the end of the period.

The payoff from the safe asset for the equity holders is less than the expected payoff from the risky asset.

Payoff to safe asset = 1.25 - 0.77 = 0.48

Expected payoff to risky asset = $0.5 \times 0 + 0.5 \times (1.8 - 0.77) = 0.52$

The debt holders would want to prevent the firm from undertaking the risky project because they would obtain 0.77 if the firm undertakes the safe project and $0.5 \times 0.77 = 0.39$ on average if it chooses the risky one. This is where asymmetric information plays an important role. If possible, the debt holders would write covenants that would prevent the firm from doing the risky project. If there is asymmetric information, this would not be possible and the firm would choose the risky project. It would do this for any level of debt greater than 0.64. Below that level, the firm would choose the safe project.

Financial innovation can solve this problem by developing securities other than debt and equity.[18] If the debt is *convertible,* so that the bondholders would receive 49% of the equity if the equity price was more than 1, this would ensure it is not worth it to the equity holders to choose the risky project. If the equity holders did undertake the risky project and it was successful, the bondholders would convert their bonds into 49% of the equity of the firm. In this case, they would receive $0.49 \times 1.8 = 0.88$. If they did not convert, they would receive 0.77. The initial equity holders would receive $0.51 \times 1.8 = 0.92$. They would no longer have an incentive to choose the risky project in the first place, since their expected payoff would be $0.5 \times 0.92 = 0.46$, which is less than the 0.48 they would receive from undertaking the safe project.

In another seminal contribution, Stewart Myers pointed out a second agency problem (conflict of interest between various parties with competing claims on the firm's cash flow).[19] In the previous example, the firm was willing to undertake a bad, risky project. Here the firm will not undertake a good, safe project. Consider the same safe project as the previous example, in which the investment is 1 and the payoff is 1.25. Because the interest rate is 10% and this project earns 25%, it is clearly a desirable undertaking. However, if there is existing debt of 0.3 and the project needs to be financed, it might not be possible for the firm to raise the necessary funds.

The problem is that the equity holders would receive 1.25 - 0.3 = 0.95 when the project pays off, so they would not be willing to put in 1 unit at the initial date to fund the project. The bondholders who are owed the 0.3 in debt would be willing to put up the funds if they could be sure the project really was the safe one, since this would allow them to recover part of their initial debt as well as the subsequent debt. However, if there is asymmetric information that prevents the bondholders from observing the project quality and it could be the risky one, they will not provide the finance. Therefore, the project would not be undertaken.

Again, financial innovation can solve the problem. If the debt converts to 10% of the equity when the stock price falls below 0.2, the equity holders will be willing to put up the funds. They would receive $0.9 \times 1.25 = 1.125$. This allows them to obtain a 12.5% return on their initial investment. This is preferable to the 10% interest rate (abstracting the effects of risk).

Stephen Ross has suggested that the interaction of agency issues and marketing costs is an important driver of financial innovation.[20] Agency considerations lead borrowers to contract with commercial banks. A shock, such as a change in regulation or taxes, can change the amount of lending they wish to do. As a result, they sell some of these low-grade assets by approaching investment banks to market these assets using financial innovations to reduce the costs of selling them.

Robert Merton has also stressed agency costs.[21] In addition, he points to the role of transaction costs savings and improvements in liquidity as important benefits of financial innovations such as commercial paper, financial futures, options, and swaps.

Subsequent chapters offer specific examples of innovations to solve agency problems.

Taxes and Regulation

Miller has argued that much of the innovation that occurred in the 1970s and early 1980s came in response to government regulation and features of the tax code.[22] However, these types of restrictions had caused innovation even before that. In the middle of the nineteenth century, the popularity of preferred stock in England arose from the fact that corporations were prohibited from borrowing more than one-third of their total share capital. More recently, in the 1960s, the U.S. Interest Equalization Tax, which excluded most foreign issuers from the U.S. market, significantly spurred the development of Euromarkets (markets for dollar securities and deposits outside the United States).

Another classic example of innovation in response to the tax code is zero-coupon bonds, which offer a single payment at the end of the bond's life that includes both principal and interest.[23] Before the Tax Equity and Fiscal Responsibility Act of 1982 (TEFRA), the tax liability on zero-coupon bonds was allocated on a straight-line basis—the annual interest deduction was the amount to be repaid at the due date minus the issue price, divided by the number of years until repayment. This rule ignored the effect of interest compounding and created an opportunity for corporations to avoid taxes by issuing long-term zero-coupon bonds to tax-exempt investors. When interest rates were high in the early 1980s, the potential tax benefits from this type of security became significant, and corporations raced to issue these bonds. Although TEFRA closed this loophole, the market for zero-coupon bonds continued. Investment banks first satisfied the demand for these securities, and then the Treasury provided strips of government securities (in which bonds were broken into principal and interest components).

Edward Kane has stressed that the "regulatory dialectic" is an important source of innovation.[24] In this process, regulation leads to innovations, which lead in turn to new regulations, and so on. One example is bank capital requirements, which prompted banks to introduce capital notes and preferred stocks that would count toward their capital. Similarly, the first swaps occurred in the 1960s; they were currency swaps, motivated by a desire to avoid British exchange controls.

Tools for Financial Innovation

Now that we've considered how the Modigliani–Miller propositions and agency theory laid a theoretical framework for financial innovation, we outline a number of other models that propelled the field forward. We begin with the Capital Asset Pricing Model (CAPM), the first model that made it possible to properly quantify a security's risk, and the Black–Scholes option pricing model, which opened a whole new way of thinking about finance and allowed new financial products to be engineered in a way that had not been possible before. Finally, we look at Monte Carlo simulation techniques, which can evaluate the properties of options and complex new financial instruments when the assumptions of the Black–Scholes model are not satisfied.

The CAPM

In 1952, Harry Markowitz introduced the idea of thinking about the risk of portfolios of securities in terms of the mean and standard deviation of returns.[25] An efficient portfolio is one in which the standard deviation is minimized for a given expected return. The portfolio efficiency locus gives the possible trade-off between risk and return.

What does this really mean? Markowitz's innovation enabled people to formally consider diversification and the important role it could play in reducing the risk of a portfolio. He showed that a portfolio's risk, as measured by its standard deviation, depended on the standard deviations and covariances (or the correlations) of the returns of the stocks in a portfolio. In other words, if a portfolio contains many independent stocks, so that the covariances of their returns are zero, the portfolio's risk is eliminated. However, in practice, stock returns are not independent, because the business cycle affects most companies to some extent. Not all risk can be eliminated.

It would be another 12 years before the next step was taken, enabling William Sharpe and John Lintner to independently derive the CAPM.[26] The crucial innovation was to not only consider risky stocks, but to also introduce a risk-free government bond. They showed that, in this case, all investors will hold a combination of the risk-free asset and the market portfolio, consisting of all the risky securities that exist, so that they can achieve the maximum possible degree of diversification. Risk-averse people will hold a high proportion of their wealth in the risk-free government bond, while less-risk-averse people will hold more in the market portfolio. Sharpe and

Lintner were also able to derive a simple relationship between the expected return on a stock and its risk as measured by its beta (β), which depends on its correlation with the market portfolio. The formula follows:

$$r = r_F + \beta(r_M - r_F),$$

Here, r is the expected return on the stock, r_F is the return on the risk-free government security, r_M is the expected return on the market portfolio, and

β = Covariance (Stock, Market)

(Standard deviation of M)^2

β is important for determining the stock's expected return because it measures the contribution of the stock to the risk of the market portfolio. If the amount of the stock in the market portfolio increases slightly, it indicates how much the risk of the market portfolio would change. The other way to think about β is that it measures the slope of the regression line of the stock's return against the market returns. It shows how much the return of the stock increases on average for every 1% increase in the return on the market portfolio.

The CAPM revolutionized the way people thought about risk. They no longer focused on the standard deviation of a stock's returns, but rather on its contribution to the risk of a portfolio as measured by its β. The risk that is unique to the firm is not included in the measure because this risk is diversified away. Instead, β focuses on the risk of the firm that covaries with the market.

The Black–Scholes Model

The year 1973 saw two seminal events: the opening of the Chicago Board Options Exchange and the publication of two groundbreaking papers (one by Fischer Black and Myron Scholes, and the other by Robert Merton) on valuing options.[27] In 1997, Scholes and Merton were awarded Nobel prizes for their work (unfortunately, Black had died in 1995, so he was not eligible).

Why was their work so pivotal? Options might be significant, but it was really the broader ideas introduced by these economists that proved to be game changing. These concepts are applicable in many different contexts and have revolutionized the practice of finance.

The two crucial components of their theory are **arbitrage** and **dynamic trading**. These allow **financial engineering**, which involves the manufacture of securities and portfolios with any desired payoffs.

We consider these ideas in the context of options, the field in which they were first introduced. Options are used in many settings and are useful because they allow **insurance.** For example, options on foreign exchange enable firms to eliminate the undesirable effects from fluctuations in exchange rates. In addition to options on foreign exchange, options can be used on stocks. Using options together with stocks and bonds allows investors to design a desirable set of portfolio payoffs. For example, if you are worried about the possibility of a fall in stock prices, you can buy options to insure against the downside risk. Markets for options on stocks are among the most active in the world. Although we focus on options on stocks, the methodologies can be applied to other types of options, such as those on foreign exchange.

First off, what exactly is an option? Purchasers of a **call** option have the right, if they want, to *buy* a share of the stock from the seller of the option at a prespecified exercise price on or before the maturity date. Purchasers of a **put** option have the right to *sell* a share of the stock to the seller of the option at a prespecified exercise price on or before the maturity date.[28]

The Black–Scholes formula and its many extensions have been found to work well in practice.[29] Despite what appear to be strong assumptions and the abstract nature of the model, the empirical evidence strongly supports the Black–Scholes model and its extensions.

The basic idea behind the Black–Scholes model is to create a dynamic trading strategy using stock and risk-free bonds to create the equivalent to a call. Calls are not the only items that can be dynamically synthesized—in fact, almost any kind of asset can be dynamically created. This is why the model has revolutionized finance. You can always create any arbitrary pattern of payoffs using an appropriate dynamic trading strategy. The methodology enables investors to evaluate and price new financial products, which is why its discovery represented a quantum leap forward for financial innovation. It is difficult to believe that the Chicago Board Options Exchange would have been so successful without the discovery of the Black–Scholes formula.

Monte Carlo Methods

The assumptions of the Black–Scholes model are very strong. Phelim Boyle later pointed out that Monte Carlo techniques could be used to value options in many situations in which the Black–Scholes assumptions were not satisfied.[30] The method involves considering a particular random path of the stock price and evaluating the value of the option of interest at each point. This is done many thousands or hundreds of thousands times. The initial price of the option is found by averaging across all these different possible paths and then discounting this value back at the risk-free rate. The methods are very powerful because they enable analysts to incorporate a wide range of deviations from the Black–Scholes model. For example, they allow option prices to be evaluated when there are jump processes.

Just as the analytical approach of the Black–Scholes model can be applied to securities other than options, Monte Carlo simulations can be applied in many situations. The methods are particularly useful when there are multiple sources of risk.

Conclusions

This chapter set forth a framework for thinking about financial innovation. The concepts and theoretical models that comprise this toolkit have been empirically applied across a range of financial products and in real markets. In the ideal world of Modigliani and Miller, in which capital markets are perfect and there are no taxes, financial innovation has no role to play. But the act of translating this abstract model into the empirical rough-and-tumble world of real markets has produced important insights and applications. Only in a world with frictions can financial innovation improve the situation. Whenever markets are incomplete, agency problems arise between parties, or regulations and taxes present hurdles, there will be an incentive to innovate and create value by reducing the frictions.

In the following chapters, we show how this plays out in the real world and how creative practitioners have put these concepts to work in financing new businesses, increasing homeownership, funding medical solutions, solving environmental problems, and spurring economic development in emerging markets.

The recent crisis notwithstanding, a clear and well-documented link between finance and growth has held true over time. By moving these formulas and theories into practice, financial innovators have transformed industrial organization and corporate strategy over the centuries. Today they are still striving to open new frontiers in the twenty-first-century economy.

Endnotes

[1] Franco Modigliani and Merton H. Miller, "The Cost of Capital, Corporation Finance and the Theory of Investment," *American Economic Review* 48, no. 3(1958): 261–297.

[2] Jacques Bughin, "Black–Scholes Meets Seinfeld," *McKinsey Quarterly* (May 2000); Eduardo S. Schwartz, "Patents and R&D As Real Options," *Economic Notes* 33, no. 1 (February 2004): 23–54.

[3] J. Christina Wang, "Financial Innovations, Idiosyncratic Risk, and the Joint Evolution of Real and Financial Volatilities," *Proceedings*, Federal Reserve Bank of San Francisco (November 2006).

[4] Thomas E. Copeland, John F. Weston, and Kuldeep Shastri, *Financial Theory and Corporate Policy*, 4th ed. (New York: Addison-Wesley, 2005).

[5] For a full analysis of firms' choice of capital structure, see Chapters 17 and 18 of Richard A. Brealey, Stewart C. Myers, and Franklin Allen, *Principles of Corporate Finance*, 10th ed. (New York: McGraw-Hill, 2010).

[6] Merton Miller, as quoted by Matt Siegal in "How Corporate Finance Got Smart: The Modigliani–Miller Theorem Turns 40," *Fortune* (25 May 1998).

[7] Franco Modigliani and Merton H. Miller, "Corporate Income Taxes and the Cost of Capital: A Correction," *American Economic Review* 53 (1963): 261–297.

[8] For example, see Alan Kraus and Robert Litzenberger, "A State-Preference Model of Optimal Financial Leverage," *Journal of Finance* 28 (1973): 911–922; James Scott, "A Theory of Optimal Capital Structure," *Bell Journal of Economics and Management Science* 7 (1976): 33–54; and E. Han Kim, "A Mean-Variance Theory of Optimal Capital Structure," *Journal of Finance* 33 (1978): 45–63.

[9] This section draws on Franklin Allen and Douglas Gale, *Financial Innovation and Risk Sharing* (Cambridge, MA: MIT Press, 1994); and Peter Tufano, "Financial Innovation," in George M. Constantinides, Milton Harris, and René Stulz, eds., *Handbook of the Economics of Finance, Volume 1a, Corporate Finance* (New York: Elsevier-North Holland, 2003).

[10]In effect, such a contingent security would be a credit default swap in which there is a payoff when a company defaults. See Chapter 3, "Innovations in Business Finance," for a full discussion of these instruments.

[11]Robert A. Jarrow and Maureen O'Hara, "Primes and Scores: An Essay on Market Imperfections," *Journal of Finance* 44 (1989): 1263–1287.

[12]See Deborah G. Black, "Success and Failure of Futures Contracts: Theory and Empirical Evidence," Salomon Brothers Center for the Study of Financial Institutions Monograph Series in Finance and Economics, Graduate School of Business Administration, New York University (1986); and Darrell Duffie and Matthew Jackson, "Optimal Innovation of Futures Contracts," *Review of Financial Studies* 2, no. 3 (1989): 275–296.

[13]Jerome Detemple and Lawrence Selden, "A General Equilibrium Analysis of Option and Stock Market Interactions," *International Economic Review* 32 (1991): 279–303.

[14]See Jennifer Conrad, "The Price of Option Introduction," *Journal of Finance* 44 (1989): 487–498; and Jerome Detemple and Philippe Jorion, "Option Listing and Stock Returns: An Empirical Analysis," *Journal of Banking and Finance* 14 (1990): 781–801.

[15]James C. Van Horne, "Of Financial Innovation and Excesses," *Journal of Finance* 40 (1985): 621–631.

[16]See Franklin Allen and Douglas Gale, *Financial Innovation and Risk Sharing* (Cambridge, MA: MIT Press, 1994); and Darrell Duffie and Rohit Rahi, "Financial Market Innovation and Security Design: An Introduction," *Journal of Economic Theory* 65 (1995): 1–42.

[17]Michael C. Jensen and William H. Meckling, "Theory of the Firm: Managerial Behavior, Agency Costs, and Ownership Structure," *Journal of Financial Economics* 3 (1976): 305–360.

[18]See Richard Green, "Investment, Incentives, Debt, and Warrants," *Journal of Financial Economics* 13 (1984): 115–136; and Amir Barnea, Robert Haugen, and Lemma Senbet, *Agency Problems and Financial Contracting* (Englewood Cliffs, NJ: Prentice Hall, 1985).

[19]Stewart C. Myers, "Determinants of Corporate Borrowing," *Journal of Financial Economics* 5 (1977): 147–175.

[20]Stephen Ross, "Institutional Markets, Financial Marketing, and Financial Innovation," *Journal of Finance* 44 1989): 541–556.

[21]Robert C. Merton, "The Financial System and Economic Performance," *Journal of Financial Services Research* 4 (1990): 263–300.

[22]Merton H. Miller, "Financial Innovations: The Last Twenty Years and the Next," *Journal of Financial and Quantitative Analysis* 21 (1986): 459–471.

[23]Zero-coupon bonds are discussed further in Chapter 3.

[24]Edward J. Kane, "Technology and the Regulation of Financial Markets," in Anthony Saunders and Lawrence J. White (eds.), *Technology and the Regulation of Financial Markets: Securities, Futures, and Banking* (Lexington, MA: Lexington Books, 1986): 187–193.

[25]Harry M. Markowitz, "Portfolio Selection," *Journal of Finance* 7 (1952): 77–91.

[26]William F. Sharpe, "Capital Asset Prices: A Theory of Market Equilibrium under Conditions of Risk," *Journal of Finance* 19 (1964): 425–442; and John Lintner, "The Valuation of Risk Assets and the Selection of Risky Investments in Stock Portfolios and Capital Budgets," *Review of Economics and Statistics* 47 (1965): 13–37.

[27]Fischer Black and Myron Scholes, "The Pricing of Options and Corporate Liabilities," *Journal of Political Economy* 81 (1973): 637–654; and Robert C. Merton, "Theory of Rational Option Pricing," *Bell Journal of Economics and Management Science* 4 (1973): 637–654.

[28]Strictly speaking, these are American options. European options allow exercise only on the date of maturity. The Black–Scholes model applies to European options.

[29]See the Appendix for the formula and the assumptions underlying it.

[30]Phelim P. Boyle, "A Monte Carlo Approach to Options," *Journal of Financial Economics* 4 (1977): 323–338.

3

Innovations in Business Finance

For the layperson, few subjects are more daunting than business finance, which seems laden with inscrutable concepts, mysterious jargon, and mathematical formulas. Experienced practitioners might as well be speaking a language of their own.

But even the most sophisticated applications have a clear-cut principle at their core: This is the business of financing business—finding ways to propel growth, create jobs, and bring new ideas to the marketplace. Companies need to select the appropriate capital structure (a mix of various types of short- and long-term debt and equity) to finance their operations and growth. Whether the question is extending credit to an entrepreneur who wants to open a neighborhood shop or helping a multinational corporation restructure its debt burden in a cash crunch, every business needs the right kind of financing at the right time in order to succeed.

The recent financial crisis drove home this simple truth. To the untrained observer, corporate finance might have once seemed to be an academic exercise—the dry rearranging of figures on a balance sheet. But as U.S. credit markets swung from freewheeling to frozen, business financing was revealed to be the lifeblood of the U.S. economy. Highly leveraged firms scrambled to find the right fixes that would enable them to stay afloat, while small companies struggled to get the loans they needed for equipment, supplies, and payroll. The credit crunch immediately translated into job losses and sparked a deep recession. It became abundantly clear that the economy can't function when individual companies lose the ability to manage their cash flow and obligations in a manner that matches the circumstances.

Even in good times, corporate finance provides the tools that keep commerce humming. In bad times, however, these tools can make all the difference in determining whether an enterprise survives or shutters its doors.

Under normal conditions, business investment is mostly financed by internal cash flow (in accounting terms, depreciation and retained earnings). But the ability to raise external financing spells the difference between stagnation and growth, entropy and innovation. Internal cash flows generally cannot meet the total capital needs of firms and projects, especially for those enterprises focused on future developments and expansion, not only on current operations.

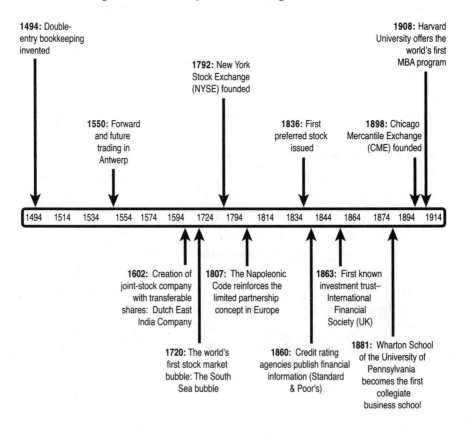

The ability of firms to access capital through the equity and corporate bond markets is critical to driving growth. That door slammed shut in the face of a financial hurricane in 2008. As the Great Recession descended, the tap ran dry and economic growth hit a wall.

Small businesses, a crucial engine of jobs and economic growth, were particularly hard hit by these events. A 2009 survey found that more than one-third of small business respondents were unable to get the financing they needed to run their operations. A similar number reported worsening terms for lines of credit and credit cards.[1]

Uncertainty, the enemy of capital markets, always increases during economic crises. Suppliers become reluctant to ship materials to any enterprise struggling under a heavy debt load; many demand cash on delivery because they fear becoming a long-term creditor of a

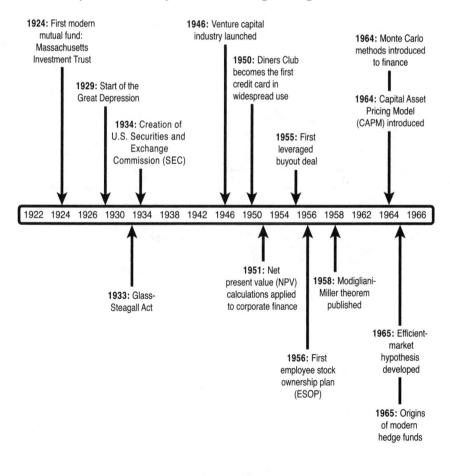

company whose debt is selling at a deep discount. Formerly routine credit transactions become increasingly unavailable, even to solvent firms, because suppliers worry that their bills might not be paid.

But necessity remains the mother of invention. Just as the painful recession of the 1970s gave rise to a great wave of innovation in designing capital structure, the same story will be written one day about the solutions devised to resolve today's extreme economic challenges. Many businesses caught in this perfect storm have managed to navigate through it by coming up with shrewd approaches to restructuring. Especially during periods of rising defaults, creative approaches to financing and refinancing can enable firms to survive, reorganize, and reinvent themselves to adapt to new market conditions. The innovations that emerge in this field today will be the

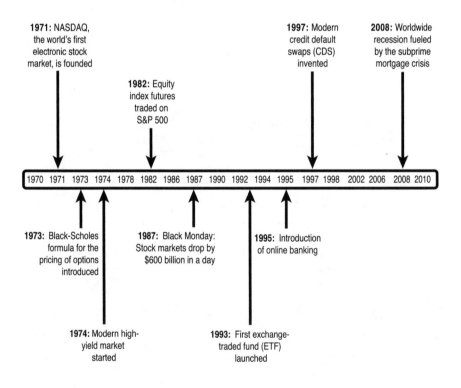

signposts that lead us out of the Great Recession and back to productive lending and real job growth.

Capital Structure Matters

Growth—those pioneering, building, or restructuring strategies that corporations employ to reinvent themselves, forge new markets, or even conjure up wholly new industries—occurs largely on the cutting edge of the total population of firms and projects. Small, risky, and rapidly growing firms tend to rely more heavily on stock issues and access to private and public capital markets. The innovations applied to devising new capital structures are critical in providing firms with the right mix of securities and financing resources they need to fund real investment and expansion.

Leverage in capital structure is inherently neither good nor bad. For some companies, debt is an important and effective part of their capital structures; other companies in volatile industries should avoid debt entirely. The key is finding an optimum and flexible ratio of debt and equity as market conditions change.

The demand for capital and the typical debt-equity ratio vary widely across industries. Oil companies, utilities, and the chemical, transportation, telecommunications, forest products, and real estate development industries all rely heavily on debt for external financing. Pharmaceutical companies tend to have negative debt ratios, with liquid assets (holdings of cash and marketable securities) exceeding their outstanding debt. Debt ratios are low when profitability, growth opportunities, and business risk are high.[2] Lower debt means firms have financial slack that allows them to take advantage of good investment opportunities or withstand any unexpected shocks.

In a perfect world (or, at least, that theoretical Neverland imagined by economists, where all things work without friction), gaps in capital structure would always be bridged. Firms would have access to capital based only on their business risk and not on the cost of available financing. That is not, however, how the capital markets currently work. In theory, capital should always flow to its most efficient and best use—yet it doesn't. In the economic models we build, we'd like to assume that capital markets would be competitive, frictionless, and complete. Alas, they are not. Ideally, the risk characteristics of every security issued by a firm could potentially be matched by purchase of another existing security or portfolio. But the pattern of financial crises and the reality of trading desks in a panic prove that things don't always play out that way.

The practice of finance strives to continually improve conditions to more closely resemble that ideal world of theory, striving to make it a reality in the rough-and-tumble, trial-and-error environment of the marketplace—a setting in which we learn as we go and sometimes even manage to tease out solutions by empowering firms, entrepreneurs, and innovators.

As entrepreneurs pursue their ideas and ambitions in hopes of seeing an eventual payday for their personal risk taking and sweat equity, financial capital comes in to coinvest, bringing with it similar expectations about the future. The process of creating capital structures that align the interests of owners and investors mobilizes the resources of the capital markets and sets creativity in motion.

As Bradford Cornell and Alan Shapiro have shown, innovations in business finance frequently center on selling off parts of a firm's cash flow pie in order to grow that pie. As a firm needs more money to grow, it sells off future cash flows generated by its current and future projects. It can do this through selling all rights directly through equity or, as we shall see, repackaging those cash flows into debt instruments, equity-participating debt instruments, or hybrid products that combine characteristics of both debt and equity. (The boundaries between those categories are increasingly blurring as the world of corporate capital structures grows ever more complex).[3] Innovations have emerged to match the needs of firms and investors, increase liquidity, reduce transaction costs, and overcome information asymmetries between those inside the firm and outside investors.

Corporate managers and investment managers now have a wide range of tools at their disposal as they go about the business of accessing capital.[4] This chapter does not delve into technical textbook definitions, nor does it attempt to provide a comprehensive catalog of all the strategies, formulas, and concepts that comprise this field. Instead, it traces how their increasingly sophisticated development and application has fueled more than two centuries of dramatic U.S. economic growth.

One crucial point merits reiterating: Like a road paver's jackhammer or a miner's pick, a financial tool is nothing more than an instrument for shaping other objects (in this case, the real economy). Some of these tools remain exotic instruments that are (or should be) used only by the most expert specialists. Others have become common features of the financial landscape. Just as it's not smart to try your hand at shaving with a lawnmower, it is critically important to choose the right financial tool, customize it to the situation at hand, and use it with care (see Table 3.1).

TABLE 3.1   Types of Innovations for Business and Corporate Finance

Products and Services	Processes and Operations	Organizational Forms
Contracts promising future delivery introduced (1200)	Double-entry bookkeeping invented (1494)	Earliest business school opened in Verona (1284)
First preferred stock issued (1836)	First Modigliani–Miller theorem published (1958)	New York Stock Exchange (NYSE) founded (1792)
Emergence of modern high-yield market (1974)	Capital Asset Pricing Model (CAPM) introduced (1964)	Napoleonic Code reinforces the limited partnership concept in Europe (1807)
Equity index futures traded on S&P 500 (1982)	Monte Carlo methods introduced to finance (1964)	Chicago Mercantile Exchange (CME) founded (1898)
Exchange-traded funds (ETFs) introduced (1989)	Efficient-market hypothesis developed (1965)	Origins of modern hedge funds (1965)
Modern credit default swaps (CDS) invented (1997)	Black–Scholes formula for options pricing introduced (1973)	NASDAQ, world's first electronic stock market, founded (1971)

The Birth of U.S. Corporate Finance: Enter Alexander Hamilton

Private corporate finance has public roots, reaching all the way back to the nation's infancy. When public buildings, roads, or other enterprises required funding, Americans generally refused to put up with new taxes (in a refrain that has been with us for centuries). On occasion, they would resort to borrowing long and short term; but more often, in the early days, the need for capital was satisfied by running lotteries. According to one study, 158 of them were held between 1744 and 1774. The Revolutionary War effort itself received support from lotteries, as did the construction of the nation's capital city and its first universities.[5]

At a time when capital was scarce, Alexander Hamilton, the first U.S. Secretary of the Treasury, had a notion that lotteries could be used to fund businesses. Given the economic climate of his day, it was not surprising that he considered lotteries the obvious and most efficient method of raising needed capital.[6] But in the long run, lotteries would not be enough.

As many historians have recounted, Hamilton's clashes with Thomas Jefferson were notoriously fierce. One of their biggest bones of contention was Hamilton's belief that government should take a more active role in the economy. When Hamilton took the Treasury's helm in 1789, the new nation was groaning under the weight of $54 million in debt inherited from the Confederation government. If credit ratings had been given in those days, the United States might have been BBB. Interest rates were high, the political situation was dicey, and capital was hard to come by for both continuing businesses and new ventures. Lenders were unwilling to assume risks, and borrowers were unwilling or unable to pay the high interest rates they demanded.

Hamilton's actions can still serve today as a template for nations in financial distress. He dismissed out of hand any suggestion of default or bankruptcy, insisting that America's reputation would never recover from such actions. Instead, he proposed a multipart program to establish the nation's credit, creating a climate that would give borrowers and lenders the confidence to exchange business debts.

Hamilton set to work restructuring the young nation's sovereign debt through a debt-for-debt exchange. He focused first on repaying some $11.7 million in foreign debt, a move he executed by issuing new certificates in place of the old, depreciated ones. Two-thirds of the newly issued bonds would pay 6% interest from the origination date of January 1, 1791 (at a time when similar European bonds paid between 4% and 5%). The other third would pay interest after 1800.[7] In modern parlance, the latter were zero coupons for the first nine years and sold at a discount to reflect this, sparing the government from the burden of making those interest payments during a shaky period.

Next came a recommendation that the federal government should assume state debts (to bind the states to the union). This proposal elicited howls of outrage from states that had no or little debt, while thrilling those states that relished the opportunity to have someone else pay their bills. This plan angered Hamilton's opponents, who organized to defeat the program.[8]

To advance his plans, the secretary recommended the creation of a Bank of the United States to serve as the government's depository and fiscal agent. The bank, through its branches, would provide a national currency in which borrowers and lenders alike could have confidence. The First Bank of the United States was founded in 1791 and lasted until 1811. The 1792 Mint Act established a bimetallic standard, ensuring that the government would pay its debts in legal tender instead of the dreaded paper money.

As expected, prices rose on Confederation and state bonds in late 1790, as it became clear that Hamilton's plan would win the day. In fact, bondholders were so sure of the success of the Hamilton program that, by January 1, 1791, those 6% certificates were selling at 20% above par, and interest rates declined down the line.

By creating the system of public credit, Hamilton was able to promote the public good by making investment safer and easier. This laid a foundation for the development of large-scale business finance. His bold moves constituted the first of many institutional breakthroughs in creatively financing U.S. economic expansion.[9]

The Nineteenth Century Ushers In Rapid Innovation

Hamilton's First Bank of the United States was followed by the Second Bank of the United States, which lasted from 1816 to 1836, and there was considerable distrust of the concentration of power these institutions represented. In a report on the Second Bank, John Quincy Adams wrote, "Power for good is power for evil, even in the hands of Omnipotence."[10]

The controversy came to a head in the debate on rechartering the Second Bank in 1832. Although Congress passed the bill, President Andrew Jackson successfully vetoed it. A strong bias toward decentralizing the banking system emerged, along with an aversion to powerful financial institutions of any kind. As a result, the U.S. banking system remained highly fragmented throughout the nineteenth century. Unlike every other industrializing country, the United States failed to develop nationwide banks with extensive branching networks. But this vacuum strengthened the role of financial markets and created a wide-open playing field for financial innovation.

In the last half of the nineteenth century, the New York market grew in prominence, due in part to bonds issued during the Civil War and the active trade in them during the following decades. This era witnessed a host of innovations, including the development of the market for commercial paper, which allowed corporations with a strong financial position to borrow short term in the markets more cheaply than they could borrow at a bank.[11]

As the nation emerged from Reconstruction, the Herculean task of building railways to span the sprawling North American continent offered another proving ground. The vast scale of the undertaking, the enormous capital it entailed, and the constant reorganizations of the railroad companies themselves came to define the great period of American development and innovation that we turn to in the following section.

As Peter Tufano has documented, many of the standard contract forms we still use today—preferred stock, convertible bonds, warrants, and bond covenants—were instruments developed and refined during this period of rapid technological invention and commercialization.[12] Preferred stock was used to raise capital for railroads between 1843 and 1850; it constituted 42% of the capitalization of trusts, mergers, and recapitalizations from 1890 to 1893, and 13% of the total value of securities issued between 1919 and 1927. Income bonds, a type of debt security in which only the face value of the bond is promised to the investor (with coupon payments occurring only with sufficient income earned), were advantageous for distressed railroads facing reorganization during the late nineteenth century. Convertible bonds and notes, devised in the late

1850s, accounted for 13% of bonds issued from 1914 to 1929.[13] This era saw major strides in the means and methods available for supplying capital.

J.P. Morgan and the Twin Transformations of Industry and Finance

The close of the nineteenth century saw the rise of financial capitalism. Investment banking became a powerful force in the American economy after the Civil War—and J.P. Morgan was the living, breathing symbol of this era.[14]

Born into a family of London bankers, Morgan made his first important splash in 1879, successfully selling 250,000 shares of New York Central stock for the Vanderbilt interests. This move demonstrated that Morgan had "placement power," meaning that he could distribute large amounts of securities without disturbing the market. This ability, earned by providing results for customers, was—and remains—the key to an investment banker's prowess.

During the next 15 years, Morgan's attention was focused on railroad reorganizations: working with the Northern Pacific, arranging a truce between the Pennsylvania and the New York Central, and restructuring the Baltimore & Ohio and the Chesapeake & Ohio. By the early 1890s, he had a hand in reviving the defunct Richmond & West Point Terminal Co., which he folded into the Southern Railway Co. and then into the Erie and the Philadelphia & Reading Railroad.

In the course of these projects, banks began to develop close relationships with clients. Indeed, the practice was known as "relationship banking." Bankers served on their clients' boards of directors and were kept on retainer for their advice on a wide variety of matters beyond financing.

By the early 1890s, the railroad system was mature, and its presence helped to create manufacturing companies that could operate nationwide. Railroads, telecommunications, and financial enterprises were once the only private firms using the capital markets to sell major bond issues, but now a handful of industrial companies began to approach the market. When they did, debt financing rather than stock issues prevailed, since the investing public remained skeptical about common stocks.

At first, these industrial companies did not seek out the services of investment banks. Companies hoping to raise funds through borrowing turned to "loan contractors," who arranged loans based on collateral. Some commercial banks would finance local enterprises, and occasionally a broker would canvass his investors to discover whether there was any interest in making loans. Several individuals, such as Charles Ranlett Flint and John W. "Bet a Million" Gates, were promoters who would go from one deal to another, bringing parties together and then presenting the results to an investment banker to arrange the financing. In any case, manufacturing operations in this period were modest affairs, usually owned and managed by their founders. Common stock offerings for industrial companies were rare.

By the early twentieth century, investment bankers had replaced promoters and loan contractors as the principal source of financing for industrial companies. In addition, they extended their influence throughout the economy, forming alliances with commercial banks and insurance companies. Into the Morgan orbit came First National Bank, Chase National, Banker's Trust, and Guaranty Trust.

The investment bankers' clients were governments and big business, and the resulting alliance dominated corporate America until the 1980s. In the course of his long and productive life, Morgan led the restructuring of many railroads and industrial corporations and even swooped in to help save government finances during the currency crisis of 1896, the railroad crisis in 1898, and the credit crunch of 1907. Yet he did little to provide small businesses and individuals with greater access to capital. As Alvin Toffler and Bradford DeLong have described, Morgan's organizational strategies and financial methods were geared toward large-scale industrial consolidation and concentration—in striking contrast to the financial innovations and corporate strategies that were to generated broader entrepreneurial capitalism during later periods.[15]

An Age of Creative Destruction

As the curtain fell on the nineteenth century and a new era dawned, advances in financing paved the way for the shift from steam power to electrification, from coal to oil, and from rail to auto. These shifts drove innovation and expansion, and built new fortunes. From 1880 to 1913, the gold standard spread, joint stock banks competed with merchant banks, and the world witnessed an explosion of new corporations and stock offerings. Futures markets in organized commodity and currency exchanges grew, and corporations tried on new organizational forms, including holding companies, trusts, and other corporate or trading entities.

Almost overnight, it seemed, finance made it possible for marvelous new inventions to hit the market: electric generators, dynamite, photographic film, light bulbs, electric motors, internal combustion engines, steam turbines, aluminum, prestressed concrete, and rubber tubing.[16] By the 1920s, the U.S. Patent and Trademark Office was granting record numbers of patents. This epoch of technological progress was marked by the emergence of major corporations built on these advances—and by a new realization that investing in intangibles could lead to very real returns.[17] The growth in the number of investors, along with the increased willingness to take risks for capital gains, drove financial innovation.

Innovation materializes at the nexus between finance and technology. From this intersection, Joseph Schumpeter constructed his complex but compelling theory of business cycles. The gales of "creative destruction," he observed, rendered old investors, ideas, technologies, skills, plants, and equipment obsolete in the continuous drive to improve productivity, efficiency, and standards of living. This period of history proved that human knowledge and creativity could be monetized through innovation and catalyzed by finance, leading Schumpeter to map out his ideas of dynamic entrepreneurial capitalism and cast aside the static equilibrium models that the economists of his day favored.[18]

Business failures also hastened the development and adoption of new securities. Between the Civil War and the Great Depression, the United States lurched through 20 recessions and 15 major bank panics and financial crises.[19] The reorganization of railroads and the improvisation of financing that often accompanied restructuring related to bankruptcies opened new avenues for innovations in business finance. As costs outstripped their original estimates in the building of railroads and industrial plants, preferred stocks enabled near-bankrupt firms to raise additional funds. Long-maturity bonds arose in the late nineteenth century and were used repeatedly for reorganizations through the Great Depression.

Another innovation at the beginning of the twentieth century came in the form of warrants. These were usually issued with bonds or stocks and essentially consisted of an option that allowed the holder to buy stock at a predetermined amount for a limited amount of time. They were first deployed when the American Power and Light Company issued 6% notes in 1911. They were sporadically used until 1925, when they enjoyed wide popularity for several years.[20] Warrants would reemerge as valuable tools in the 1960s, as we shall see later in this chapter.

Many decades later, during the credit crunch and business crises of the 1970s and 1980s, the financial innovations of this earlier period would resurface as useful building blocks. Expanding on these earlier advances, financiers found new ways to allow for balance sheet and operational restructuring. Firms came to enjoy flexibility in adapting their capital structures to market conditions: selling debt or equity, for example, or exchanging one for the other when market conditions were most receptive, without tax consequences, to strengthen their balance sheets. Having the opportunity to deleverage (that is, to reduce debt) was a fundamental reason why relatively few companies defaulted in the 1970s and 1980s. Many companies whose debt was considered extremely risky in the 1970s—such as Westinghouse, Tandy, Chrysler, and Teledyne—found ways to manage their capital structures and return to profitability. In the early 1980s, firms such as International Harvester, Allis-Chalmers, Mattel, and Occidental Petroleum were able to deleverage by issuing equity in exchange for debt. They were able to attract investors, maximize shareholder value, and often forestall bankruptcy, thus preserving jobs even as the economy stalled.

A. P. Giannini and the Democratization of Capital

Through the efforts of Morgan and others, a great number of financial innovations increased access to capital for larger enterprises. Corporate and industrial power was concentrated in these behemoths and centralized in Wall Street banks. But soon the doors were destined to swing wider.

The initial attempt to pry open capital access to the broader public began in commercial banking—and it was the brainchild of a man who seemed to be the polar opposite of the august J.P. Morgan. A continent away from Wall Street, Amademo Peter Giannini was born in California in 1870, the son of an Italian immigrant farmer.[21] Giannini attended school until the age of 14, when he joined his stepfather in the fruit and vegetable trade. There he gained the hands-on experience in small business that would shape his worldview.

In 1903, Giannini took over his deceased father-in-law's properties, including a minority interest in the Columbus Savings Association. Suddenly, the young vegetable merchant was a banker. In 1909, he formed the Bank of Italy—the institution that would later become Bank of America.

In those days, American banking was dominated by East Coast titans who catered to institutions, corporations, and the upper crust. These banks made loans to only the most creditworthy customers— and modest, immigrant-run enterprises need not apply.

From the first, Giannini focused on small depositors and borrowers, intending to open banking to the masses. His turning point came with the 1906 San Francisco earthquake and fire. When the larger banks had to close down in the aftermath of the disaster, he pitched his tent on a pier and made loans to distressed businessmen on the spot. The legend of A.P. Giannini was born.

Within a few years' time, he was opening branches in other parts of California, beginning with San Jose, all concentrating on the same small depositors and borrowers that had made the San Francisco bank so successful. Giannini made no secret of his ambition to go national (and even international); in 1928, he even changed the bank's name to Transamerica. The success of this upstart riled Wall

Street and Washington, but despite their efforts to cook up regulations to thwart him, Giannini's bank had become the largest in America by 1945.

Giannini's popularization of small business loans and home mortgages began to shape emerging public policies regarding capital access. His move to democratize commercial banking contributed to the explosive growth of California's agricultural economy and its real estate and entertainment industries (he even bankrolled the first Disney films).

Another revolution of access was also taking place around this time as the first form of mutual funds opened a new channel of capital for business finance. John Elliott Tappan was among the handful of financial innovators seeking higher yields for thrifty small savers. He devised a new method of mobilizing funds, selling face-amount certificates that could be purchased by ordinary folks paying monthly installments over several years. Paying a higher compound interest rate than was available from banks or other traditional financial intermediaries, Tappan founded Investors Syndicate. (Later called Investors Diversified Services, the firm would eventually be acquired by American Express, then spun off to become Ameriprise Financial.[22]) His instruments were backed by first mortgages and became a modern, liquid alternative to real estate or land for urban Americans who no longer earned their income from agriculture. His financial innovations informed the development of the life insurance industry, opened the market to small investors, and paved the way for the modern-day mutual fund industry.[23]

The 1950s: Rise of the Capital Markets and the Birth of Venture Capital

The first reliable census of stockholders took place in 1952, when a NYSE-sponsored study reported 6.5 million individual shareholders.[24] It was in this period that Charles Merrill became to stocks what Giannini was to deposits and business loans. By popularizing ownership of securities, he spawned continuous waves of financial innovation between World War II and the end of the twentieth century.

Merrill began his efforts before World War I but met no real success until after World War II. In those somnolent years, he revolutionized the brokerage community, convincing the broad middle class that investing in stocks was a sensible and even prudent move.

This was no easy task. The average Joe had not participated in the raging bull market of the 1920s but had plenty of all-too-vivid memories of the crash and the Great Depression. Most Americans simply had no interest in stocks—and lacking a broad base of investors, many fledgling companies couldn't hope to attract financing. The banks and bond markets both shunned start-ups. Bond buyers of this period were not inclined to gamble on young firms with great ideas but no proven track record. Most established investment banks were conservative through and through when it came to deciding where to put their clients' money. Institutional investors had no interest in pioneering broader ownership or more innovative financing. When Merrill commenced his campaign for "people's capitalism" after World War II, only 11% of the U.S. population owned equities. Within two decades, that number had risen to one in six Americans, including more than 30.9 million shareholders.[25]

Merrill got his start during a time when small new investment banks and regional firms began underwriting local issues of manufacturers in emerging industries. With the demise of the Consolidated Exchange in the 1920s, the New York Stock Exchange had taken center stage. However, the Curb Exchange (later rechristened the American Stock Exchange in 1953) gained greater respectability, especially as a secondary market for issues of innovative companies. More than 30 organized exchanges arose outside of New York City in major cities; significant over-the-counter (OTC) markets took hold as well. New sources of reliable business information became available. Class-A common stock—a post–World War I innovation—achieved new popularity in the mid-1950s, offering investors noncumulative participating dividends without voting rights. Securities design for such Class-A common stock incorporated and required new information about company performance and cash flows into new contracts and monitoring of firm performance.[26]

Until common stock offerings became more viable in the 1950s, the only course of action for young companies and potential startups came from the earliest forms of private equity and venture capital.

Two seminal figures in the development of these markets were George Doriot, a former general affiliated with Harvard Business School, and MIT president Karl Comptom, who effectively launched the venture capital industry in 1946 with the founding of American Research and Development (ARD), a publicly traded closed-end fund marketed mostly to individuals.

Doriot had a nose for sniffing out the most promising entrepreneurs, and he found two in Kenneth Olson and Harlan Anderson, who wanted to start a firm to manufacture small computers. They had no money, no credit, and, apparently, no hopes when they incorporated Digital Equipment. But Doriot was willing to help out. In 1956, he offered to invest $70,000 in the company in return for a 60% stock interest; Olson and Anderson eagerly accepted.

By 1958, the first venture capital limited partnership was formed: Draper, Gaither, and Anderson. Start-ups soon had another option, too, in risk-capital pools federally guaranteed under the Small Business Investment Companies (SBIC) program. Soon growth equity and leveraged buyouts were scaling up, trying to overcome the fundamental problems of business finance: illiquidity, uncertainty, and information gaps, and the macroeconomic cyclicality of business formation.[27] They were able to do so by incorporating reporting that was required by active investors; these included close monitoring of operations, active board involvement, and intervention to protect both minority shareholder and creditor interests. As *Sputnik* galvanized interest in government commitments to new technology, firm financings began anew.[28]

Initial public offerings (IPOs) became another important tool for new and old businesses alike to access the capital markets. In 1956, Ford went public by selling 10 million shares to raise $658 million.[29] IPO activity picked up briskly after that and became a full-fledged fad by 1960.

At first, most offerings were made by old-line investment banks that wouldn't touch a company with less than a five-year record of successful operations. These banks had reputations to safeguard and weren't about to trade them for quick one-time profits. Then, as the mania gathered steam, marginal underwriters sprouted to peddle low-grade merchandise.[30] They were more salesmen than bankers, small-timers who operated on shoestrings and weren't in business for the long haul. Their operations were legitimate enough but were laced with dubious practices (a common enough occurrence when worthwhile movements hit the mania stage). The later absorption of IPOs into white-shoe investment banking would not happen until the high-tech boom that began in the 1980s.

The IPO craze fell out of favor as a bull market ground to a halt in 1968–1969. Once more it became difficult for start-ups to obtain financing. But this time the situation was mitigated by the continuing growth of venture capital. By the 1970s, VC had become firmly established as a crucial source of funding for up-and-coming firms in new industries.

From Recession to a Revolution in Corporate Finance

During the 1950s and 1960s, when inflation was low, interest rates were stable, and the United States faced little international competition, financial planning was not a top concern for corporate managers. Financing, for many companies, involved little more than balancing the corporate checkbook.

This was, however, an unusually fruitful period for high-level theoretical thinking that laid the groundwork for further financial innovation. In 1958, professors Franco Modigliani and Merton Miller (both of whom would later win Nobel prizes) published a groundbreaking article titled "The Cost of Capital, Corporation Finance, and the Theory of Investment." The Modigliani–Miller (or M&M) theorem posits that, under perfect market conditions, the value of a firm is independent of its capital structure. This theorem launched a new way of thinking about capital structure, and a generation later, researchers are still analyzing how real-world frictions impact the theorem's idealized assumptions.

The early 1960s also saw the introduction of the Capital Asset Pricing Model (CAPM), a formula for pricing securities based on the expected rate of return plus a risk premium, and Monte Carlo methods for valuing complex instruments by shifting uncertain variables in simulated outcomes and averaging the results. These conceptual breakthroughs (along with the 1973 Black–Scholes option pricing model, which paved the way for an explosion of activity in new derivative markets) were explained in greater detail in Chapter 2, "A Framework for Financial Innovation: Managing Capital Structure." Their appearance greatly broadened the possibilities and technical sophistication of corporate finance.

Moving beyond the realm of theory, the pace of real-world financial innovation quickened sharply in the 1970s, born out of a bitter recession in which interest rate spikes and skyrocketing energy prices followed hard on the heels of a stock market collapse.

Many firms needed to restructure themselves in order to survive; others were eager to commercialize exciting new technologies despite the tough environment. As the downturn took hold in 1974, banks curtailed lending to all but the largest and highest-rated companies, while the most innovative firms—those with the highest returns on capital and the fastest rates of growth—were shut out. This pent-up need for capital provided the impetus for another leap forward in the field of corporate finance.

Building on the research of W. Braddock Hickman and others, who discovered that below-investment-grade debt earned a higher risk-adjusted rate of return than investment-grade bonds, financier Michael Milken realized that premium high-yield bonds more than compensated investors for the added risk of default.[31] He soon built a vast market for high-yield debt that provided innovative companies with the ability to finance growth and the flexibility they needed to manage their capital structures in changing times.

High-yield debt (known pejoratively as "junk bonds") was not an entirely new concept, but the market for it had shriveled up for most of the twentieth century. Before the 1970s, virtually all new publicly issued bonds were investment grade—and only the debt of large ultra-blue-chip companies fell into this category. Until this time, the only publicly traded junk bonds were issues that had once been investment grade but had become "fallen angels," undergoing downgrades as the issuing company fell into financial distress. The interest payments on these bonds were not high, but with the bonds selling at pennies on the dollar, their yields were tempting. Companies deemed speculative grade were effectively shut out of the capital market and forced to rely on more expensive and restrictive bank loans and private placements (which involve selling bonds directly to investors such as insurance companies).

Milken realized that the debt market for fallen angels and troubled securities could have a wider purpose: It could be utilized to create securities for up-and-coming companies that simply needed access to capital. After all, tens of thousands of publicly traded firms (in fact, 95% of the publicly traded companies with more than $35 million in revenues) were not being served by the corporate bond market.[32]

The "junk bond revolution" began in 1977, when Bear Stearns underwrote the first new-issue junk bond in decades and Drexel Burnham Lambert developed new-issue high-yield bonds for seven companies once shunned by the corporate bond market. Companies could now issue bonds that were below investment grade from their inception.

Because high-yield bonds are deemed to be riskier than other types of debt, they typically promise higher yields than investment-grade bonds. It began to dawn on investors that junk bonds could actually outperform investment-grade bonds over time, and they flocked to this new market. From 1979 to 1989, the high-yield debt market grew almost 20-fold, to almost $200 billion.[33] Junk bonds financed the successful restructuring of numerous manufacturing firms, including Chrysler.[34] The subsequent use of these instruments as a component in hostile takeovers eventually produced a strong backlash, but the primary function of the high-yield market was providing capital for corporate growth, expansion, and survival.[35]

Financial instruments had traditionally been lumped into categories based on whether they related to debt or equity, but in recent decades those distinctions have blurred. Changes in the corporate bond market and the growth of structured finance in fixed-income asset classes enabled greater flexibility in managing corporate capital structures, and a wide array of products emerged to help corporations lower the cost of capital and account for various types of risk.

Bond-warrant units offer a prime example. Corporations could exchange these hybrid securities (combining equity and debt components) for the assets of companies they were seeking to acquire. This type of instrument was first used in the 1960s in deals such as Loews

Theatres' acquisition of cigarette manufacturer Lorillard; the transaction involved Loews exchanging $400 million in 15-year, 6.875% bonds and 6.5 million warrants.[36] Almost $1.5 billion of these types of transactions were completed in the late 1960s and early 1970s.[37]

Recession gave way to recovery in the early 1980s, but stock prices, though rising, were still considerably below replacement costs. Companies were hesitant to embark on new common stock offerings that might dilute the holdings of existing shareholders. Interest rates were declining but remained historically high, making the prospect of long-term borrowing equally unappealing.[38] Bond-warrant units proved to be a good tool for resolving this dilemma. They made the dilution of ownership more palatable because they were exercisable above the current market price; they substantially reduced borrowing costs while allowing companies longer time horizons for repayment.

Dozens of non-investment-grade companies had opted to issue bond-warrant units by 1983; cumulatively, they raised almost $3 billion through this avenue.[39] Golden Nugget sold $250 million in these instruments to expand operations in 1983; three years later, MGM sold $400 million in 10% bond-warrant units to refinance the bank debt used in its acquisition of United Artists.[40]

MCI stands out as one of the largest such offerings in this time period. Its management had been consumed with the never-ending task of raising short-term capital to build an ambitious long-distance network; however, in 1983, the company issued $1 billion in 10-year bond-warrant units with a coupon of 9.5%, substantially less than what U.S. Treasuries were yielding at the time. Now the company had the capital—and the freedom—to focus on creating a cutting-edge fiber-optic telephone network even though the profits it would generate remained further down the road.[41]

As with MCI, other growth-oriented companies needed to finance the buildout of new technology infrastructure. They needed the right capital structure to survive and thrive until that investment could pay off. Zero-coupon, payment-in-kind (PIK), and split-coupon securities emerged as additional financial tools for the task. These debt securities are sold below face value because they promise no periodic cash interest payments. Instead, the interest is internally calculated based on time to maturity and credit quality. The buyer of such a bond receives the rate of return by the gradual appreciation of the security, which is redeemed at face value on the maturity date. In the case of a PIK, the issuer is given the option to make interest payments in additional securities or in cash, providing flexibility in regulating cash needs for the enterprise.

In April 1981, J.C. Penney made a public issue of zero-coupon bonds.[42] This offering, along with a tax benefit that existed at the time, boosted the popularity of these instruments. Although the tax loophole was quickly closed when firms started taking advantage of it on a large scale, the market for zero coupons nevertheless continued as investors found their payment characteristics desirable because of a lack of reinvestment risk. Investment banks initially stripped government securities to satisfy this demand, but eventually the Treasury stepped in and took over this role.[43]

Firms such as McCaw Cellular, Turner Broadcasting, and Viacom International were burning through current cash flow to expand their cellular telephone networks, cable television programming, and cable television systems, respectively—so they turned to the high-yield market to finance growth. In 1988, McCaw issued $250 million in 20-year discounted convertible debentures paying no cash interest for 5 years, freeing up cash flow for expansion. (The firm later merged with AT&T in 1994.) Turner Broadcasting issued $440 million in zero-coupon notes that deferred interest payments until maturity. Viacom issued $370 million in PIK securities, with the flexibility to pay interest in additional securities rather than cash.[44] Time-Warner, News Corporation, and other firms used similar financing strategies to transform the way we use media, communications, and information technology.

Commodity-linked securities also came into vogue during this time period. In 1980, Sunshine Mining issued the first silver-backed, commodity-indexed bonds in 100 years.[45] By linking these securities to the price of silver, Sunshine could pay about half the interest rate of a straight debt issue (about 3% less than what U.S. Treasuries were paying at the time). Investors shared in the profits when the price of silver rose—and this paid off handsomely at various points. Meantime, Sunshine lowered its cost of long-term capital.

All of these innovations in corporate high-yield debt instruments involved some form of risk reallocation. Zero-coupon bonds enable interest to be effectively reinvested and compounded over the life of the debt issue. Interest-rate risks can be managed through adjustable-rate notes and floating-rate notes, while commodity-linked bonds address price and exchange-rate risks. Securities can be structured to reduce the volatility of cash flow to the extent if interest or principal payments are associated with changes in a company's revenues; the debt-service burden is shifted from times when the firm is least able to pay, to times when it is most able to pay. Currency risk can similarly be managed through tools like dual-currency bonds, indexed currency option notes, principal exchange rate linked securities (PERLS), and reverse principal exchange rate linked securities (reverse PERLS).

The advent of information-processing technology (such as credit scoring) and asset-pricing models (such as CAPM, which enables analysis of asset prices based on risk and rates of return of a particular financial asset compared to the overall stock market) gave rise to products that could enhance liquidity. An infinite variety of features attached to bonds and notes reduced agency costs, transaction costs, taxes, and regulatory bottlenecks. This remarkable surge of creativity in the high-yield debt market ultimately spawned additional ideas for preferred stock, convertible debt, and equity innovations.[46]

The Rise of Private Equity and the Decade of the Leveraged Buyout

Private equity came into its own in the 1980s. George Fenn, Nellie Liang, and Stephen Prowse argue that this was due to the widespread adoption of the limited partnership as the means of organizing the private equity partnership. Thanks to this organizational innovation, private equity, once the province of wealthy families and industrial corporations, was now dominated by professional managers acting as general partners (largely on behalf of institutional investors who provide finance as limited partners). This partnership form relied on high-powered incentives to overcome extreme informational asymmetries and incentive problems. Between 1980 and 1995, funds invested in the organized private equity market grew from $4.7 billion to more than $175 billion.[47]

Private equity firms employ a wide range of strategies. Though perhaps best known as a force behind leveraged buyouts (discussed later in this section), they also invest in anything from distressed debt to real estate. Perhaps most important, venture capital (VC) is a subset of private equity. Fenn, Liang, and Prowse argue that the growth in private equity has enabled more funds to flow, both to classic start-up companies and to established private companies.[48] Between 1980 and 1995, venture capital outstanding grew from $3 billion to $45 billion. VC financed the rise of many of America's most innovative firms, including Genentech, Microsoft, Oracle, Intel, and Sun. It is fair to say that venture capital played a crucial role in making the United States a leader in high-tech industries, particularly biotechnology and computers.[49]

Nonventure private equity also increased substantially during the 1980s, when blockbuster leveraged buyouts (LBOs) dominated the business headlines, culminating with the $31 billion takeover of Nabisco by Kohlberg Kravis Roberts (KKR). In this type of acquisition, the financial sponsor or a private equity firm uses a significant amount of debt to purchase the target company, sometimes using the target company's assets as collateral. LBOs, management buyouts, and employee buyouts can, at their best, produce corporate makeovers that result in greater efficiency and competitive advantage.[50] Although LBOs boomed during the 1980s, severe competition at the end of the decade reduced the profitability of deals as funds were forced to pay more for firms. This led to a fall in the number of LBOs for several years.

The rise of the LBO sparked another set of innovations regarding corporate governance.[51] In response to the increasing number of hostile bids that occurred during this period, a number of antitakeover techniques were developed. Initially, these involved charter amendments, such as supermajority voting provisions that might require, for example, that 80% of shareholders approve a merger. Another example is staggered terms for board members, which can delay transfer of effective control for a number of years.

An important characteristic of charter amendments is that shareholder approval is required. In 1982, an alternative anti-takeover defense was developed to protect the El Paso Company from a raid: the issuance of what came to be known as poison pill securities. There are a number of variations on these, including preferred stock plans, flip-over plans, and back-end plans.

Preferred stock plans were the exclusive tool of choice for fending off takeovers until 1984. With these, the potential target issues a dividend of convertible preferred stock to its shareholders, granting them certain rights if an acquiring party purchases a large position (30% in one plan) in the firm; the board of directors can choose to waive these rights. The preferred stockholders can require the outside party to redeem the preferred stock at the highest price paid for common or preferred stock in the past year. If a merger occurs, the acquiring firm must exchange the preferred stock for equivalent securities that it must issue. These preferred stock plans made it more difficult for raiders to acquire firms by removing an incentive for shareholders to bid early on, because they can always be sure of obtaining the highest price paid.

Crown Zellerbach used the first flip-over plan as a poison pill in July 1984. The first step in executing this strategy is the issue of a common stock dividend consisting of a special form of "right." This gives the holder the right to purchase common stock at an exercise price well above its current market price. It can be exercised starting 10 days after an outside party obtains or bids for a substantial amount (such as 20%) of the target firm's stock for up to 10 years. Ordinarily, nobody would want to exercise these rights because the exercise price is well above any likely market price. However, if a merger occurs, they "flip over" and allow the holder to buy shares in the merged firm at a substantial discount. This makes hostile mergers extremely costly, but friendly mergers are still possible because a company can repurchase the rights for a nominal fee unless they have been triggered.

The back-end plan was also introduced in 1984. When acquiring a target, firms often made a "two-tier bid": They initially paid a high price for a majority of shares and then used their voting power to force a merger at a lower price, so the remaining shareholders did worse than those who initially tendered. This structure provides an incentive for shareholders to tender. Back-end plans are similar to flip-over plans, except the rights issued put a minimum on the amount acquirers must pay in the second part of a two-tier offer.

Consolidation of Innovation in the 1990s and 2000s

After the rapid advances of the 1970s and 1980s, financial innovation for corporations shifted into lower gear. The last two decades have produced incremental rather than revolutionary advances in business finance.[52] Many of the new instruments were structured products issued by financial institutions instead of new securities to raise funds for corporations. (For example, structured equity products are medium-term notes that have payments based on an individual company's stock price, a stock index, or multiple indices.) During this period, most of the truly exciting innovation was concentrated in the fields of housing finance and environmental finance (these topics are discussed in subsequent chapters).

There were, however, some noteworthy developments in business finance. One of the most important was the expansion of credit-scoring techniques from consumer loans to small business loans. Credit scoring involves assigning a single quantitative measure to borrowers, indicating their creditworthiness. Originally, it was thought that commercial loans were too heterogeneous to use credit scores, but it turned out that the personal credit history of small business owners was very useful in predicting repayment performance for loans less than $100,000. The adoption of this methodology has significantly changed the way small businesses finance themselves.[53]

Another important (and soon-to-be-notorious) innovation was the credit default swap (CDS). These instruments allow investors to buy protection, or insurance, against default. In exchange for a regular premium, they provide a payment if a corporation defaults on its bonds. However, credit default swaps are not restricted to corporate debt. They can also be purchased on government debt and other types of debt (including mortgage-backed securities) issued by a variety of institutions. JPMorgan Chase invented credit default swaps in the mid-1990s; the first arrangement involved selling the credit risk of Exxon to the European Bank of Reconstruction and Development.[54]

The "spread" of a CDS is the annual amount of protection the buyer must pay the seller over the life of the contract or until a default occurs. It is expressed as a percentage of the notional amount of protection. A 1% spread on a notional amount of protection of $100 million of a corporation's bonds would imply a payment of $1 million a year from the buyer to the seller. In the event of a default by the corporation the credit default swap was written on, the seller would pay the buyer $100 million, minus the value of the bonds at the time the payment is made.

The great advantage of credit default swaps is that they allow credit risk to be hedged. For example, the holders of the bonds of a corporation or companies doing business with the corporation could insure against their default. Unfortunately, CDS also provided a tempting vehicle for speculation. The CDS market quickly ballooned, and by the end of 2007, the total notional amount of CDS contracts outstanding was $62 trillion.[55]

During the financial crisis that erupted in 2008, credit default swaps came under severe criticism for magnifying systemic risk. One of the major sellers of CDS was the insurance company AIG. When its capital was impaired by a fall in the value of the mortgage-backed securities it held, the company was downgraded. Its CDS contracts required the company to post a substantial amount of collateral when this happened, which it was unable to do. Rather than allowing AIG to default, the government intervened and took it over. In the end, the federal bailout enabled AIG to pay out $105 billion in counter-party payments.[56] This move elicited howls of protest, but the government felt compelled to act in order to contain the systemic risk entailed by a potential AIG default, which might have sparked a chain of further defaults among other holders of AIG CDS. The danger of a meltdown of the entire financial system seemed too great.

Going forward, the future of the CDS market is unclear. At the end of the first half of 2009, the total notional amount outstanding had been halved to $31 trillion.[57] However, apart from the AIG fiasco, credit default swaps worked reasonably well. The CDS written on Lehman Brothers were settled smoothly when it defaulted—and the same was true for 11 other credit events that triggered payments on CDS.[58]

Before the financial crisis, the CDS market had been essentially unregulated as a result of the Commodity Futures Modernization Act of 2000. This will undoubtedly change. There have been many calls for CDS to be traded on an exchange instead of in the over-the-counter market, to improve the transparency of counterparty risk. The market is likely to survive in some form but will probably not see a return to its 2007 peak for some time to come.

The media has frequently singled out credit default swaps as culprits in the financial crisis—but they are simply products, not to be confused with the individuals who misused them. It is a simple fact that new financial products will sometimes fail. At the very least, they present a learning curve and may require serious refinement. But many critics have taken things further, arguing that the way to prevent crisis is to turn back the clock. In our view, we can't allow this way of thinking to win the day. Sustained long-term growth requires continuous financial innovation so that small and big businesses alike can obtain the funds they need and grow and prosper.

Conclusions

In the last few decades, corporate finance has added new layers of complexity. And yet, for all of the sophisticated computer models and mathematical formulas that have been thrown at the task, devising the best way to finance an individual firm remains something of an art. As Michael Milken, one of the innovators profiled in this chapter, once said:

> *There is no optimum capital structure—X percent equity and Y percent debt—that can be applied to different organizations, or to the same corporation at different points of time. Just as you can't make real money by putting a dollar bill on a copying machine, you can't successfully copy the financing technique that once worked for a particular company and transfer it to another time or another company .... [F]inance is a continuum with infinite variations and hybrids. It takes deep understanding of a company, its environment, and the financing tools available to build sustainable growth that will reward shareholders and create jobs.*[59]

Finding the right variables to suit the situation can make all the difference in transforming an innovative start-up into an iconic company. That kind of undertaking equates to more than just a profitable investment. It builds lasting value.

The story of America's economic expansion is inextricably bound to the advances made in business financing. It is a chronicle of empowering entrepreneurs, launching new industries, and bringing breakthrough technologies to market. Innovative financing strategies have made it possible for companies to meet a host of challenges, from building railways that would span a continent to creating a revolutionary system of commerce in cyberspace.

It's possible to get lost in the complexity of this field. Business finance is a moving target, constantly evolving to keep up with new markets, new needs, and changing conditions. But today, as we try to shake off the stagnation of the Great Recession, it all boils down to a simple goal: enabling companies large and small to create jobs for a return to prosperity.

Endnotes

[1]National Small Business Association, "2009 Mid-Year Economic Report": 6.

[2]Stewart C. Myers, "Capital Structure," *Journal of Economic Perspectives* 15, no. 2 (Spring 2001): 81–102.

[3]Bradford Cornell and Alan C. Shapiro, "Financing Corporate Growth," in *The Revolution in Corporate Finance, 4th ed.*, J. M. Stern and D. H. Chew, Jr., eds. (London: Blackwell Publishing Ltd., 2003): 260–277.

[4]Much of the discussion in this chapter is based on Glenn Yago and Susanne Trimbath's *Beyond Junk Bonds* (New York: Oxford University Press, 2003). See also James R. Barth, Daniel E. Nolle, Hilton L. Root, and Glenn Yago, "Choosing the Right Financial System for Growth," Milken Institute Policy Brief 8 (February 2000).

[5]Charles T. Clotfelter and Philip J. Cook, *Selling Hope: State Lotteries in America* (Cambridge: Harvard University Press, 1989); and Robert Sobel, *The Money Manias: The Eras of Great Speculation in America, 1770–1970* (New York: Beard Books, 2000).

[6]Much of the discussion regarding Hamilton is drawn from Ron Chernow's *Alexander Hamilton* (New York: Penguin Press, 2004). See also Robert E. Wright, *The First Wall Street: Chestnut St., Philadelphia and the Birth of American Finance* (Chicago: University of Chicago Press, 2005); and Robert E. Wright and David J. Cowen, *Financial Founding Fathers: The Men Who Made America Rich* (Chicago: University of Chicago Press, 2006).

[7]Theodore M. Barnhill, William F. Maxwell, and Mark Shenkman (eds.), *High-Yield Bonds* (New York: John Wiley & Sons, 1999); and Stuart C. Gilson, *Corporate Restructuring: Case Studies* (Cambridge, MA: Harvard Business School Press, 2000).

[8]Glenn Yago, *Junk Bonds* (New York: Oxford University Press, 1993).

[9]Michael D. Bordo and Carlos A Vegh, "What If Alexander Hamilton Had Been Argentinean? A Comparison of the Early Monetary Experiences of Argentina and the United States" (working paper no. 6862, National Bureau of Economic Research, December 1998).

[10]Richard H. Timberlake, *The Origins of Central Banking in the United States* (Cambridge, MA: Harvard University Press, 1978).

[11]H. G. Guthmann and H. Dougall, *Corporate Financial Policy*, 4th ed. (Englewood Cliffs, NJ: Prentice Hall, 1962): 465–466.

[12]Peter Tufano, *Three Essays on Financial Innovation*, Ph.D. dissertation, Harvard University (1989).

[13]*Ibid.*

[14]This discussion is derived from Robert Sobel, *The Pursuit of Wealth: The Incredible Story of Money Throughout the Ages* (New York: McGraw Hill, 2000); Ron Cherow, *The House of Morgan: An American Banking Dynasty and the Rise of Modern Finance* (New York: Atlantic Monthly Press, 1990); and Jerry W. Markham, *A Financial History of the United States* (Armonk, NY: M. E. Sharpe, 2002).

[15]J. Bradford DeLong, "Did J.P. Morgan's Men Add Value? An Economist's Perspective on Financial Capitalism," in *Inside the Business Enterprise*, Peter Temin, ed. (Chicago: University of Chicago Press, 1991); and Alvin Toffler, *Power Shift* (New York: Bantam, 1990).

[16]Larry Neal and Lance E. Davis, "Why Did Finance Capitalism and the Second Industrial Revolution Arise in the 1890s?" in *Financing Innovation in the United States: 1870 to the Present*, Naomi Lamoreaux, Kenneth Sokoloff, and William Janeway, eds. (Cambridge: MIT Press, 2007).

[17]Tom Nicholas, "Why Schumpeter Was Right: Innovation, Market Power, and Creative Destruction in 1920s America," *Journal of Economic History* 63 (2003): 1023–1057. See also Tom Nicholas, "Stock Market Swings and the Value of Innovation, 1908–1929," in *Financing Innovation in the United States, 1870 to Present*, Naomi Lamoreaux, Kenneth Sokoloff, and William Janeway, eds. (Cambridge: MIT Press, 2007).

[18]Thomas K. McCraw, *Prophet of Innovation: Joseph Schumpeter and Creative Destruction* (Cambridge, MA: Harvard University Press, 2007).

[19]G. W. Schwert, "Business Cycles, Financial Crises, and Stock Volatility,"(working Paper no. 2957, National Board of Economic Research [NBER], March 1990).

[20]Arthur Stone Dewing, *A Study of Corporation Securities* (New York: Ronald Press, 1934).

[21]This discussion is largely based on Felice Bonadio's *A. P. Giannini: Banker of America* (Berkeley: University of California Press, 1994).

[22]Ameriprise Financial, "Key Facts & Milestones," www.ameriprise.com/about-ameriprise-financial/company-information/key-facts.asp.

[23]Ken Lipartito, *Investing for Middle America: John Elliott Tappan and the Origins of American Express Financial Advisors* (New York: St. Martins Press, 2001).

[24]Robert Sobel, *Dangerous Dreamer: Financial Innovators from Charles Merrill to Michael Milken* (New York: John Wiley & Sons, 1993).

[25]*Ibid.*

[26]Tufano, *Three Essays on Financial Innovation*, Ph.D. dissertation, Harvard University (1989).

[27]Josh Lerner, Felda Hardymon, and Ann Leamon, *Venture Capital and Private Equity: A Casebook* (New York: John Wiley & Sons, 2009).

[28]Mary O'Sullivan, "Finance and Innovation," in *The Oxford Handbook of Innovation*, eds. J. Fagerberg, D. Mowery, and R. Nelson (New York: Oxford University Press, 2004).

[29]Douglas Brinkley, *Wheels for the World: Henry Ford, His Company, and a Century of Progress* (New York: Harper Collins, 2003). See also T. Loughran and J.R. Ritter, "Why Don't Issuers Get Upset About Leaving Money on the Table in IPOs?," *Review of Financial Studies* 33, no. 6 (2002): 401–419.

[30]This discussion is based upon the elaboration of market revival in the 1960s by Sobel, *The Pursuit of Wealth* (see endnote 14).

[31]W. Braddock Hickman, *Corporate Bond Quality and Investor Experience* (Princeton: Princeton University Press, 1958).

[32]*Ibid.* Yago (1993).

[33]Sean Monsarrat, "Economist, Defying Conventional Views, Calls Junk Bonds Corporate Scapegoat," *The Bond Buyer* (28 September 1990). See also data from the Salomon Center, NYU's Stern School of Business, as published in Edward Altman, "Are Historically Based Default and Recovery Models in the High-Yield and Distressed-Debt Markets Still Relevant in Today's Credit Environment?," *Bank i Kredyt* no. 3 (2007) (available at SSRN, http://ssrn.com/abstract=1011689).

[34]Thomson Reuters, SDC database.

[35]Edward Altman and Scott Nammacher, *Investing in Junk Bonds: Inside the High-Yield Debt Market* (New York: John Wiley & Sons, 1987).

[36]*Moody's Industrial Manual*, 1970 ed. (New York: Moody's Investor Services, 1970).

[37]*Ibid.* Yago and Trimbath (2003).

[38]Phil Molyneux and Nidal Shamroukh, "Diffusion of Financial Innovations: The Case of Junk Bonds and Note Issuance," *Journal of Money, Credit, and Banking* (August 1996): 502–526.

[39]*Ibid.* Yago and Trimbath (2003).

[40]"Briefs: Debt Issues," *New York Times* (15 April 1983 and 1 July 1983).

[41]James L. Rowe, Jr., "MCI Offer Doubled to $1 Billion; Notes Are Placed Before Scheduled Sale on Monday," *Washington Post* (2 August 1983).

[42]"Zero-Coupon Issue Is Sold by Penney," *New York Times* (22 April 1981).

[43]Franklin Allen and Douglas Gale, *Financial Innovation and Risk Sharing* (Cambridge, MA: MIT Press, 1994).

[44]Thomson Reuters, SDC database.

[45]"Sunshine Mining Sets First Offer Backed by Precious Metals Since the Late 1800s," *Wall Street Journal* (5 February 1980).

[46]John Finnerty, "An Overview of Corporate Securities Innovation," *Journal of Applied Corporate Finance* 4, no. 4 (1992): 23–39; and Stephen A. Ross, "Institutional Markets, Financial Marketing, and Financial Innovation," *Journal of Finance* 44, no. 3 (1989): 541–556.

[47]George W. Fenn, Nellie Liang, and Stephen Prowse, "The Private Equity Market: An Overview," *Financial Markets Institutions and Instruments* 6, no. 4 (July 1997): 1–105.

[48]George W. Fenn, Nellie Lang, and Stephen Prowse, "The Economics of the Private Equity Market," *Federal Reserve Bulletin* (January 1996).

[49]Andrew Metrick, *Venture Capital and the Finance of Innovation* (Hoboken, NJ: John Wiley & Sons, 2007).

[50]Glenn Yago, Mike Bates, Wendy Huang, and Robert Noah, "Tale of Two Decades: Corporate Control in the '80s and '90s," Milken Institute Research Report 21 (November 2000). See also Zoltan Acs, Randall Morck, and Bernard Yeung, "Productivity Growth and Firm Size Distribution," Milken Institute Research Report (June 1996).

[51]The discussion of leveraged buyouts and poison pill provisions draws on Franklin Allen and Douglas Gale's *Financial Innovation and Risk Sharing* (Cambridge, MA: MIT Press, 1994).

[52]Enrique Schroth. "Innovation, Differentiation, and the Choice of an Underwriter: Evidence from Equity-Linked Securities," *Review of Financial Studies* 19, no. 3 (2006): 1041–1080.

[53]Jalal Akhavein, W. Scott Frame, and Lawrence J. White, "The Diffusion of Financial Innovations: An Examination of the Adoption of Small Business Credit Scoring by Large Banking Organizations," *Journal of Business* 78, no. 2 (2005): 577–596.

[54]John Lanchester, "Outsmarted: High Finance vs. Human Nature," *The New Yorker* (1 June 2009). Available at www.newyorker.com/arts/critics/books/2009/06/01/090601crbo_books_lanchester.

[55]International Swaps and Derivatives Association (ISDA), Market Survey (2007).

[56]Lex column, "AIG's Billions," *Financial Times* (FT.com) (16 March 2009). Available at www.ft.com/cms/s/2/a2b7095a-1237-11de-b816-0000779fd2ac.html.

[57]ISDA Market Survey (2009).

[58]Colin Barr, "The Truth about Credit Default Swaps," *CNN/Fortune* (16 March 2009). Available at http://money.cnn.com/2009/03/16/markets/cds.bear.fortune/index.htm; accessed November 10, 2009.

[59]Michael Milken, "The Corporate Financing Cube," *Milken Institute Review* (Fourth Quarter 2002).

4

Innovations in Housing Finance

Homeownership rates in the United States reached an all-time high during the first six years of the twenty-first century, reaching across lines of class, ethnicity, and race. During the boom, American home buyers were offered a dizzying array of mortgage products, many with novel features: fixed or floating interest rates, rate lock-ins, rate resets, new choices of term and amortization, interest-only options, prepayment penalties, and easily dispensed home equity loans.

But, as we learned all too painfully, any victory laps for the financial and social policy achievements represented by wider homeownership were destined to be short-lived, as many new mortgage products failed with severe consequences. Overcomplexity and dangerous levels of leverage eventually swamped housing finance markets—and mortgage credit, as it turned out, was the canary in the coal mine signaling the broader financial crisis that was soon to follow.

An ocean of ink has since been spilled as analysts and pundits have weighed in on why our regulatory system consistently fails to detect and rein in asset bubbles. Now that our financial architecture has proven to be inadequate in today's brave new world of intricate global connections, it is clear that we need a new wave of financial and policy innovation to prevent a repeat of recent history.

Gimme Shelter: The History of Innovation in U.S. Housing Finance

As demographic and social shifts have generated an ever-greater demand for housing, financial innovations have evolved to keep pace. The advances that expanded homeownership (and access to housing more generally) have been a lynchpin of greater economic and social mobility in industrializing economies. If the past offers any template for the future, it is not unreasonable to hope that new innovations emerging from the current financial crisis will restore and sustain historical trends of homeownership as a critical, but not unique, part of income and wealth creation.

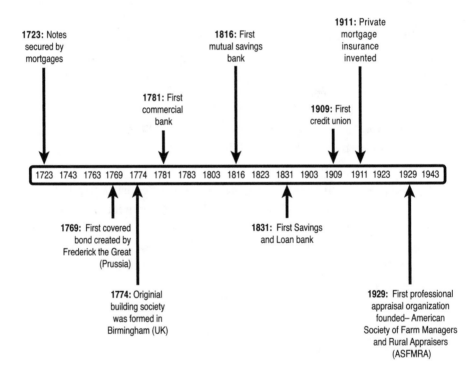

The ideal of homeownership is entwined with the democratization of capital and our ideals of economic and social mobility. Being an owner has always been part of the American Dream. In the United States, ever since passage of the Land Ordinance of 1785 and the Land Act of 1796, the government had provided assistance to settlers in the form of low-priced land.[1] Other legislation followed, such as the Preemption Act of 1841, which permitted would-be settlers to stake claims on most surveyed lands and purchase up to 160 acres for a minimum price of $1.25 per acre.

The Homestead Movement, which advocated parceling out land in the Midwest, the Great Plains, and the West to settlers willing to cultivate it, was consistent with Jeffersonian ideals; it was geared

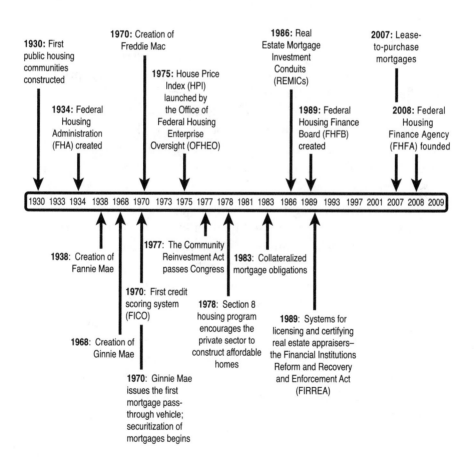

toward opening opportunities for would-be farmers in an age when this occupation was still considered the norm.[2] Critical to this process was lending through mortgages. (These instruments had actually been in use since the twelfth century, when mortgages—literally, "dead pledges"—emerged as agreements to forfeit something of value if a debt was not repaid. Either the property was forfeited, or "dead," to the borrower if he defaulted, or the pledge became "dead" to the lender if the loan was repaid.[3])

In 1862, President Lincoln signed into law the Homestead Act. Under its terms, any citizen or person intending to become a citizen who headed a family and was over the age of 21 could receive 160 acres of land, eventually obtaining clear title to it after five years and payment of a registration fee. As an alternative, the land could be obtained for payment of $1.60 an acre after six months.

Lincoln had a strong ethical vision uniting capital ownership and labor productivity; his policies aimed to create, as Eric Foner writes, free soil, free labor, and free men. Lincoln spoke of "the prudent, penniless beginning in the world, who labors for wages for a while, saves a surplus with which to buy tools or land for himself ... and at length hired another new beginning to help him. This just and generous and prosperous system ... opens the way to all."[4] Enabling wider access to capital was a theme that echoed throughout many of Lincoln's economic policies.

From homesteading to homeownership was a quick development, accompanied by the rise of urban industrial centers and the need to finance the communities within them. The origins of home finance grew out of two early-nineteenth-century institutional innovations: mutual savings banks and building and loan societies. Mutual savings banks were owned by their depositors rather than by stockholders; any profits belonged to the depositors, whose savings typically were invested in safe vehicles, such as early municipal bonds. Building and loan associations, by contrast, were explicitly created to promote homeownership. Building societies were corporations, with members as shareholders who were required to make systematic contributions of capital that were then loaned back for home construction.[5]

Meeting the Growing Demand for Housing Finance

Aspirations for homeownership that emerged in the nineteenth-century immigrant working classes eventually became an integral part of the American Dream. Over time, owning a home came to represent both physical and financial shelter. By the twentieth century, owning a home was a clear symbol of middle-class status, a goal that lower-income households strove for in order to supplement their incomes and economic security.[6] The structural shift in demand that typically sparks financial innovations appears in the housing market in the form of the early twentieth century's urbanization and rapid population growth.

The demand for capital rose steadily due to these long-term trends but occasionally spiked in the wake of critical events like Chicago's Great Fire of 1871 or the San Francisco earthquake of 1906. Both of these episodes sparked new regulatory oversight of homebuilding and new innovation in commercial banking practices to boost housing market expansion.

After the San Francisco earthquake, A.P. Giannini, founder of the Bank of America (originally the Bank of Italy), reinvented commercial banking to support new customers entering agricultural, business, and housing markets—customers who had been rebuffed by the typical lending practices of the day. Giannini was determined to democratize commercial banking. From the first, he focused on small depositors and borrowers, opening banking to the masses. He advertised for depositors and made certain that local businessmen knew that the Bank of Italy was prepared to offer them its services in personal and business loans, as well as innovations in home mortgages.[7] (For more on Giannini, see Chapter 3, page 65.)

The development of the modern mortgage industry, mortgage guarantee insurance, and homeownership as a policy goal was a natural extension of the spirit of the nineteenth-century Homestead Movement. But prior to Giannini and then the New Deal guarantee system, mortgage financing was limited in scope, with terms that seem unrecognizable and prohibitive today: high down payments, variable interest rates, and short maturities (five to ten years), with "bullet" payments of the full remaining principal due all at once when the mortgage's term expired.[8]

TABLE 4.1   Types of Innovations in Housing Finance

Products and Services	Processes and Operations	Organizational Forms
First covered bond created by Frederick the Great (Prussia, 1769)	First professional appraisal organization founded (1929)	Original Building Society formed in Birmingham, England (1774)
Private mortgage insurance invented (1911)	First credit scoring system invented (FICO; 1970)	First savings and loans bank founded (1831)
Ginnie Mae issued the first mortgage pass-through vehicle (securitization; 1970)	House Price Index (HPI) launched by the Office of Federal Housing Enterprise Oversight (1975)	First credit union founded (1909)
Collateralized mortgage obligations introduced (1983)	Systems for licensing and certifying real estate appraisers created under the Financial Institutions Reform and Recovery and Enforcement Act (1989)	Federal Housing Administration (FHA) established (1934)
Lease-to-purchase mortgages introduced (2007)	Automated underwriting of mortgages begins (1990)	Fannie Mae created (1938)

Despite these financial constraints, homeownership grew from 10 million units in 1890 to 30 million units in 1930, especially during the boom of the 1920s. However, the financial capacity of the market was limited, as reflected in the high interest rates on loans—rates that were indicative of lending institutions' relative lack of ability to hedge the interest rate risk and default risk associated with mortgages. Volatility (price fluctuations) and the absence of a nationwide capital market for housing (in which risks could be dispersed over a greater number of investors) produced high costs for home buyers and contributed to cyclical ups and downs. As existing residential real estate markets became saturated, the inability to finance new construction constrained growth.[9]

At the close of World War I, the "Own Your Own Home" movement was launched to reward returning veterans by helping them finance their homes. By 1932, Herbert Hoover oversaw the creation of the Federal Home Loan Banking System to reorganize the thrift industry and establish a credit reserve model based on the Federal Reserve.

In President Franklin Roosevelt's first year in office, the housing market—like the rest of the economy—was in a downward spiral, with home mortgage defaults in urban areas around 50%. Many insufficiently capitalized private mortgage insurance companies failed during the Depression years. Sweeping government interventions were necessary to restore confidence and draw private investors back into the market. Since the federal government was not in the business of holding long-term mortgages, it created institutional responses to make the mortgage market function.[10]

The Roosevelt administration embarked on a major overhaul. Initially, the government offered federal charters to the existing private savings and loan associations and gave them the mission of providing funds for mortgage loans. It also insured their deposits, creating the Federal Deposit Insurance Corporation (FDIC) to stabilize the banking industry and encouraging savers to place their funds in mortgage lending institutions. Mortgage insurance programs were instituted to reduce the risk faced by lenders. This era saw the establishment of the Home Owner's Loan Corporation (later supplanted by Fannie Mae), the Federal Housing Administration (FHA), and the Federal National Mortgage Association (FNMA) to increase the supply of mortgage credit and reduce regional disparities in credit access. These moves, together with federal income tax provisions allowing homeowners to deduct mortgage interest and property tax payments, contributed to a sharp rise in homeownership—from 48% to 63% of all households between 1930 and 1970.[11]

The system of mortgage finance that resulted was characterized by long-term, fixed-rate, self-amortizing loans (provided mainly by savings and loan associations and mutual savings banks out of funds in their short-term deposit accounts). This was indeed the first mortgage revolution.[12]

Social policy and financial objectives converged to spur further innovation in the decades that followed. As millions of servicemen streamed home after World War II, they unleashed a vast pent-up demand for housing. Soon the Baby Boom was under way, and the great American migration to the suburbs commenced. The need for housing finance soon outstripped the capacity of depository institutions or the government. Gradually, capital market solutions began to emerge, including new innovations to enhance the liquidity of lenders. Fannie Mae was transformed into a private shareholder-owned corporation in 1968, and two years later, Freddie Mac was founded. Together these government-sponsored enterprises (complemented by Ginnie Mae, which remained within the federal government) vastly increased the liquidity, uniformity, and stability of the secondary market for mortgages in the United States. The traditional reliance upon thrifts and commercial banks as sources of mortgage credit changed; funding became increasingly available through securities backed by mortgages and traded in the secondary market.

The Savings and Loan (S&L) Crisis

One of the key pieces of regulatory residue left over from the Great Depression was the ability of the government to impose deposit rate ceilings on lending institutions. This rule, Regulation Q, remained in effect until it was finally phased out in the early 1980s. It eventually caused banks and thrifts to experience "disintermediation," or sudden withdrawals of funds by depositors when short-term money market rates available elsewhere rose above the maximum rate those institutions were allowed to pay on deposits.

S&Ls (also known as thrifts) were therefore locked into using short-term deposits to fund long-term mortgages, a mismatch that plagued the industry through a series of later financial crises. Without alternative funding sources, a loss of deposits could restrict credit access to new home buyers. Thrifts were restricted from matching what the market was paying through new savings vehicles (such as mutual funds, Treasuries, or money market accounts).

By the 1960s, the ability of depository institutions to fund long-term, fixed-rate mortgages was compromised by inflation, which pushed up nominal interest rates and eroded the balance sheets of those institutions. The maturity mismatch problem came to a head during the late 1970s and 1980s, culminating in the liquidity crises and insolvencies that became collectively known as the savings and loan crisis.

The crisis came about due to poorly designed deposit insurance, faulty supervision, and restrictions on investments to hedge the interest rate and credit risks faced during this period. The sharp rise in interest rates in the late 1970s (caused by the appreciation of the dollar against other currencies) caused a twist in the term structure of interest rates (the yield curve) that generated losses. From 1979 to 1983, unanticipated double-digit inflation coupled with dollar depreciation led to negative real interest rates. As financial institutions extended their lending base and their capital ratios worsened, conditions weakened in the industry. Monetary policy tightened, short-term rates soared, loans were squeezed, and a crisis was underway.[13] Regulatory restrictions on S&Ls amplified the crisis, and hundreds of institutions went under, at a distressingly high cost to U.S. taxpayers.

Securitization Changes the Face of Housing Finance

The S&L crisis crystallized a major structural challenge in U.S. mortgage markets. The danger inherent in funding short-term liabilities with long-term assets in markets with interest rate volatility became a lesson well learned.

Historically, lenders had used an "originate to hold" model for home mortgages: Institutions originated loans based on careful due diligence and then serviced and held the loans in their portfolios. But starting in the 1970s, securitization (an "originate to distribute" model) took hold. Under this new model, lenders packaged pools of loans into securities that were sold in the secondary market. Upon getting the loans off their balance sheets, lenders gained liquidity and were able to make additional loans at lower cost to consumers.

In 1970, Ginnie Mae issued the first mortgage pass-through security (granting investors an interest in a pool of mortgages and "passing through" the regular payments of principal and interest, providing a flow of fixed income). By the 1980s, Freddie Mac had introduced collateralized mortgage obligations (CMOs), which separate the payments for a pooled set of mortgages into "strips" with varying maturities and credit risks; these could be sold to institutional investors with specific time horizons in their investment needs and different risk preferences. It became common for firms to slice the risk associated with this type of investment vehicle into different classes, or tranches: senior tranches, mezzanine tranches, and equity tranches, each with a corresponding credit rating. Investors in these different tranches absorb losses in reverse order of seniority; because equity tranches carry a higher risk of default, they offer higher coupons in return.

Local and international institutional investors purchased these mortgage-backed securities (MBS), introducing new and broader sources of funding into the housing market. From 1980 to Q3 2008, the share of home mortgages that were securitized increased dramatically (see Figure 4.1).

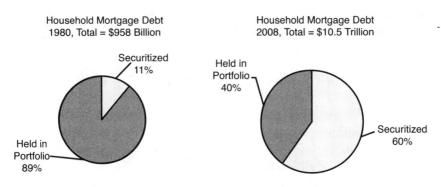

Figure 4.1   The mortgage model switches from originate-to-hold to originate-to-distribute.

Sources: Federal Reserve, Milken Institute.

The rise of securitization made mortgage credit and homeownership available to millions of Americans. Securitization, combined with deep and liquid derivatives markets, eased the spread and trading of risk.[14]

The momentum created by securitization truly caught fire when new information technology was introduced in the 1990s, vastly improving the ability of mortgage issuers to gather and process information.[15] The costs of loan origination were drastically reduced, with greater accessibility of data on credit quality and the value of collateral. Today lenders share information with credit bureaus, title companies, appraisers and insurers, servicers, and others. It has been estimated that the mortgage industry increased its labor productivity about two and a half times with the proliferation of data processing and Internet services.[16]

Despite the power of the information technology that has been introduced into mortgage markets, it's worth remembering that old adage "garbage in, garbage out." These new tools are powerful, but their ultimate effectiveness is totally dependent on the accuracy and quality of the data inputs. During the housing boom, many lenders used information technology solely to increase volume, neglecting its capacity to help them more carefully sift through risk factors.

Notwithstanding the current mortgage crisis, the innovations of securitization and financial policy made mortgages cheaper and more accessible while fueling the broader housing markets.[17] With fewer institutional and regulatory barriers to operation, the mortgage market became more efficient. Yet a critical ingredient was missing: the proper alignment of incentives. This would prove to be a fatal Achilles' heel, since originators had nothing to gain by maintaining high underwriting standards on loans that were immediately sold into structured finance products in the capital markets. Harmonizing the interests of borrowers, originators, lenders, and investors is an issue that urgently needs to be addressed by future financial innovations in this market.

The Current Housing Crisis: What Happened and Why?

From the initial rumblings in the subprime market to the government's unprecedented bailout programs, the turmoil in the U.S. financial sector sent shockwaves throughout the global economy beginning in 2007. Federal and state governments continue to struggle with appropriate legislative and regulatory responses. As of these writing, financial institutions, corporations, and individual households are still engaged in a massive wave of deleveraging. The capital markets are sorting out competing financing models—and the U.S. housing market remains in need of serious repair.

The genesis of the housing bubble emerged from the ashes of the dot-com bust. To alleviate the downturn, the Federal Reserve drastically reduced interest rates, and the era of easy credit was under way. Other nations with massive foreign reserves were drawn to invest in the United States, and, with Treasuries offering only meager returns, they began to eye mortgage-backed securities as a "safe" vehicle offering higher yields. The appetite for these securities proved to be insatiable, and the mortgage market was soon awash with liquidity.[18]

With mortgages so cheap and painless to obtain, homeownership reached a record high of 69.2% in mid-2004 (see Figure 4.2). Housing prices rose in accordance, posting sizable gains across the country—including huge double-digit year-over-year increases in frenzied markets such as Las Vegas, Los Angeles, Phoenix, and Miami. Real estate began to look like a surefire investment, open to almost everyone. But this game of musical chairs could continue only as long as home prices continued to climb and refinancing channels were open.

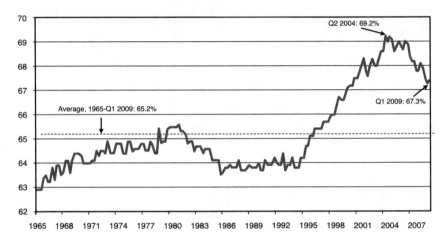

Figure 4.2   Credit boom pushes homeownership rate to historic high

Sources: U.S. Census Bureau, Milken Institute.

Thirty-year fixed-rate loans were once the only game in town, but less traditional home mortgage products started to appear in greater numbers in the early 2000s, with new variations on interest rate structures and amortization and payment schedules. Hybrid mortgages offered fixed rates for a short period of time, then reset periodically over the remaining term of the mortgage. These products have perfectly legitimate uses under the right circumstances, but they were too often handed out inappropriately, especially to consumers who—in a classic example of information asymmetry—didn't fully understand the terms.

As the originate-to-distribute model took hold, lenders no longer had to retain all the functions associated with a mortgage. Not only could these institutions sell off the loan, but they could contract with outside originators and loan servicers. Soon there emerged a new class of originators who earned fees without retaining any credit risk. Between 1987 and 2006, mortgage brokers' share of originations grew from 20% to 58%.[19]

With no ongoing responsibility for risk, originators had little economic incentive to ensure that borrowers were particularly creditworthy. As a result, subprime borrowers with shakier credit histories or inadequate income were able to obtain mortgages with little or no down payment—and that lack of equity eventually pushed them underwater when prices declined, increasing their incentive to default. This freewheeling environment saw the proliferation of complex mortgage products that embedded ever-higher levels of borrower, lender, and market risk. Subprime mortgage originations grew almost fourfold between 2001 and 2005, and total outstanding subprime mortgages increased at an average of 14% annually between 1995 and 2006.[20]

As described earlier, securitization did successfully increase liquidity and lower the cost of capital in the home mortgage market for decades. But during the boom, increasingly intricate and opaque securitized products appeared on the market, while the underlying valuation, credit analysis, and transparency of the underlying mortgages deteriorated. These complex securities were purchased by all manner of international and institutional investors, spreading the risk widely throughout the system.

Given the ready liquidity and the huge demand for mortgages triggered by historically low interest rates and rising home prices, lenders relaxed underwriting standards even further. Novel types of loans were not confined to the subprime market; some products offered to higher-end borrowers in the prime and near-prime markets carried such flawed incentives that they, too, would also eventually exhibit higher delinquency rates. Interest-only loans and loans requiring little or no down payment or income verification became commonplace.

Many buyers were attracted by the low initial monthly payments offered by adjustable-rate mortgages (ARMs), and lenders loved these products, too, since they shifted interest rate risk to borrowers. The largest share of ARMs went to subprime borrowers (as seen in

Figure 4.3). Many borrowers and lenders operated under the assumption that housing prices would continue to rise indefinitely. Don't worry about rate resets and your ability to afford higher monthly payments down the road, the thinking went—as long as home prices kept rising, magically creating more equity, borrowers would always have time to refinance before the interest rate on their ARMs jumped.

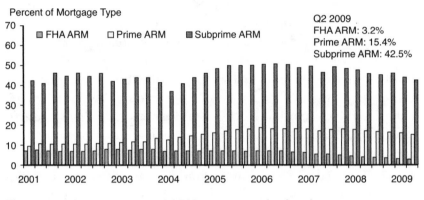

Figure 4.3   Largest share of ARMs goes to subprime borrowers

Sources: Mortgage Bankers Association, Milken Institute

The vast majority of subprime loans (almost 68% in 2007[21]) were securitized, which means that a huge share of this credit risk was passing through the capital markets to investors. Complex and highly leveraged mortgage-backed products were developed to meet demand: collateralized debt obligations (CDOs), CDOs of CDOs, and even CDOs of CDOs of CDOs. The convoluted structures of these securities, and the investors' lack of familiarity with the original loans, limited their ability to evaluate risk. Instead, they relied heavily on rating agencies to evaluate the quality of the underlying loans.

But an inherent conflict marred the rating process, in that agencies received fees from the very issuers they rated—yet another instance of misaligned incentives. Rating agencies relied on and applied historically low mortgage default rates to hand out AAA ratings to many questionable securities. The sterling ratings were illusory, of course. Too many of the underlying loans were held by highly leveraged borrowers who were operating on the false assumption that home prices would continue to rise forever. As we look to repair the system going forward, it is crucial to revamp the role and the compensation structure of the rating agencies.

Congress, too, bears some culpability. Beginning in 1992, it pushed Fannie Mae and Freddie Mac to increase their focus on affordable housing. While the goal of expanding homeownership was undertaken with good intentions, it ultimately led to unintended consequences as these two government-sponsored enterprises (GSEs) took on riskier portfolios. These two firms did not make loans directly, but they injected greater liquidity into a lending sector that was already becoming overheated. Even when problems became apparent, Congress and HUD regulators failed to rein in Fannie and Freddie until it was too late; both went into conservatorship in the fall of 2008, at a vast cost to taxpayers. Many observers have attributed this lapse in oversight to the fact that Fannie and Freddie spent millions on lobbying and campaign contributions over the years.

For anyone who was willing to look at historical patterns, it was plain to see that a serious housing bubble had formed. The ratios of median home prices to median household income and to rents had become seriously distorted—a fact that should have sounded a clear alarm bell to market participants and regulators alike. The increase in housing prices during the bubble years was simply too extraordinary to be sustainable (see Figure 4.4).

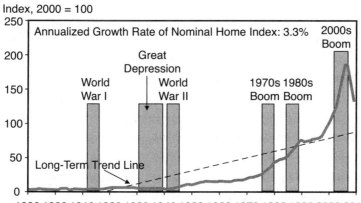

Figure 4.4   The recent run-up of home prices was extraordinary

Sources: Shiller (2002), Milken Institute

Some observers *did* correctly observe that a dangerous bubble had formed. In 2005, Paul Krugman warned that "the U.S. economy has become deeply dependent on the bubble."[22] That same year, *The Economist* estimated that the total value of residential property in developed economies had risen by more than $30 trillion in just five years to over $70 trillion—an increase equivalent to 100% of those countries' combined GDPs. This supercharged growth not only dwarfed any previous house-price boom, but it exceeded the U.S. stock market bubble of the late 1920s (which grew to 55% of GDP). As *The Economist* called it, "it looks like the biggest bubble in history."[23] Economist Nouriel Roubini earned the nickname "Dr. Doom" for correctly predicting the crisis that was brewing. Hedge fund manager John Paulson took home $3.7 billion in 2007 compensation by, as *The New York Times* put it, "betting against certain mortgages and complex financial products that held them."[24] But surprisingly few on Wall Street shared Paulson's prescience or his willingness to short subprime securities, betting on a decline in the price of these assets. Although it is easy to dismiss it today, the prevailing notion that home prices would not fall was persuasive to many people. Huge asset bubbles tend to encourage optimistic groupthink. Future efforts to contain systemic risk must take this behavior into account.

The collapse in home prices began in 2005 and accelerated dramatically by mid-2007. Forty-six states posted price declines in the fourth quarter of 2007.[25] Delinquencies and foreclosures were skyrocketing, while new sales began to plummet. Many homeowners, especially those who bought late in the boom when prices were high, found themselves underwater. Other borrowers with ARMs had little or no equity in their homes and were unable to refinance when their payments reset.

Just as homeowners carried record levels of debt, financial firms were operating with unprecedented levels of leverage (see Figure 4.5). With too little capital supporting risky loans, neither homeowners nor institutions could absorb sudden, substantial losses.

As it turned out, mortgage-backed securities were just the tip of the iceberg. In fact, trillions of dollars were at stake in the form of insurance coverage and the complex derivatives known as credit default swaps (CDSs) that were based on these securities. (CDSs are contracts that allow investors to hedge against defaults on debt

December 2008

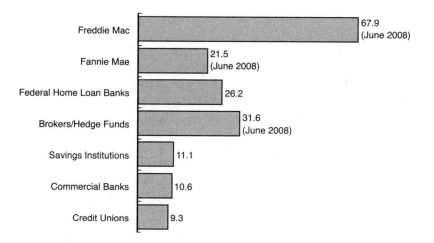

Figure 4.5   Leverage ratios of different types of financial firms.

(Note: All ratios are as of December 2008 unless otherwise noted in parentheses.)

Sources: FDIC, OFHEO, National Credit Union Administration, Bloomberg, Google Finance, and Milken Institute

payments.) Some financial firms even traded massive swaps on mortgage-backed securities in which they had no underlying stake at all. Because these trades were made over-the-counter and not through a central exchange, investors' fears were exacerbated. Uncertainty and a loss of public confidence are the greatest enemies of any well-functioning financial market.[26]

Studies have shown that around 40% of the approximately $1.4 trillion of total exposure to subprime mortgages issued over the period 2005–2007 was held by U.S. commercial banks, securities firms, and hedge funds.[27] Contrary to the conventional wisdom that prevailed during the bubble, overly complex, opaque securitization didn't manage to disperse risk—in fact, tremendous risk was concentrated on the highly leveraged balance sheets of financial institutions and intermediaries. As the financial crisis took hold, lending effectively ground to a halt as liquidity dried up and firms hoarded cash. The fallout seeped into the general economy as credit spreads widened, provoking widespread fear and massive government interventions. The very nature of the new global economy caused ripple effects to travel far and wide, regardless of whether countries had great advances in financial innovation (as in the United States) or relatively lower levels of financial innovation (like Japan, Germany, France, Spain, or Italy).

The core macroeconomic trends that drove the crisis had been underway for quite some time. Massive asset bubbles, first in tech stocks and then in housing, formed in the context of a major decline in the U.S. savings rate. The monetary policies of central banks, particularly the Federal Reserve, were too loose for a long period of time, focusing on the danger of consumer price inflation while ignoring the problem of asset price inflation. And for a number of years, investors and consumers alike made bad decisions based on faulty asset prices derived from the bubble.

We believe that loose monetary policy, combined with the ready availability of funds because of global imbalances, inflated the bubble in property prices, which we consider to be the most important cause of the crisis. It was the bursting of this bubble that precipitated the problems with mortgage-backed securities.

Another important factor to recognize is the existence of the government safety net and the prospect of government bailouts for many financial institutions, which created moral hazard. This encouraged risk-taking by banks and institutions such as Fannie Mae and Freddie Mac. In particular, they were willing to take on large amounts of leverage, which magnified their losses and made these institutions much more vulnerable in a downturn. With the exception of Lehman Brothers, the financial firms were indeed correct in their belief that the government would bail them out when they got into trouble. In the wake of such extraordinary government intervention, moral hazard of this type is likely to be an even more important problem as we move forward. Financial innovators urgently need to address this issue in order to diminish the systemic risk caused by excessive risk-taking.

To what extent did the recent crisis result from the failure of financial innovation? Some pundits were quick to claim that was the case, but in fact, it came about because so many individuals and institutions cast aside the fundamental principles that must be in place for innovations to succeed.

New financial products always create learning curves for issuers, consumers, and investors. Mitigating this problem requires special emphasis on designing the right incentives, requiring all parties to have "skin in the game," and increasing transparency—all factors that were neglected during the housing bubble.

The recent crisis in the housing market was a wrenching turn of events, but in the big picture, financial markets are laboratories that are constantly undergoing renewal—and they will eventually recover and adjust.

Avoiding the Mistakes of the Past

It's said that those who do not understand history are doomed to repeat it. In order for capital to flow again, we must identify solutions that resolve past mistakes. We should avoid the following pitfalls:

- **The misperception that asset prices will always continue to rise and the false sense of security built on that belief.** During the dot-com boom, investors were swept up in a mania, buying stocks of companies with no proven track record as they chased an entire sector on a wild ride upward. The resulting correction was exponentially more painful because the frenzy had become so widespread.

  The same events played out just a few years later in the housing market. As long as prices rose, the originate-to-distribute model seemed to convey little risk. Borrowers thought they could always refinance and capitalize on their increased equity. Investors in mortgage-backed securities relied on rating agency evaluations of the loan pools—but rating agencies didn't account for the possibility of a price correction in their models and assumed the number of defaults in any pool would be small due to diversification.

  But what goes up *can* go down. Regulators and the financial sector alike must take a clear-eyed view of the sustainability factors behind rising markets and break the cycle of tunnel vision that seems to take hold when asset bubbles are forming. The lure of the profits to be made when there is a huge demand for a product is a powerful thing, but an unrealistic comfort with risk can be dangerous for the stability of the financial system.

- **A lack of transparency in mortgages and in securitized pools.** As home prices skyrocketed, many consumers took out second mortgages, often without informing the first lien holder. At a Milken Institute Financial Innovations Lab held in October 2008, Tom Deutsch of the American Securitization Forum provided some startling statistics on 2006 residential mortgage-backed securities. While expected performance of loans within a securitized pool may have been based on a traditional 80% loan-to-value (LTV) ratio, the *combined* LTV (CLTV) was often closer to 90%. In the subprime market, the first lien LTV averaged 88%, and only 55% of loans had full documentation. In many cases, the full CLTV could not be determined, as the second liens were "silent seconds." The vast majority of these mortgages were packaged into CDOs with less collateral than recorded.[28]

  Once the loans were securitized, investors had no way of knowing the true composition of the pool. To their and the market's detriment, they did not pursue trying to uncover this information, but relied too heavily on the opinions of rating agencies. When delinquencies and defaults began to climb, the lack of transparency became even more problematic. Borrowers looking for loan modifications often had a hard time discovering exactly with whom they should be negotiating. Murky pools of assets could not be sold, and banks lost confidence in each other's balance sheets. This asymmetric information about counterparty risk led to liquidity hoarding and a breakdown of the interbank credit market.

  Securitization has already proven it can work, but increased transparency will be key to rebooting the market.

- **Misaligned incentives.** During the housing boom, incentives became misaligned at several points, reducing the likelihood of positive outcomes. When risk is too easily passed along, it can snowball. When borrowers were not required to make substantial down payments, thus giving them an equity stake in a home from the very beginning, they tended to take on loans that were too large to handle. Mortgage brokers were paid fees for originating a greater volume of loans, not for originating *appropriate* loans to creditworthy borrowers. Lenders simply sold off loans in the secondary market without retaining an interest, thus losing all incentive to apply more prudent underwriting standards. Securitization pools were rated by agencies that were paid by the very institutions that issued the securities in question, leaving them inclined to simply please their clients by issuing favorable grades. Clearly, the incentive structure needs to be revisited at every stage of the game. If every participant retains a slice of risk, it will discourage recklessness.

- **Ineffective regulation.** Regulators have been wholly inadequate in the face of major asset bubbles. Gaps and overlaps between U.S. regulatory agencies left the government with no consistent, strategic approach to addressing the emerging crisis.

  Moving forward, regulatory efforts should focus more intensely on containing systemic risk, strengthening capital requirements for banks, promoting greater transparency in the market, and modifying incentive structures to discourage excessive risk-taking. And regulators, like institutions, should be held accountable if they fail to perform their responsibilities. More effective enforcement of the regulations that were already on the books could have mitigated the crisis. The convoluted U.S. regulatory structure itself must be addressed if we have any hope of taking a more holistic, integrated approach to addressing asset bubbles and systemic risk.

- **The dysfunctional role of ratings agencies.** The government is making efforts to bring greater competition among rating agencies by designating other firms Nationally Recognized Statistical Rating Agencies. More generally, the government should avoid encouraging investors from relying excessively on ratings from such firms when making investment decisions.

Beyond the Crisis: Finding the Way Forward

There is nothing quite like a crisis to focus the financial innovation process. A major transformation of mortgage products and markets emerged out of the Great Depression. Similarly, the most recent systemic crisis (although it was an event of far smaller magnitude) is generating long-overdue debate about the role financial innovation can play in improving housing finance and preventing future market failures.

Many of these new ideas focus on capital market solutions: fixing what went wrong with the originate-to-distribute model and proposing ways to revive the securitization market. Others center on devising new ways to expand access to affordable housing in the current environment with lower risk.[29]

Capital Market Solutions

Rebooting securitization is the first step toward restoring the health of the mortgage market. It will require a return to fundamental analysis, due diligence, and sound underwriting, plus a new commitment to transparency and full disclosure about structured finance products. Additional data reporting is needed for disclosure on the vast number of loans in residential mortgage-back securities, including regular reporting of performance over time, full information on second liens, and loan comparisons. Requiring lenders to retain a certain share of each loan or even making provisions for possible repurchase obligations might also make structured finance more viable in the future.

Covered bonds, a financial innovation that dates back to eighteenth-century Prussia *(pfandbriefe)*, are widely used in Europe (in fact, they are one of the largest sectors of the European bond market), and they are gaining favor as a way to help resolve the current crisis in the United States. These securities are issued by banks and backed by a dedicated group of loans known as a "cover pool"; each country's laws outline the requirements for inclusion. If the issuing bank becomes insolvent, the assets in the cover pool are set aside for the benefit of the bondholders. Covered bonds closely resemble mortgage-backed securities, but the underlying loans remain on the balance sheet of the issuing bank. The bank therefore retains the control necessary to change the makeup of the loan pool to maintain its credit quality and to change the terms of the loans. MBS, on the other hand, are typically off-balance-sheet transactions in which lenders sell loans to special-purpose vehicles that issue bonds, thus removing the loans (and the risk) from the lender.[30]

Another idea that provides greater flexibility in managing mortgage risk hails from Denmark. In this model, when a lender issues a mortgage, it is obligated to sell an equivalent bond with a maturity and cash flow that exactly matches the underlying home loan.[31] The issuer of the mortgage bond remains responsible for all payments on the bond, and, in an interesting twist, the mortgage *holder* can buy back the bond in the market and use it to redeem their mortgage. When interest rates rise and home prices fall, borrowers are empowered to reduce the amount they owe as bond prices fall.

In the Danish model, the bond's terms match the interest rate and maturity of the loan. Bonds are collateralized with pools of identical mortgages: generally fully amortizing, fixed-rate, 30-year loans with recourse and issued with an 80% LTV ratio. The issuer keeps the mortgage on its books, and if the borrower fails to pay, it buys the mortgage out of the pool at the lower of par or market price. Originators retain the credit risk, leaving the investors to bear only interest-rate risk. This approach combines characteristics of both covered bonds and securitization. Like standard covered bonds, the Danish instruments keep credit risk with the loan originators. Similar to securitization, the system creates tradable instruments, facilitating liquidity.

All bonds are tradable and transparent; the price can be tracked daily. Borrowers can monitor movement and, if interest rates rise, can take advantage of the buyback option. This enables borrowers to repurchase their own loans, providing flexibility. If a mortgage's rate rises, the corresponding bond declines in value, allowing the borrower to purchase it at a reduced rate and gain equity in the home. Borrowers can then obtain a new, smaller mortgage with a higher coupon. This approach limits negative equity in periods of declining home values. The buyback option is exercised frequently: In the period 2001–2005, as yields fell from 6–7% to 4–5%, almost 100% of mortgages were prepaid and refinanced. It is interesting to note that while Denmark has been experiencing a downturn and falling home prices, it has not undergone the waves of defaults and foreclosures seen in the United States. During the global credit crisis, the country's mortgage banks continued to sell bonds and issue mortgages at virtually the same pace as before.[32]

Affordable Housing Solutions

The fact that we experienced specific mortgage product failures (such as negative amortization mortgages and ARMs that created perverse incentives to default) does not negate the overall social objective of making decent housing affordable to all.

Currently, homeownership in the United States is an all-or-nothing proposition: You can rent, with 0% ownership, or you are on the hook for 100% of the risk and reward. **Shared equity** is a concept that implies reduced assets in exchange for reduced liability. One approach attempts to balance wealth generation for individual owners with the goal of preserving affordable housing. Some form of subsidy, either a tax benefit or direct subsidy, reduces the price of the home in exchange for a share of appreciation. There may be limits on the resale of the property and/or the appreciation of housing values. An alternate approach is the private-sector shared equity model, in which investors provide a share of the housing cost in exchange for a portion of appreciation. Both approaches foster access to homeownership at reduced levels of debt, while lenders reduce their risk by maintaining a share of ownership.

Three models generally make up the shared equity or fractional equity approach: limited equity cooperatives, community land trusts, and deed-restricted housing. These and other products on the drawing board have the potential to mitigate the blight and disrepair left behind in so many American neighborhoods by the recent wave of foreclosures. They could be sustainable and durable strategies for ensuring occupancy, promoting ongoing maintenance, and avoiding further foreclosures.

One of these models, the community land trust (CLT), involves establishing a nonprofit organization to hold land, with the mission of making any housing built on that land perpetually affordable to the designated community. CLTs are often used to extend homeownership in times of rising housing costs by keeping the rights to the underlying land in the hands of a separate entity and not passing along appreciated values to new purchasers. Currently, CLTs are operated or being established in roughly 200 communities in the United States[33]; there were 5,000–9,000 units as of 2006.[34]

Similarly, land banks attempt to lower housing costs through addressing the issue of land aggregation and development.[35] A land bank enables state and local governments to acquire, preserve, convert, and manage foreclosed and other vacant and abandoned properties. By permitting the relevant agency (public or nonprofit) to aggregate and obtain title to these properties, the model creates a useable asset that can reduce blight, generate revenue, and facilitate affordable housing. It is thus a solution to both the affordable housing challenge and the foreclosure challenge.

Another model is the shared-equity mortgage, in which the lender agrees as part of the loan to accept some or all payment in the form of a share of the increase in value (appreciation) of the property.[36] The shared-equity mortgage is a deferred-payment loan that spreads risk more effectively and increases affordability. In lieu of monthly payments, borrowers repay a lump sum upon termination.[37] If the value of the house has risen, that sum represents a share of the appreciated value, greater than what would be owed under a traditional mortgage. But if the value declines, the borrower pays back only the original principal. The borrower has saved monthly payments as well as interest expenses; the lender loses the periodic interest payments but gains upside if the house increases in value. In effect, the lender has obtained equity in the property.

A related variation is the home equity fractional interest security (HEFI), designed by John O'Brien of the University of California, Berkeley, Haas School of Business. This fractional ownership arrangement would allow the homeowner to purchase only a certain percentage of a home while bringing in a passive coinvestor to finance the rest. This coinvestor shares in the potential gains and losses as the home price rises or falls. In the short term, this model could be used to head off foreclosures. For distressed homeowners, the proceeds from the HEFI security would be used for partial satisfaction of an existing lien or consideration for forbearance or mortgage restructuring by an existing lender. As O'Brien describes it, "The HEFI security represents a passive investor interest in a home—analogous to a share of stock, which represents a passive investment in a company. Institutional investors, such as those who manage pension and endowment funds, are interested in HEFIs to achieve diversification beyond stocks and bonds."[38]

Fighting the Foreclosure Battle:
The Genesee County Land Bank

In the heart of Genesee County, Michigan, lies the city of Flint—a town that has seen more than its share of hard times. Flint's fortunes declined along with the ailing U.S. auto industry, and, in recent years, its population has dwindled as residents left town to find opportunities elsewhere. Not only does Flint have a high unemployment rate, but its city government was actually in receivership from 2002 to 2004. As foreclosure rates have skyrocketed, block after block has been marred by abandoned properties—tangible signs of economic pain.

County Treasurer Dan Kildee led an unconventional effort to meet the foreclosure crisis head-on. The county's land assembly, tax collection, and foreclosure process has been reorganized to more easily gain control of rapidly depreciating property. Rather than selling the receivables of tax liens from foreclosed property, the county borrows the receivables and acquires, manages, demolishes, and redevelops tax-foreclosed properties. This reduces the inventory of vacant property, lowers land-acquisition costs, enables parcel consolidation and urban planning, and creates a potential benefit to new homeowners by lowering overall development costs.

Attracting Private Capital Back into the System

Until the recent financial crisis, the private sector played a major role in funding residential real estate. But in the wake of the mortgage-market meltdown, the U.S. government has increasingly replaced the private sector as the major source of real estate funding.

Lending institutions have curtailed credit to the real estate sector as they recapitalize their balance sheets, and investors have cut back on purchases of mortgage-backed securities. At the same time, the securitization of mortgages by private firms has collapsed along with private-investor participation. Much of the funding now available for real estate is being provided by the government through its control of Freddie Mac, Fannie Mae, the FHA, the Veterans Administration (VA), and Ginnie Mae, and through purchases of mortgage-backed

By operating at a county-wide level, the land bank is able to pool a large number of properties and cross-collateralize them, reducing risk and enhancing positive impacts on urban revitalization and homeownership.

In Genesee County, several legislative changes were required, including reforming the tax foreclosure process, providing land bank authorities with a variety of development tools, and enabling land bank properties to be classified as brownfields (abandoned commercial properties that may require cleanup; its development may qualify for government assistance). The particular adjustments would vary by locale, but in Michigan, a Land Bank Fast Track Authority was created to make the process more efficient. Land bank properties are tax-exempt, are all considered brownfields, can sell at less than fair market value, and are subject to an expedited 90-day quiet title auction to establish ownership by the land bank.

The Genesee County Land Bank was the state's first, funded by tax foreclosure fees, land sales revenue, and tax capture. A Michigan State University study of 400 Genesee County Land Bank properties found that the process increased the value of the surrounding landscape by $112 million, at a cost of only $3.5 million.[39]

securities by the Federal Reserve. Most of the funding, moreover, currently goes only to the most creditworthy individuals.

This dramatic shift in funding poses a major problem that has yet to be addressed: a growing gap in the availability of credit to the real estate markets. The government has been focused on stemming the tide of home foreclosures through various loan modification efforts while also providing its own credit to the housing sector. But these actions are not designed to get real estate markets functioning normally again, and, in any event, the financial resources of the government are much smaller than those of the global capital markets and cannot sustain the financing of growing housing demand. Sole dependence on the Federal Reserve and other public entities or GSEs to support the real estate sector after the recession could threaten national economic growth and stability. The government's stabilization and emergency stimulus plan should be supplemented with a plan to address the restoration of the historical partnership with private investors that was a major policy innovation of the past century. This is essential to promote a well-functioning financial system and sustainable and stable long-term economic growth.

Conclusions

With foreclosure and delinquency rates still at sky-high levels and more than one-fifth of U.S. home mortgages under water,[40] scorched housing markets are still struggling to recover as of this writing. In this chapter, we've outlined the factors that led to spiraling prices (including lax monetary policy, excessive leverage, and irrational optimism) and market failures (including overly complex products, the ability of lenders to pass along risk, a lack of transparency, and the failure of rating agencies). While all these factors were dangerously distorting the market, U.S. regulators failed to take action. This is partly due to the procyclicality of regulation (the tendency for regulation to be loose during good times but much more stringent in financial downturns). It's also due to a lack of accountability and the convoluted, overlapping structure of the various enforcement agencies. The federal government is currently debating ways to remedy this structural deficiency by streamlining the regulatory structure and creating a greater focus on systemic risk.

Progress is often born out of moments of crisis. Just as sweeping financial and policy innovations emerged from the Great Depression to provide housing opportunities, new financial products and policies are already being developed in response to the current housing meltdown. We've examined alternatives that could reduce the number of foreclosures in times of declining real estate prices, and distribute risk among loan originators and the ultimate owner of the mortgage while giving upside potential and downside protection to homeowners. It is crucial to reboot the market for mortgage-backed securities, but this time with greater transparency, following models used in the corporate bond market.

Historically, real estate has proven to be one of the riskiest asset classes. Safely facilitating access to affordable housing is a continuing objective of financial innovation. The expansion of homeownership may be a radioactive topic in the wake of the meltdown, but it's a task that has never been more urgent. Stabilizing the housing market is critical to stabilizing the broader economy.

Endnotes

[1] Joyce Appleby, *Liberalism and Republicanism in the Historical Imagination* (Cambridge, MA: Harvard University Press, 1992).

[2] Richard Rosenfield, *American Aurora: A Democracy-Republic Return* (New York: St. Martin's Press, 1997).

[3] Jim Duffy, "What Is a Mortgage, and Why Does It Matter?," FHA Mortgage Blog (16 September 2009). Available at www.myfhamortgageblog.com/2009/09/what-is-a-mortgage-and-why-does-it-matter/; accessed September 28, 2009.

[4] Quoted in Eric Foner, *Free Soil, Free Labor, Free Men: The Ideology of the Republican Party before the Civil War* (New York: Oxford University Press, 1970). See also Foner, *Politics and Ideology in the Age of the Civil War* (New York: Oxford University Press, 1980).

[5] James R. Barth, Susanne Trimbath, and Glenn Yago, *The Savings and Loan Crisis* (Norwell, MA: Kluwer Academic Publishers, 2004).

[6] Margaret Garb, *City of American Dreams: A History of Home Ownership and Housing Reform in Chicago, 1871–1919* (Chicago: University of Chicago Press, 2005).

[7] Felice Bonadio, *A. P. Giannini* (Berkeley: University of California Press, 1994).

[8] Marc A. Weiss, "Marketing and Financing Home Ownership: Mortgage Lending and Public Policy in the United States, 1918–1989," in *Business and Economic History* 2, no. 18 (1989):109–118. See also William W. Bartlett, *Mortgage-Backed Securities: Products, Analysis, Trading* (New Jersey: Prentice-Hall, 1989).

[9] Ben. S. Bernanke, *Housing, Housing Finance and Monetary Policy*, speech delivered at the Federal Reserve Bank of Kansas City's Economic Symposium, Jackson Hole, Wyoming (21 August 2007). Text available at www.federalreserve.gov/newsevents/speech/bernanke20070831a.htm.

[10] William S. Haraf and Rose-Marie Kushmeider (eds.), *Restructuring Banking and Financial Services in America* (Washington: American Enterprise Institute Publishing, 1988).

[11] Congressional Budget Office, "The Housing Finance System and Federal Policy: Recent Changes and Options for the Future" (October 1983): ix.

[12] Richard K. Green and Susan M. Wachter, "The Housing Finance Revolution," paper presented at the Federal Reserve Bank of Kansas City's 31st Economic Policy Symposium: Housing, Housing Finance and Monetary Policy, Jackson Hole, Wyoming (31 August 2007).

[13]Barth, Trimbath, and Yago, *The Savings and Loan Crisis* (Norwell, MA: Kluwer Academic Publishers, 2004).

[14]Andreas Lehnert, Wayne Passmore, and Shane Sherlund, "GSEs, Mortgage Rates, and Secondary Market Activities," *Journal of Real Estate Finance and Economics* 36, no. 3 (April 2008): 343–363.

[15]Eric S. Belsky, Karl E. Case, and Susan J. Smith, "Identifying, Managing, and Mitigating Risks to Borrowers in Changing Mortgage and Consumer Credit Markets," Joint Center for Housing Studies, Harvard University (2008).

[16]Mark S. Doms and John Krainer, "Innovations in Mortgage Markets and Increased Spending on Housing," (working paper no. 2007–05, Federal Reserve Bank of San Francisco, 2007): 4–5.

[17]Heitor Almeida, Murillo Campello, and Crocker Liu, "The Financial Accelerator: Evidence from International Housing Markets," *Review of Finance* 10, no. 3 (2006): 321–352. See also Paul Bennett, Richard Peach, and Stavros Persitiiani, "Structural Changes in the Mortgage Market and the Propensity to Refinance," Federal Reserve Staff Report no. 45 (September 1998).

[18]The research and analysis throughout the section is based on James R. Barth, Tong Li, Wenling Lu, Triphon Phumiwasana, and Glenn Yago, *The Rise and Fall of the U.S. Mortgage and Credit Markets: A Comprehensive Analysis of the Market Meltdown* (New Jersey: John Wiley & Sons, 2009).

[19]Wholesale Access and Milken Institute data, as cited in Barth, et al., *The Rise and Fall of the U.S. Mortgage and Credit Markets: A Comprehensive Analysis of the Meltdown*.

[20]*Ibid.*

[21]*Ibid.*

[22]Paul Krugman, "That Hissing Sound," *New York Times* (8 August 2005).

[23]"In Come the Waves," *The Economist* (16 June 2005).

[24]Jenny Anderson, "Wall Street Winners Get Billion-Dollar Paydays," *New York Times* (16 April 2008).

[25]Freddie Mac data, as cited in as cited in Barth, et al., *The Rise and Fall of the U.S. Mortgage and Credit Markets*.

[26]*Ibid.*

[27]David Greenlaw, Jan Hatzius, Anil K. Kashyap, and Hyun Song Shin, "Leveraged Losses: Lessons from the Mortgage Market Meltdown," U.S. Monetary Policy Forum Report no. 2 (2008).

[28]Betsy Zeidman, James Barth, and Glenn Yago, "Financial Innovations for Housing: Beyond the Crisis," Milken Institute Financial Innovations Lab Report (November 2009).

[29]This discussion draws from Zeidman, Barth, and Yago, "Financial Innovations for Housing: Beyond the Crisis."

[30]PIMCO, "Bond Basics: Covered Bonds." Accessible at http://europe.pimco.com/LeftNav/Bond+Basics/2006/Covered+Bond+Basics.htm.

[31]Alan Boyce, "Can Elements of the Danish Mortgage System Fix Mortgage Securitization in the United States?" Presentation at the American Enterprise Institute, Washington, DC (26 March 2009).

[32]"A Slice of Danish: An Ancient Scandinavian Model May Help Modern Mortgage Markets," *The Economist* (30 December 2008).

[33]National Community Land Trust Network, "Overview." Accessible at www.cltnetwork.org/index.php?fuseaction=Blog.dspBlogPost&postID=27.

[34]John Emmeus Davis, "Shared Equity Homeownership: The Changing Landscape of Resale-Restricted, Owner-Occupied Housing," National Housing Institute (2006).

[35]Don T. Johnson and Larry B. Cowart, "Public Sector Land Banking: A Decision Model for Local Governments," *Public Budgeting and Finance* 17, no. 4 (1995): 3–6.

[36]John Emmeus Davis, "Shared Equity Homeownership: The Changing Landscape of Resale-Restricted, Owner Occupied Housing," National Housing Institute (2006).

[37]Andrew Caplin, Noel B. Cunningham, Mitchell Engler, and Frederick Pollock, "Facilitating Shared Appreciation Mortgages to Prevent Housing Crashes and Affordability Crisis," The Brookings Institution (2008).

[38]John O'Brien, "Revolutionary Help for Homeowners," *Christian Science Monitor* (26 November 2008).

[39]Nigel G. Griswold and Patricia E. Norris, "Economic Impacts of Residential Property Abandonment and the Genesee County Land Bank in Flint, Michigan," MSU Land Policy Institute Report 2007–05 (April 2007).

[40]Daniel Taub, "Fewer U.S. Homeowners Owe More Than Properties Are Worth," Bloomberg (9 November 2009).

5

Environmental Finance:
Innovating to Save the Planet

The now-famous "inconvenient truth" of the twenty-first century is that our collective failure to value our natural resources has placed the planet in real peril. Pollution, deforestation, and climate change are taking a fearsome toll on biodiversity, nature's astounding variety of plant and animal species.

Back in 1997, a group of economists and biologists estimated that humans derive trillions of dollars each year in benefits from ecosystem services that they don't pay for—benefits that total between 55% and 185% of global GDP.[1] In purely economic terms, this equation is unsustainable.

Under the weight of our consumption, the world's stocks of natural capital—that is, ecosystems and the benefits and resources they provide—have dramatically shrunk in the past century. Vast swaths of coral reefs lie bleached and lifeless in the Caribbean and around Australia, while tropical rainforests have been leveled in the Amazon and Indonesia. The International Union for the Conservation of Nature (IUCN) released a report in 2008 warning that 25% of all wild mammal species are in danger of disappearing.[2] Scientists have estimated that there are anywhere from 5 million to 30 million species on Earth, but we have identified only some 1.5 million to date. Less than half a million have been analyzed to determine their potential economic uses.[3]

The burning of fossil fuels and massive deforestation are also hastening global warming, which brings with it more volatile and extreme weather, along with the potential for rising seas, the spread of infectious disease, and fertile soil turning to desert. Together these trends portend massive destruction of real assets.

The stark reality of the situation presents a crystal-clear call to action: We must speed the convergence of environmental and capital markets and seize the opportunity to build a more sustainable economy. We have the ability to create new markets that value air, water, and natural resources. We can fund new clean technologies and find more equitable and sustainable ways to generate jobs, income, and wealth in the future.

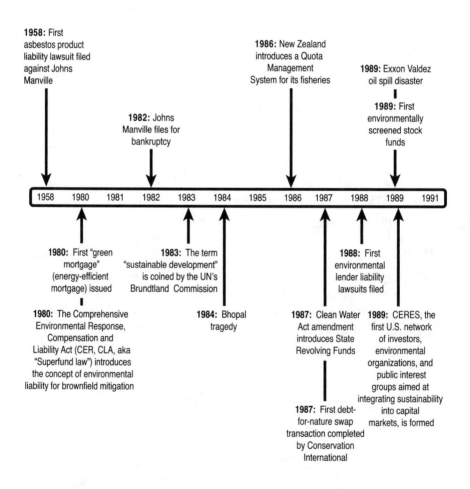

To achieve this paradigm shift, we will need to apply financial technologies to the valuation and pricing of environmental externalities (such as air and water pollution) and common-property resources (such as biodiversity). The first step is building an adequate pricing mechanism, mobilizing proven innovations for developing environmental markets. The price discovery made possible through innovative environmental finance signals the real market value of natural resources, and thereby stimulates inventive conservation practices and new clean technologies that will facilitate growth. This process requires a new approach to financial decision making that monetizes formerly hidden assets.

From experience with curtailing acid rain via the sulfur dioxide–allowance market to the implementation of the Clean Water

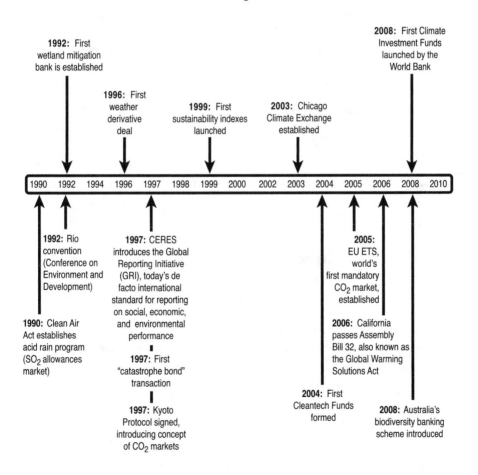

Act, market-based solutions have proven consistently more effective in protecting the environment than government regulation alone. Project financing, public–private partnerships, and tradable permits have come to supplement or replace conventional command-and-control regulation and purely tax-based instruments. This approach can minimize the aggregate costs of achieving environmental targets while providing dynamic incentives for the adoption and diffusion of greener technologies.

Market-based financial and public policy instruments emerged in the 1980s and have steadily gained momentum. Tradable permit systems have been deployed to phase down use of leaded gasoline, end the use of ozone-depleting chlorofluorocarbons, and even reduce air pollution in the smoggy skies above Los Angeles.[4] New attempts are being made to attach an economic value to public goods such as biodiversity. In fact, the United Nations Environment Programme has launched a Finance Initiative as a formal mechanism for mobilizing the financial sector to take a more active role in protecting the environment.

This chapter demonstrates that it is possible, and urgently necessary, to apply principles of finance and economics—efficient use of scarce capital, price transparency, and lowered transaction costs—to environmental issues. Aligning the interests of consumers, producers, and the general public can have a powerful effect. A crucial point to underline is that economic growth appears to be a necessary condition for environmental protection. Growth is not the enemy of conservation.

Market Failures and the Environment

Economists call them "externalities." When someone engages in wasteful production or consumption, they may cause negative impacts on others who had absolutely nothing to do with the original activity. These costs are never accounted for by the parties actually engaged in and most directly affected by that activity. Negative externalities are a type of market failure, leading to the misallocation of resources, and environmental degradation is perhaps the prime example of this concept.

It is possible, of course, to ban or tax environmentally destructive behavior, but doing so can weigh down economies and cause other market distortions. The most efficient way to resolve externalities is to internalize them—to embed them into the economic decision making and transactions of market actors by adequately pricing them. Achieving this shift requires clearly defined property rights and some kind of market mechanism.

One way to understand externalities is to revisit the famous "tragedy of the commons," a theory explored by biology professor Garrett Hardin in 1968.[5] In a later article, Hardin noted that satellite photos taken over Africa in 1974 captured this concept unfolding. They revealed a dark patch covering 390 square miles. It turned out to be nothing more than a fence enclosing fertile grasslands; but outside the fence, the soil was barren and lifeless.

> *The explanation was simple: The fenced area was private property, subdivided into five portions. Each year the owners moved their animals to a new section. Fallow periods of four years gave the pastures time to recover from the grazing. The owners did this because they had an incentive to take care of their land. But no one owned the land outside the ranch. It was open to nomads and their herds .... Their needs were uncontrolled and grew with the increase in the number of animals. But supply was governed by nature and decreased drastically during the drought of the early 1970s. The herds exceeded the natural "carrying capacity" of their environment, soil was compacted and eroded, and "weedy" plants, unfit for cattle consumption, replaced good plants. Many cattle died, and so did humans.*[6]

Air, fishing grounds, and drinking water ... these resources belong to everyone but are owned by no one, so they are used heedlessly. But eventually, the principle of diminishing marginal returns kicks in: As more and more people exploit a natural resource, the benefits they derive from that resource increase at a declining rate. Even though it is in everyone's interest to preserve shared resources, larger societal goals do not typically motivate individual market actors as they pursue their narrow self-interest. Resources may be destroyed by the combined actions of multiple parties intent on maximizing their own consumption rather than conserving for the future. Without direct ownership, people have little incentive to preserve a resource.[7]

It is not so much that the market fails; rather, it does not exist. The public and social costs of private production can be priced and paid for through a market exchange; creating that platform is critical to conservation. The problem inherent in doing so is that buyers and sellers lack information about available supply and demand of environmental goods and services without any guarantee of uniformity. But this issue can be overcome—just as market mechanisms were established for corn, rice, wheat, railroads, or manufacturing debt and equity in the past. The crucial ingredient is a system of well-defined, enforceable, and transferable property rights.

Property Rights and Professor Coase

The absence of property rights can hinder the very essence of a market economy—and perhaps, in this case, threaten human survival. Environmental problems often stem from the absence or incompleteness of property rights. When rights to resources are defined and easily defended, all market actors have an incentive to avoid pollution problems. The externality of air pollution, for instance, can be solved by establishing property rights over clean air so that residents are entitled to a fee if nearby smokestacks belch soot into their "property."

The first to suggest that a system of well-defined property rights could overcome the problem of externalities was Ronald Coase, in a ground-breaking 1960 article that won him the 1991 Nobel Prize for economics.[8] If property rights can be established for clean air and water, Coase maintained, individuals and firms will be forced to pay for any negative impacts they impose on others. This would provide incentives for more eco-friendly behavior and investments in improved technology, while also creating efficient economic returns. The "Coase theorem" stresses the importance of clearly defining property rights and using their transferability to allocate resources. By creating a property right in water or air, or embedding the costs of environmental impacts in business decisions, the public and social costs of private production can be priced and traded.

New Directions in Environmental Finance

While innovators in labs and factories are racing to harness renewable sources of energy and make our daily lives more energy efficient, financial innovators have been also been pushing the envelope in the environmental field, searching for new ways to apply economic concepts to protecting public goods.

Water withdrawals from sources such as groundwater have tripled over the last 50 years, and with continued population growth, demand is rising exponentially.[9] Product and process technologies affecting water desalination, recycling, filtration and treatment, metering, and infrastructure stand ready to be taken to scale. The pressure of ever-growing demand is simultaneously driving the creation of new markets and public payment mechanisms in watershed ecosystem services.

Another nascent market is being formed to value biodiversity. These measures have often taken the form of government regulations, fines, and tax breaks, but now there is a movement to apply the principles of cap-and-trade (in which the government sets a cap on pollution or usage and then allocates permits to businesses and other entities, allowing them to trade permits among themselves) to diverse fields ranging from fisheries management to wetlands protection. The United States has led the way in this field, but market-based approaches are also taking hold in Australia and New Zealand and across Europe (the Netherlands, in particular, stands out for its willingness to try a wide range of different market mechanisms).[10] One ground-breaking idea actually set up a market for "woodpecker credits" to help attach a value to endangered red-cockaded woodpeckers; if developers harm their habitats in one area, they must purchase credits to offset that harm. This has given rise to a market among those who own similar land. Now that a value is attached, they have an economic incentive to protect it.[11]

Table 5.1 offers some examples of the wide-ranging innovations already being deployed in environmental finance, from strategies that help protect ecosystems as providers of public goods to tools that help launch green businesses (including access to credit and loans, venture capital, and investment guarantees; resource extraction rents and/or severance fees related to natural resource development; entry fees and concessions; and securitization of revenues generated by marketable goods and services such as ecotourism, climate regulation, erosion control, pollination, water services, carbon offsets, and the like).[12]

TABLE 5.1   Types of Innovations in Environmental Finance

Products and Services	Processes and Operations	Organizational Forms
Municipal bonds for smart growth	Feed-in tariffs for alternative energy	Alternative-energy venture capital
State revolving fund bonds	Wetland banks	Bioprospecting venture capital
Tax-exempt screened bonds	Nutrient trading	Environmental buyout funds
Clean energy bonds	Carbon sinks/carbon offsets	Biotech venture capital
Brownfield development portfolio insurance	Best-in-class environmental screening	Chicago Climate Exchange
Sewage/water treatment project finance guarantees	Debt-for-nature swaps	European Climate Exchange
Tax-exempt green bonds	Pollution monitoring	Biodiversity banks

Financing Conservation Projects

State Revolving Funds: From Seed Money to Self-Sustaining Project Financing

For many years, the United States financed environmental improvements, such as sewage treatment plants, with substantial one-time grants made by the federal government to localities. But as the demand for funding grew, policymakers and capital market experts began to think creatively about how to leverage finances: to generate, for example, $2 million of pooled capital from a one-time $500,000 grant.

In 1987, Congress passed the Federal Clean Water Act and replaced its aging grants program with state revolving funds (SRFs).[13] Under this model, each state applies for a federal capital grant, which requires a 20% local match; this pool of funding is then supplemented with capital market investment and possibly "seed money" from philanthropies. The states then make low-interest loans to local municipalities and organizations, which repay the loans from project revenue and local taxes. States may provide loans to communities, individuals, nonprofit organizations, and commercial enterprises.[14] Their repayments recapitalize the state fund, creating a sustainable resource for funding.

This model maximizes the impact and longevity of government grants. SRFs have successfully ensured a steady flow of capital into water quality and management projects in rural areas, small towns, and major cities. The Environmental Protection Agency (EPA) estimates that they have provided more than $68.8 billion in cumulative assistance, serving more than 115 million people; the agency also states that, between 1987 and 2005, the funds created more than 600,000 construction jobs and 116,000 additional jobs.[15]

The local river and stream projects receiving funding generate sustainable income (through local taxes, tourism revenue, or usage fees, for example) that repays the original loan and recapitalizes the fund. Because the loans are offered at well below market interest rates, local communities save substantially on the cost of capital. Local river authorities can also leverage their resources with capital market investment through the sale of municipal bonds that can finance multiple projects.

SRFs provide federal assistance while maintaining state and local control over spending priorities. States are granted flexibility in setting up the structure of their programs. In addition to offering low-interest loans, they may allow the funds to be used for refinancing, purchasing, or guaranteeing local debt, or purchasing bond insurance. States set their own loan terms, including interest rates and repayment periods, and can customize these terms to assist small and disadvantaged communities.[16]

A state's fund is rated on the entirety of its program, not on individual loans made to specific projects. This pooling of projects to reduce risk through diversity has been a key to success. In 2008 alone, the SRF program funded $2.7 billion for treatment facilities, $2.9 billion for sewer construction, and more than $220 million for controlling nonpoint source pollution (pollution that stems from many diffuse sources and is carried by rainwater runoff). These nonpoint source projects included sanitary landfill and brownfield rehabilitation (the cleanup of abandoned industrial sites), urban storm water–runoff management, and the improvement of agricultural water-management practices.[17]

State revolving funds have enabled new product development within the municipal bond market. By moving financing away from general obligation risks and toward revenue-bond project financing based on the business models of individual projects, it became possible to raise more funding in the capital markets. Moreover, these innovations made it possible to leverage limited government funds and to use the power of aggregating to pool risk over a large number of diverse projects. New organizational forms also arose that engage private investors in these projects. By moving away from reliance on conventional municipal bonds, the market itself was transformed by new capital structures and financial products that have results in cleaner rivers and better water management.

There are two basic SRF models. The "cash flow model" uses the fund's original equity (the federal and state contributions) to originate direct loans to the communities. Repayments are pledged to bond issuance, with more loan repayments coming in than are actually needed to pay the bond debt. The proceeds from the sale of the bonds go to fund additional loans, creating a collateralized cash flow (see Figure 5.1). The coverage from the direct loans provides added security, as well as the subsidy on the loans.

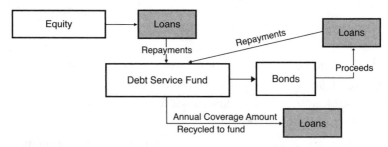

Figure 5.1   The cash flow model

Source: Susan Weil, Lamont Financial

The "reserve model" uses the original equity to create a pool that cushions the fund from any potential defaults. The size of the reserve can vary anywhere from 30% to 70% of overall transactions. Bonds are then issued, and the proceeds from these bonds provide loans to local communities for river projects (see Figure 5.2). The interest earned by the reserve subsidizes the loans.

Missouri offers a good case study of a successful reserve model. The volume of loans issued through its SRF program ranks twelfth in the nation.[18] Despite a slow start, the state had completed 150 loans to its communities, resulting in over $1.7 billion in construction, as of late 2008. The state's residents must vote to approve project financing, and thus take an active interest in the success and subsequent repayment of any loan.

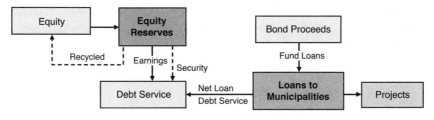

Figure 5.2   The reserve fund model

Source: Susan Weil, Lamont Financial

Missouri's SRF is a leveraged loan program with dedicated pool financing across municipalities and towns. The fund maintains a reserve at 70% of its total transactions; this is the highest reserve level in the nation, ensuring excellent bond ratings.

The recipient of one of Missouri's early SRF loans was the town of Branson, one of America's country-music capitals, with a population of just 3,700 but an influx of 5 million tourists per year. When it became clear that Branson's water infrastructure was inadequate for the needs of the community and such concentrated tourism, the city council approved a $56 million wastewater system capable of meeting stringent discharge limits and growing demand. Because the project's budget could not possibly be paid by the town's small population, the city enacted a 2% tourism tax on the cost of hotel rooms and entertainment, and a 0.5% tax on restaurant tabs. Moving debt responsibility to the tourism industry has enabled Branson to repay its SRF debt for the past 14 years.

Both the cash flow and reserve models of SRFs have worked successfully. Some states have also attempted to create a hybrid of these structures, using a set portion of the original equity for a reserve and the remainder to fund direct loans. Whatever blend is chosen, it is clear that the revolving fund has proven to be an effective financing model that eventually leads to self-sufficiency. It is important to note that loans give the recipient a stake in the financial package, creating an incentive to reduce wasteful expenditures.

Once the revolving fund idea proved its effectiveness, it served as a model for a number of other programs, with its scope being gradually broadened over time. In 1996, Congress established the Drinking Water State Revolving Fund (DWSRF) program, which mirrors the Clean Water Fund program in assistance options, state and federal responsibilities, and other structural aspects. In the DWSRF program's first decade, states were able to loan $12.6 billion for 5,555 projects around the country. Special assistance has gone to small drinking water systems and disadvantaged communities, enabling them to meet public health standards.[19] Revolving funds are also being used by the EPA to finance the cleanup of brownfields.

Using SRFs for Land Acquisition

In certain cases, the best way to improve water quality is to set aside strategically chosen parcels of land where water flows or originates, preventing pollution from development and industrial uses. By saving wetlands, we can also maintain important wildlife habitats.

New York State has deployed its SRF as a low-cost way to fund land-acquisition projects that protect water quality. In 2000, the city of Rye used a $3.1 million short-term, zero-interest loan from the Clean Water State Revolving Fund (CWSRF) to acquire and protect crucial land in the Long Island Sound Estuary.[20] This fragile ecosystem is a huge and complex watershed, where the Connecticut, Housatonic, and Thames rivers meet and mingle with ocean waters. It is also a vitally important breeding and migratory habitat for a rich variety of bird species.

Some 20 million people live within 50 miles of Long Island Sound, enjoying its scenic beaches and consuming fish and shellfish from these waters.[21] But industry, shoreline development, and heavy recreational use placed this vital watershed under stress, degrading wildlife habitats and causing frequent beach closures. Sewage plant discharge and storm water runoff deposit nitrogen into the water, creating "dead zones" where marine life cannot thrive. Extensive cleanup efforts have been underway for decades, but much more remains to be done.[22]

Long Island Sound's Comprehensive Conservation and Management Plan recommended key land acquisitions as part of the ongoing strategy for saving this vital watershed. Rye's acquisitions are an important piece of the puzzle; they will preserve and improve the waterfront, tributaries, and wetlands that lie within the city. In fact, New York State expanded its SRF to provide not-for-profit organizations with a mechanism for funding similar land-acquisition projects that protect water quality.

In California's Central Valley, local land trusts and conservancies have partnered with federal and state agencies to leverage millions of dollars (including $9.5 million in CWSRF loans) for conservation purposes. The partnership has successfully protected tens of thousands of acres of land surrounding the Valley's vernal pool wetlands, unique ecosystems that support rare plant and animal species. The Nature Conservancy (TNC) has played a crucial role in this effort: In 1999, the group pooled an $8 million loan from the state with $6 million from private and public sources in order to preserve the sprawling Howard Ranch as part of the Cosumnes River Preserve in South Sacramento County. The ranch is now off limits to new housing developments and conversion to vineyards or orchards, protecting its wetlands and delta streams. The local Sacramento Valley Conservancy later obtained a $1 million SRF loan to help set aside the Sacramento Vernal Pool Prairie Preserve.[23]

Debt-for-Nature Swaps

At first glance, a country's external debt and its ability to protect biodiversity might appear to be completely unrelated. But linking these issues creatively through debt-for-nature swaps has made progress possible on both fronts. By relieving the foreign debt burden carried by developing nations, it is possible to secure their commitment to invest in local conservation projects and save imperiled ecosystems.

Most debt-for-nature swap deals executed up to now have been designed to protect endangered tropical forests. Not only are rain forests essential to the well-being of local communities, but they have global significance due to their ability to act as "carbon sinks," absorbing the CO_2 that causes climate change.[24] Science has barely scratched the surface of the discoveries that lie hidden in these wilderness areas, which are teeming with rare and exotic plants and animals.

Yet around the globe, rain forests are under assault from a variety of factors: mining, logging, displaced farmers, cattle grazing, poverty-stricken locals gathering firewood, and new hydroelectric dams. Preserving the amazing biodiversity sheltered within these rain forests is a concern that transcends national borders.

Debt-for-nature swaps are the brainchild of Thomas Lovejoy of the World Wildlife Fund, who seized on the idea back in 1984 as a way to deal with the entwined problems of environmental degradation and the crushing sovereign debt burdens shouldered by many developing nations. When the Latin American debt crisis hamstrung the ability of many highly indebted nations across the region to focus on conservation, Lovejoy called for building an explicit link between debt relief and environmental protection.[25]

Many debt-for-nature swaps begin with a nongovernmental organization (NGO) or a "conservation investor" undertaking the purchase of a developing country's hard-currency debt titles. A commercial bank might even be willing to sell to the NGOs at a discount, since the ability of the debtor nation to repay is already considered shaky. The NGO then forgives the debt in exchange for the debtor country's commitment to fund a conservation project or set aside a crucial parcel of land. The debtor government might also be asked to use this newly freed-up financial stream to issue bonds, appointing local environmental groups to make grants from the proceeds. Conservation International conducted its first debt swap transaction in 1987, when it purchased a portion of Bolivia's foreign debt from a commercial creditor, then cancelled that debt so the Bolivian government would set aside 3.7 million acres in and around the Beni Biosphere Reserve.[26]

Bilateral debt-for-nature swaps are a slightly different animal. In this case, the debt forgiveness deal is a direct transaction between two governments. In 1991, President George H.W. Bush unveiled the Enterprise for the Americas Initiative to pursue this strategy.[27] The Environmental Foundation of Jamaica was the first fund established under this program; in exchange for forgiveness of $311 million of the island nation's bilateral debt, the foundation received funding to administer child development programs, along with projects such as water quality monitoring, waste management, reforestation, and biodiversity protection.[28]

The U.S. Tropical Forest Conservation Act (TFCA) was enacted in 1998 to further institutionalize the idea of debt-for-nature swaps. Under this program, developing countries can reduce high levels of debt owed to the U.S. government, generating funds in local currency for programs that will protect local rain forests. Hundreds of millions of dollars that once went to debt payments have now been redirected to conservation activities in more than a dozen countries, from Botswana and Bangladesh to Paraguay and the Philippines.[29]

NGOs often help broker TFCA agreements and contribute additional funding. The Nature Conservancy and Conservation International each contributed $1.26 million to facilitate a 2007 debt-for-nature swap under the TFCA, in which the United States forgave $26 million of Costa Rica's debt.[30] The debt relief will finance forest conservation in Costa Rica over the next 16 years, helping rural and indigenous communities pursue sustainable livelihoods while protecting one of the world's great natural treasures for future generations. (A portion of this funding will go to protect the La Amistad region, a tract of virgin rain forest that shelters some 90% of Costa Rica's known plant species, more than 350 species of birds, and a host of exotic animals, including giant anteaters and ocelots.)[31]

Conservation International and The Nature Conservancy also played a key role in a 2006 deal that cancelled $24 million of Guatemala's debt to the United States. The money will instead be channeled into a local fund for conservation grants to be distributed over the next 15 years. The grants will be used to protect Guatemala's cloud forests, rain forests, and coastal mangrove swamps, home to many rare and endangered species.[32]

In June 2009, the U.S. government announced the largest debt-for-nature swap secured to date under the TFCA. Conservation International helped to broker and underwrite the deal, in which the United States will forgive nearly $30 million of debt payments owed by Indonesia in exchange for commitments to protect the Sumatran rain forest, which has experienced rampant destruction.[33] The debt reduction will help to provide livelihoods for the people of the island while hopefully ensuring the survival of some critically endangered species, including tigers, elephants, orangutans, and rhinos. Over eight years, the government of Indonesia will pay the nearly $30 million to a trust, which will issue grants for forest conservation and restoration work in Sumatra. It will lead to increased protection of 13 vital areas of Sumatran rain forest that are home to hundreds of species of threatened plants and animals.[34]

Pollution Markets

The most practical solution for building a greener economy is to correct faulty pricing by making consumers and firms pay for the environmental damage they cause. Once these negative externalities are internalized, they will be incorporated in the prices of goods and services, creating real incentives for the creation and adoption of clean technologies.

One of the most compelling examples of using these principles to fix broken markets is that of cap-and-trade pollution markets. In such markets, the **cap** (or maximum amount of total pollution allowed) is usually set by government. Businesses, factory plants, and other entities are given or sold permits to emit some portion of the region's total amount. If an organization emits less than its allotment, it can sell or **trade** its unused permits to other businesses that have exceeded their limits. Entities can trade permits directly with each other, through brokers, or in organized markets. This approach leaves individual companies free to choose if and how they will reduce their emissions and by how much.

Markets can achieve abatement targets at the lowest possible cost. Firms will choose the most affordable way to comply with the pollution cap, creating competitive incentives to develop new clean technologies. This dynamic speeds innovation, creates new opportunities for innovators, and quickly lowers compliance costs. In other words, Schumpeter's theory of creative destruction (referenced in Chapter 3, "Innovations in Business Finance") clearly applies to environmental markets. Invention, innovation, and replication on a large scale are required for the development and application of physical and financial technologies alike.

The U.S. Acid Rain Program and the Sulfur Dioxide (SO₂) Market

The overriding concern for today's green movement is global warming, but back in the 1970s and 1980s, acid rain was public enemy number one. This phenomenon occurred when power plants and industrial smokestacks spewed sulfur dioxide and nitrogen oxides into the atmosphere, where they mixed with water vapor. Alarms went off when scientists observed that fish, algae, and frogs were dying off in lakes and rivers. Acid rain not only took a toll on forests, crops, and buildings—it actually ate through the paint on cars and damaged ancient archeological landmarks. The problem seemed too diffuse and complex to be tamed by a simple command-and-control solution. After all, sulfur dioxide was emanating from thousands of unique sources, falling under multiple regulators.[35]

Two economists working for the precursor organization to the U.S. EPA, Ellison Burton and William Sanjour, decided to tackle the problem from a unique angle, building on the work of Coase and others. In their quest to find a low-cost, decentralized solution for abatement, they hit upon the idea of creating an actual marketplace to control emissions. The key was to devise penalties for polluting and incentives for emitters to invest in changing their practices.[36]

The breakthrough came in 1990, when the United States passed new amendments to the Clean Air Act. With these changes, the EPA placed a national cap on emissions of sulfur and nitrogen oxides and set up a system for polluters to trade permits among themselves. Title IV of the 1990 Clean Air Act established the allowance market system known today as the Acid Rain Program, which eventually became the prototype for emissions trading in all other major pollutants. The ultimate goal was to reduce annual SO₂ emissions to about half of their 1980 levels. The cap was gradually lowered, with implementation coming in two stages of tightening operating restrictions on power plants.[37] The market for emissions allowances simply would not function and create accurate pricing without an effective regulatory cap on the total number of allowances available.

When Congress placed an overall restriction on power plant emissions nationwide in 1990, plants had a choice: They could invest in cleaner fuels or abatement technologies, or they could purchase extra emissions rights from plants that had managed to achieve their own reductions and had surplus permits to sell. The ability to buy excess rights enables older, less efficient plants to comply with the new rules. Emissions targets are met at the lowest possible cost.[38]

In the initial phase of the program, from 1995 to 1999, the allowance market encompassed only about one-fifth of the nation's plants, but it focused on the biggest polluters. Phase 2 kicked in after 2000, bringing virtually all power plants above a certain size into the market. One of the key features of this program is that "banking" is allowed; power plants can save their allowances for future use, though they cannot borrow permits from future years to pollute today. This provides additional flexibility and a much more meaningful price signal.[39]

The world sat up and took notice of the significant environmental progress achieved by this nationwide experiment in capping and trading pollutants. The initial goal was to cut annual sulfur dioxide emissions in half by 2010, but the cap-and-trade program achieved its targets three years ahead of schedule and at a fraction of the initial cost estimates.

In 1992, estimates of emissions rights ranged from $981 to $1,500 a ton. By 1998, the Chicago Board of Trade auctioned off a large number of allowances at $115 a ton[40] (though it is important to note that improved technologies for burning low-sulfur coal and lower fuel costs simultaneously contributed to lowering these costs[41]). Prices spiked from 2004 to 2006, reaching over $1,400 a ton, but soon fell just as sharply. In 2008, the SO_2 allowances saw a 65% price decline; that trend continued in 2009, with prices hitting $71 a ton by May.[42]

The program is now fully phased in, with the final 2010 SO_2 cap set at 8.95 million tons, approximately one-half of the emissions from the power sector in 1980. Actual emissions in 2008 were well below that level, at 7.6 million tons.[43] One widely cited study has estimated the cost savings of allowance trading at $784 million annually during the second phase of the program, which began in 2000. That is approximately 43% of the estimated cost of compliance under an enlightened command-and-control model of achieving reductions.[44] The EPA also states that the program has achieved billions of dollars in health care savings each year, since the emissions removed from the air have been linked to heart and lung ailments.[45] All in all, the U.S. experiment in curbing acid rain can be considered the first successful large-scale model of an environmental market.

Carbon Dioxide (CO₂) Emissions Trading

Since carbon emissions increase the threat of significant climate change, setting up a trading system for emissions permits is the equivalent of taking out low-cost global risk insurance against infinitely larger societal, economic, and health consequences. Multiple economists (including Richard Sandor and Sir Nicholas Stern, author of Britain's landmark study on global warming) have demonstrated the economic imperatives of acting to cut greenhouse gas emissions now rather than paying a crippling toll for inaction in the years to come. The benefits of decisive, early action on climate change far outweigh the costs of the irreversible impacts that may lie ahead, including volatile weather, coastal destruction, droughts, famines, species extinction, and migration.[46]

The industrialized world can make dramatic strides in bringing down CO_2 emissions by utilizing financial innovations that drive down compliance costs, penalize environmentally harmful activities, and create incentives to change that behavior. Achieving these goals will not be easy, since the fossil fuels that produce greenhouse gas (GHG) emissions underlie almost every facet of the global economy; emissions are embedded in most of our daily activities. One study estimated that setting an aggressive cap that reduces emissions to 50% below their 1990 levels by 2050 would cause a hit to GDP of 1% per year—a significant cost, but one that can be absorbed. It also estimates that the price of allowances would rise from $41 per ton of carbon in 2015 to $161 per ton in 2050, causing conventional coal-fired power generation to fall out of favor by 2040. The proposed system could also generate hundreds of billions of dollars per year in government revenue if allowances are auctioned.[47]

But the remarkable aspect of the market-based solution is that reducing our carbon footprint is not only feasible, but consistent with growth. Implementing a cap-and-trade program for GHG emissions allowances will ensure that environmental policy has only a relatively contained impact on the U.S. economy. In fact, the benefits of developing a "green economy" include the possibility of spawning entirely new industries to provide environmental services. Tackling the emissions problem by imposing taxes or regulation runs the risk of slowing down overall growth. But a cap-and-trade system simply transfers capital from one part of the economy to another, slowing "dirty" sectors while jump-starting growth in green industries.[48]

The market for carbon trades is already a reality, whether it is voluntary (such as the Chicago Climate Exchange, a financial institution that currently operates North America's only cap-and-trade system for all six greenhouse gases) or mandatory (such as the European Union Emissions Trading System, or EU ETS). Members of the Chicago Climate Exchange, which include a number of Fortune 500 companies and major utilities, make a voluntary but legally binding commitment to reduce their GHG emissions. Their reasons for joining range from bolstering their green credentials to gaining a leg up on compliance and trading competencies before such a system becomes mandatory.[49] Ten Northeastern states are establishing a cap-and-trade program for their power sectors, called the Regional Greenhouse Gas Initiative (RGGI), and California may employ a similar approach as it seeks to implement 2006 legislation (AB 32) that mandates emissions reduction. As of this writing, Congress is preparing to debate landmark legislation that would establish a mandatory national cap-and-trade system across the United States. In the meantime, the Commodity Futures Trading Commission (CFTC) has already moved to begin regulating the Chicago Climate Exchange—a clear signal that the market has reached a new level of maturity.[50]

Launched in 2005, the EU ETS became the world's first cap-and-trade system for CO_2 emissions, and it remains the largest such market to date. Its inaugural three-year trial period reveals a number of instructive lessons, as outlined in an evaluation by the Pew Center for Global Climate Change. Allowances to emitters were initially overallocated, causing price volatility. But allowance banking and borrowing, along with better information flow and a switch to allocating allowances for longer trading periods, should address this issue. Overall, however, the market has developed with remarkable speed and smoothness, especially considering the number of sovereign governments involved. It generated an accepted price for tradable allowances, and an infrastructure of institutions, registries, and monitoring processes quickly took shape. Trading volumes have grown steadily. Businesses have already begun to incorporate the price of allowances into their decisions, thus internalizing what was once an externality.[51]

The successful functioning of a cap-and-trade program starts with standardizing the commodity (the offsets). The act of trading enables price discovery and builds the infrastructure and institutions that lower transaction costs. A system of hedging and options will evolve, as it has in other markets, and global harmonization and integration will quickly follow. If China and the United States, the world's two largest sources of GHG emissions, were to form a global market, the impact would be sweeping and transformative.[52]

Flexibility encourages cost efficiency in approaching the problem of climate change.[53] A cap-and-trade system allows individual emitters to decide which clean technologies to adopt. Instead of governments choosing which innovations to back, the marketplace decides—and that competition encourages breakthroughs and cost reductions.

Apart from cap-and-trade systems, there are complementary approaches to reducing global emissions. The Kyoto Protocol included provisions dubbed "flexible mechanisms." These provisions allow industrialized economies to meet their reduction targets under the agreement by buying GHG emission credits through exchanges, by funding projects that reduce emissions in developing economies, or by buying credits from other developed countries with excess allowances.

Even if a developing nation has no GHG emissions restrictions, it now has a financial incentive to create abatement projects: the opportunity to earn "carbon credits," or offsets, which can be sold to buyers from wealthier nations. The clean development mechanism (CDM) allows *both* emerging and industrialized economies to benefit from mitigation projects in the developing world. Projects must first be approved by a developing nation's "designated national authority" and then submitted for accreditation by the Clean Development Mechanism Executive Board, which was established under the United Nations Framework Convention on Climate Change (UNFCC).[54] Standardization of the CDM trading system is critical for reducing transaction costs, as it has been for the development of every financial market employing these tools.

Markets for Public Goods

The principles and prototypes used in emissions trading have applications in other environmental challenges, creating a chorus of possibility in financial innovation.

Saving Oceans and Fisheries:
Individual Transferable Fishing Quotas

For millennia, fisheries have been considered a common property resource. Most people believed that the ocean's supply of fish was limitless. But population growth and the industrialization of fishing have depleted that stock of capital at an alarming rate. Restoring the health of fisheries is a matter of urgent global concern, since just under 3 billion people depend on fish for 15% or more of their animal protein (in some emerging nations, it accounts for around half of animal protein intake).[55] As fishermen race to exploit the last of a dwindling resource rather than restocking for the future, the tragedy of the commons comes into full play.

In 2006, marine ecologist Boris Worm issued a chilling report about the state of the world's fisheries, predicting that continued bad practices would cause a global collapse of all fish species by 2048.[56] In 2009, however, he issued an updated study with a brighter outlook, pointing to clear progress in restoring five out of ten major fisheries (including those in the United States) that have employed strong conservation-management measures. Despite these positive signs, he warns that a great deal of work still lies ahead: Many species remain threatened, and 63% of fish stocks need to be rebuilt.[57]

When it first became clear that intensive fishing could endanger renewal of the existing stock, command-and-control approaches were tried, such as imposing time limits on fishing or restricting the number of boats in a given area. But these regulations failed to accomplish much other than creating a frantic "rush to fish." Fishermen incurred higher costs, but the stock of fishing capital was never rebuilt.

Today financial innovations are being applied to the problem, with the goal of restoring stocks, improving catch standards and revenue, and bringing economic sustainability to local fishing communities. There's an old saying that fishing is like a bank account: You have to live off the interest and leave the principal intact (the fish you leave in the water being the principal here). Catch-share programs, or "limited access privilege programs" (LAPPs), allocate a dedicated percentage share of a fishery's total catch to individual fisherman, communities, or associations. Originating in Australia, New Zealand, and Iceland in the 1970s, the catch-share management model is now employed at a number of federal fisheries in the United States.

Under a traditional system, fishery managers set a maximum total catch, and individual boats rush to haul in the largest catch possible before the entire fishery reaches its limit. But the catch-share program operates like a cap-and-trade program for emissions. Scientists determine the optimal annual numbers of fish that can be safely harvested in a given area, setting the total allowable catch (TAC). Permits for shares of that total catch are then distributed to commercial fishing operations, based on their historical catch or an auction. Fishermen then have the right to buy, sell, or lease these shares through individual fishing quotas (IFQs) and individual transferable quotas (ITQs). These are limited-access permits to harvest definite quantities of fish, essentially a property right conveyed by the government to a private party.

There are currently around a dozen fisheries operating under catch-share programs in the United States. The Obama administration recently proposed increased funding to greatly expand the program to additional fisheries, with the goal of restoring depleted stock and halting ocean damage from overfishing.[58]

Catch-share programs have increased the abundance of fish and cut in half the collapse rate for fisheries. According to Christopher Costello's study of 121 fisheries that have implemented ITQs, catch-shares have halted, and even reversed, the global trend toward widespread fishery collapse.[59] Another 14-month study by the Environmental Defense Fund found that catch-shares reduced "bycatch" (the netting of creatures other than the intended species) by more than 40%, and that catch-share fisheries deploy 20% less gear to catch the same amount of fish, leading to reduced ocean habitat destruction. The model also had a positive impact on the economic viability of fishing, raising revenue per boat by 80% in what were recently struggling fishing communities.[60]

New Zealand's Fishing Tale

Surrounded by the sea and its seemingly infinite abundance, New Zealanders never thought of fish as a limited resource before the 1970s. But things began to change by the early 1980s. More and more boats were plying the waters but hauling in meager catches. It could no longer be denied that the fish were disappearing—and a way of life hung in the balance in this island nation where seafood is the number four export.

Regulations and fishing bans were tried, to no avail. When nothing seemed to work, the fishing industry and the government turned their thinking upside down: Instead of dictating fishing methods and restricting the number of boats going out, they would limit *how many* fish could be caught and put their faith in the marketplace to achieve the rest.

In 1986, the government introduced the Quota Management System, with the fishing industry firmly on board. Each year, scientists determine a maximum sustainable yield for each species and region. Based on their findings, the government sets a total allowable catch for each fishery, and individual fishing operations are given quotas for a portion of that total (usually based on their average historical catch).

The twist is that individual quotas can be leased, bought, sold, or transferred (though they cannot be traded across regions or species, or banked for the future). This provision tends to make permits migrate to the most efficient vessels.

This quota system has been tweaked since its introduction, but the basic concept is still at work today. Evidence indicates that fish populations are showing clear signs of recovery. Having forged a new way of thinking about fisheries, New Zealand is now regarded as a world leader in resource management.[61]

Wetlands Mitigation and Biodiversity Banking

Human activity has had a devastating impact on the diversity of life on Earth—and that impact is growing, whether it is caused by land development, redirecting the flow of rivers, pollution, trawling the ocean floor, burning fossil fuels, or simple overexploitation. Great profits have been made along the way, but at a terrible cost to natural ecosystems—and to poor rural populations in the developing world, who tend to suffer most acutely when "free" services such as clean water, viable fishing grounds, and forest resources disappear.

The U.N.'s Millennium Ecosystem Assessment warned that the changes in biodiversity that have been taking place over the past 50 years are unprecedented in human history. It reported that natural habitats and species are declining by 0.5% to 1.5% per year, and that more land has been converted to crops in the past 60 years than in the eighteenth and nineteenth centuries combined. One-quarter of the world's coral reefs have been destroyed or degraded in the last several decades, while more than one-third of mangrove forest was lost in the same time period, reducing coastal defenses against storms.[62]

Quantifying the very real economic benefit of ecosystem services is the first step toward internalizing these impacts in business decisions. A variety of approaches are being tried, from payments for watershed services (funded by a user tax and paid to encourage landowners to keep rivers and streams free of pollution and invasive plants) to "bio-prospecting," which involves charging companies (such as pharmaceutical firms) for the right to access and inventory areas rich in biodiversity, eventually receiving a share of the profits if the compounds and genetic materials they discover lead to new commercial products.

Some of the initial groundwork was laid in the United States by the Clean Water Act. The law states that any developer who wants to dredge or fill a sensitive wetland needs a permit from the U.S. Army Corps of Engineers or the EPA. Those agencies will try to avoid or minimize any damage to the land in question, but if they deem it cannot be avoided, the law directs developers to compensate by "creating, enhancing, or restoring" a wetland of similar function and value in the same watershed. The government thus forces developers to see wetland damage as a liability. The developer can turn to a third party to help them amass the credits they need to win approval—and thus wetland mitigation banking was born. Enforcement has to be a key component of this program, as government agencies must verify that wetland credits are truly comparable and the land is being maintained as intended in perpetuity. Although it is hard to get an accurate read on this market, it was recently estimated that there are 400 wetland banks operating in the United States in a market worth $3 billion a year. Entrepreneurial wetlands bankers constitute a major slice of this market.[63]

Once the wetland mitigation bank idea took hold, the same concept was stretched further and applied to endangered species. Instead of simply regulating landowners harboring rare species, the Endangered Species Act set up a mechanism to reward them. If a threatened woodpecker or an endangered species of fly, for example, lives on a developer's property, the developer can get a permit to harm their habitat—*if* they compensate for it by creating or preserving habitat for that species somewhere else. The necessity of getting this permit and paying this price makes developers think twice before plowing through fragile land. But if they are bent on following through, they have to pay—and other owners holding similar habitat suddenly find themselves with a valuable commodity on their hands. "Conservation banking" or "species banking" is a relatively new idea, but one that is gaining traction. The Australian states of New South Wales and Victoria have launched similar programs to protect biodiversity and native vegetation.[64]

This burgeoning field is not without its controversies and growing pains. But the effort to place a value on biodiversity has caught the attention of national and world leaders. In December 2008, the U.S. Department of Agriculture announced the formation of the new Office of Ecosystem Services and Markets. And at their 2007 meeting in Potsdam, the G8 environment ministers (along with their counterparts from newly industrializing nations) agreed to launch a major study bent on assessing the global price of biodiversity. Their statement underlined the important role financial innovations can play in saving the planet:

> We will approach the financial sector to effectively integrate biodiversity into its decision making ... and we will enhance financing from existing financing instruments and explore the need and the options of additional innovative mechanisms to finance the protection and sustainable use of biological diversity, together

with the fight against poverty. In this context, we will examine the concept and the viability of payments for ecosystem services.[65]

Conclusions

Creating a sustainable economy will require massive investment to establish new means and methods of production, alternative energy, clean technologies, and new green industries. This kind of immense demand for capital is exactly the sort of trigger that sets financial innovation in motion.

The point of departure is the identification of specific market failures that result in environmental degradation. By developing techniques to account for environmental goods and services, innovators can devise market mechanisms and capital market solutions to environmental problems, opening the door to real progress in the quest to conserve air, water, fisheries, wildlife, and biodiversity.

The tools already exist to identify and internalize environmental costs, discover prices for environmental goods and services, and finance projects that address environmental needs. New markets have been built, and they are rapidly maturing. The ability to create new capital structures and build mutually beneficial relationships with equity and debt investors has increased the available funding for all types of green projects.

This field is currently operating with the winds of momentum in its sails, as visionary thinkers respond to the most urgent challenge of our era and devise creative new strategies for minimizing our footprint on the planet.

Endnotes

[1]Robert Costanza, et al., "The Value of the World's Ecosystem Services and Natural Capital," *Nature* 387 (1997): 253–260. See also Gretchen Daily and Katherine Ellison, *The New Economy of Nature: The Quest to Make Conservation Profitable* (Washington, DC: Island Press, 2002).

[2]Juliet Eilperin, "25% of Wild Mammal Species Face Extinction," *Washington Post* (7 October 2008).

[3]Anil Markandya, et al., "The Economics of Ecosystems and Biodiversity: Phase 1 (Scoping) Economic Analysis and Synthesis," final report for the European Commission, Venice, Italy (July 2008).

[4]Robert Stavins, "The Making of a Conventional Wisdom," Belfer Center for Science and International Affairs, John F. Kennedy School of Government, Harvard University (13 April 2009). Available at http://belfercenter.ksg.harvard.edu/analysis/stavins/?tag=leaded-gasoline-phasedown.

[5]Garrett Hardin, "The Tragedy of the Commons," *Science* 162, no. 3859 (1968): 1,243–1,248.

[6]Garrett Hardin, in *The Concise Encyclopedia of Economics*, 2nd ed. (Indianapolis: Liberty Fund, 2008).

[7]Nathaniel Keohane and Sheila Olmstead, *Markets and the Environment* (Washington, DC: Island Press, 2007).

[8]Ronald Coase, "The Problem of Social Cost," *Journal of Law and Economics* 3 (1960): 1–44.

[9]"Facts and Figures" summary from "Water in a Changing World," United Nations World Water Development Report 3 (UNESCO, 2009): 8.

[10]Anil Markandya, et al., "The Economics of Ecosystems and Biodiversity: Phase 1 (Scoping) Economic Analysis and Synthesis," final report for the European Commission, Venice, Italy (July 2008).

[11]Ricardo Bayon, "A Bull Market in Woodpeckers?" *The Milken Institute Review* (first quarter 2002): 30–39.

[12]Ricardo Bayon, "Innovating Environmental Finance," Milken Institute policy brief no. 25 (March 2001).

[13]Environmental Protection Agency (EPA), "SRF: Initial Guidance for State Revolving Funds" (1988): 104.

[14]EPA, "Guidebook of Financial Tools: Paying for Sustainable Environmental Systems" (2008). Available at www.epa.gov/efinpage.

[15]EPA, "Clean Water State Revolving Fund Programs," 2008 Annual Report: Cleaning Our Waters, Renewing Our Communities, Creating Jobs (2008): 2. Available at www.epa.gov/OWM/cwfinance/cwsrf/.

[16]EPA, "Financing America's Clean Water Since 1987: A Report of Progress and Innovation" (1987): 7–8. Available at www.epa.gov/OWM/cwfinance/cwsrf/.

[17]EPA, "Clean Water State Revolving Fund Programs, 2008 Annual Report: Cleaning Our Waters, Renewing Our Communities, Creating Jobs (2008): 18.

[18]Presentation by Steve Townley, Finance Officer of the Missouri Environmental Improvement and Energy Resources Authority, at a Milken Institute Financial Innovations Lab held 5 November 2008 in Israel.

[19]EPA, "Drinking Water State Revolving Fund 2007 Annual Report: Investing in a Sustainable Future" (March 2008): 3. Available at www.epa.gov/safewater/dwsrf/index.html#reports.

[20]EPA fact sheet, "Using the Clean Water State Revolving Fund" (2002). Available at www.epa.gov/owow/wetlands/facts/contents.html.

[21]EPA, "Long Island Facts, Figures, & Maps." Available at www.epa.gov/NE/eco/lis/facts.html.

[22]Audubon Society, Long Island Sound Campaign, "Lifeline to an Estuary in Distress" (DATE).

[23]EPA fact sheet, "Using the Clean Water State Revolving Fund" (2002). Available at www.epa.gov/owow/wetlands/facts/contents.html.

[24]Jeffrey Q. Chambers, Niro Higuchi, Edgard S. Tribuzy, and Susan E. Trumbore, "Carbon Sink for a Century," *Nature* 410, no. 6827 (March 2001): 429.

[25]Thomas A. Sancton, Barry Hillenbrand, and Richard Hornik, "Hands Across the Sea," *Time* (2 January 1989). Available at www.time.com/time/magazine/article/0,9171,956635-2,00.html.

[26]Conservation International, www.conservation.org/sites/gcf/Documents/GCF_debtfornature_overview.pdf.

[27]USAID, www.usaid.gov/our_work/environment/forestry/intro_eai.html.

[28]Environmental Foundation of Jamaica, www.efj.org.jm/Current_Projects/current_projects.htm.

[29]USAID, www.usaid.gov/our_work/environment/forestry/tfca.html.

[30]Marc Lacey, "Costa Rica: U.S. Swaps Debt for Forest Aid," *New York Times* (17 October 2007).

[31]The Nature Conservancy, www.nature.org/wherewework/centralamerica/costarica/misc/art22576.html.

[32]"Biggest U.S. Debt Swap for Nature Will Conserve Guatemala's Forests," USAID press release (2 October 2006).

[33]"Largest TFCA Debt-for-Nature Agreement Signed to Conserve Indonesia's Tropical Forests," U.S. State Department press release (30 June 2009).

[34]"U.S. to Forgive $30 Million Debt to Protect Sumatra's Forests," Conservation International press release (30 June 2009).

[35]Joel Kurtzman, "The Low-Carbon Diet: How the Market Can Curb Climate Change," *Foreign Affairs* (September–October 2009): 114–122.

[36]*Ibid.*

[37]EPA, Overview: The Clean Air Act Amendments of 1990, Title IV: Acid Deposition Control. Available at www.epa.gov/air/caa/caaa_overview.html#titleIV.

[38]Richard L. Sandor and Jerry Skees, "Creating a Market for Carbon Emissions: Opportunities for U.S. Farmers," *Choices, Magazine of the American Agricultural Economics Association* (first quarter 1999): 13.

[39]Keohane and Olmstead, Markets and the Environment, *Markets and the Environment* (Washington, DC: Island Press, 2007).

[40]Richard L. Sandor and Michael J. Walsh, "Some Observations on the Evolution of the International Greenhouse Gas Emissions Trading Market," in *Emissions Trading: Environmental Policy's New Approach*, Richard Kosobud, ed. (New York: John Wiley & Sons, 2000).

[41]Curtis Carlson, Dallas Burtraw, Maureen Cropper, and Karen Palmer, "Sulfur Dioxide Control by Electric Utilities: What Are the Gains from Trade?" (discussion paper no. 98-44-REV, Resources for the Future, 2000): 4.

[42]EPA, Clean Air Markets, Emissions, Compliance, and Market Data, www.epa.gov/airmarkets/progress/ARP_1.html.

[43]*Ibid.*

[44]Carlson, et al., "Sulfur Dioxide Control by Electric Utilities: What Are the Gains from Trade?" (discussion paper no. 98-44-REV, Resources for the Future, 2000): 4.

[45]EPA, www.epa.gov/acidrain/effects/health.html.

[46]Nicholas Stern, *The Economics of Climate Change: The Stern Review* (Cambridge, UK, and New York: Cambridge University Press, 2007).

[47]Robert N. Stavins, "A U.S. Cap-and-Trade System to Address Global Climate Change," (discussion paper no. 2007-13, The Brookings Institution, October 2007).

[48]Kurtzman, "The Low-Carbon Diet: How the Market Can Curb Climate Change," *Foreign Affairs* (September–October 2009).

[49]Chicago Climate Exchange, Overview, www.chicagoclimatex.com/content.jsf?id=821.

[50]Simon Lomax, "CFTC Plans to Regulate Chicago Climate Exchange, Gensler Says," Bloomberg (27 August 2009).

[51]A. Denny Ellerman and Paul L. Joskow, *The European Union's Emissions Trading System in Perspective*, Pew Center for Global Climate Change (May 2008).

[52]*Ibid.*

[53]Michael J. Walsh, "Maximizing Financial Support for Biodiversity in the Emerging Kyoto Protocol Markets," *The Science of the Total Environment* 240, nos. 1–3 (1999): 145–156.

[54]Available at http://cdm.unfccc.int/index.html.

[55]"The State of the World's Fisheries and Aquaculture 2008," United Nations Food and Agriculture Organization.

[56]Boris Worm, et al., "Impacts of Biodiversity Loss on Ocean Ecosystem Services," *Science* 314, no. 5800 (2006): 787–790.

[57]Boris Worm, et al., "Rebuilding Global Fisheries," *Science* 325, no. 5940 (2009): 578–585.

[58]Alison Winter, "Obama Administration Proposes Major Spending for Fishery Cap-and-Trade Plan," *New York Times*, 11 May 2009.

[59]Christopher Costello, Steven D. Gaines, and John Lynham, "Can Catch Shares Prevent Fisheries Collapse?," *Science* 321, no. 5896 (2008): 1678–1681.

[60]"Sustaining America's Fisheries and Fishing Communities: An Evaluation of Incentive-Based Management," Environmental Defense Fund (2007): 4, 18.

[61]James Sanchirico and Richard Newell, "Catching Market Efficiencies: Quota-Based Fisheries Management," Resources for the Future (Spring 2003); Boris Worm, et al., "Rebuilding Global Fisheries," *Science* 325, no. 5940 (2009): 578–585; and Richard Newell, James Sanchirico, and Suzi Kerr, "Fishing Quota Markets," Resources for the Future (discussion paper 02-20, August 2002).

[62]United Nations Millennium Ecosystem Assessment, Findings (2005). Available at www.millenniumassessment.org/en/SlidePresentations.aspx.

[63]Ricardo Bayon, "Using Markets to Conserve Biodiversity," *State of the World 2008*, Worldwatch Institute.

[64]*Ibid.* See also Bayon, "A Bull Market in Woodpeckers?" *The Milken Institute Review* (First quarter 2002).30–39.

[65]"Biodiversity and Ecosystem Services: Bloom or Bust?" United Nations Environment Program Finance Initiative (March 2008): 7.

6

Financing the Developing World

"Like slavery and apartheid, poverty is not natural," declared Nelson Mandela. "It is man-made and it can be overcome and eradicated by the actions of human beings." This challenge lies at the heart of development finance, a field that has until recently been largely passed over by financial innovation.

The goal of ending global poverty has proven elusive for so long that it is painful to contemplate the failed efforts and squandered opportunities. But the broader picture is not uniformly bleak. The World Bank reports that the percentage of people around the world living in extreme poverty dropped by half between 1981 and 2005. Half a billion people who once struggled to survive on less than $1.25 a day have been lifted out of poverty in one of the greatest success stories of our times.[1]

Perhaps the most dramatic strides have been made in China, which just 30 years ago was one of the poorest countries in the world. Since 1990, it has grown at an average rate of more than 10% a year in real terms. In 2008, its $7.9 trillion GDP (adjusted for purchasing power) stood second only to the United States' (at $14.3 trillion). India, too, has seen sweeping change; since 1990, it has grown at more than 6% a year in real terms. It is now the fourth-largest economy in the world, with a GDP adjusted for purchasing power of $3.3 trillion (trailing the third-largest economy, Japan, which posts a GDP of $4.4 trillion).[2]

The grip of poverty has been loosened and a new middle class has emerged—not only in China and India, but also in emerging nations such as Brazil, Malaysia, and South Korea. Their trajectories make it clear that the most direct route to poverty reduction is the creation of real, broad-based economic growth that generates jobs. It is no coincidence that the World Bank found the most remarkable strides were made in East Asia. As the region's economy came roaring to life, ignited by increased international trade, the extreme poverty rate was slashed from nearly 80% to 18% in just 24 years.[3]

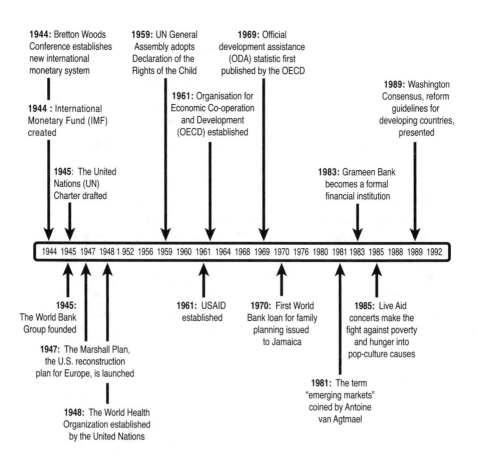

But that progress, heartening as it is, has not penetrated to all the desperate corners of the globe. In places like sub-Saharan Africa, where a dire health crisis hinders productivity, little progress has been made. The proportion of the population in sub-Saharan Africa living on less than $1.25 a day decreased from 55.7% in 1990 to 50.3% in 2005. However, because of population growth, the number of people in the region living in extreme poverty actually *grew* by 100 million over this period.[4]

Spurring on the kind of economic growth that can overcome the development gap is the central task of our generation. Traditional

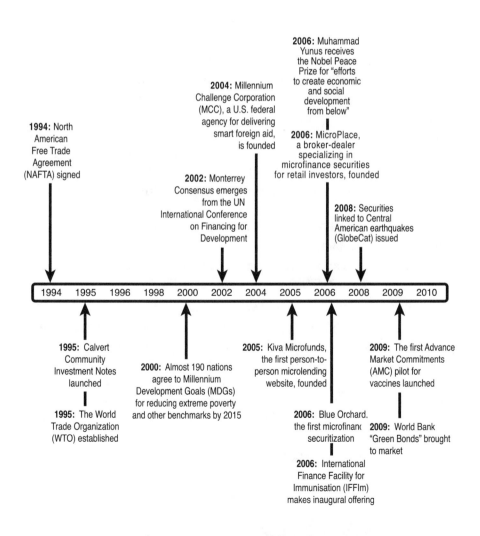

foreign aid—disbursement of loans, grants, and other assistance by individual governments or multilateral agencies—is very much focused on issues of poverty reduction and global health; there is no doubt it has a continuing and vital role to play. But a wave of financial innovation is urgently needed to supplement this model and truly integrate developing nations into the global economy.

Growth cannot be sustained by low savings rates, undeveloped financial systems, and inadequate financial intermediation between savers and investors (both locally and internationally). Sound banking systems and transparent markets are the underpinnings of sustainable development. Financial innovators will need to actively participate in the effort to build solid financial institutions and expand access to credit and financial services in order to responsibly fuel higher rates of growth.

In addition to financial infrastructure, the developing world has an overwhelming need for physical and social infrastructure—and vast flows of capital will need to be mobilized to support this effort. Nobel laureate Gary Becker and others have repeatedly shown the importance of human capital investments in determining income, so it is no surprise to see that the earnings of more educated individuals rise faster than earnings of the less educated.[5] Dramatically expanding access to education is crucial to ensuring that gains are more widely and equitably shared across entire populations, thus reducing not only the gaps between nations, but *internal* inequalities as well. Focusing on the factors that could increase human capital productivity (not only education, but inputs such as health, housing, communication, and transportation) will enable the developing world to take advantage of greater trade and inflows of technology and capital.

The dramatic gains against poverty seen in the last three decades could have happened only in a more open and integrated world economy. As the World Bank's Commission on Growth and Development noted, "Growth is not an end in itself. But it makes it possible to achieve other important objectives of individuals and societies. It can spare people *en masse* from poverty and drudgery. Nothing else ever has."[6]

TABLE 6.1   Types of Financial Innovations for Development

Products and Services	Processes and Operations	Organizational Forms
The official development assistance (ODA) statistic first published by the OECD (1969)	Launch of the Marshall Plan, U.S. funding for postwar European reconstruction (1947)	International Monetary Fund (IMF) created (1944)
Muhammad Yunus launches microlending revolution (1976)	Washington Consensus, reform guidelines for developing countries, presented (1989)	United Nations (UN) charter drafted; World Bank Group founded (1945)
International Finance Facility for Immunisation (IFFIm) established (2006)	North American Free Trade Agreement (NAFTA) signed (1994)	World Health Organization established by the UN (1948)
First advance market commitments (AMC) pilot for vaccines offered (2009)	189 countries sign the Millennium Development Goals, pledging to halve extreme poverty and hunger by 2015 (2000)	Organisation for Economic Co-operation and Development (OECD) established (1961)
First World Bank "Green Bonds" issued (2009)	Kenya's M-PESA mobile payment service uses cellphones to bring financial services to millions who were previously "unbanked" (2007)	World Trade Organization established (1995)

Paradigm Shifts in Development Finance

Whenever an international summit is convened, or whenever a new American president takes office, wistful memories of the Marshall Plan are invoked as a road map for turning around the developing world. That dutiful policy reference echoes from John F. Kennedy's "Alliance for Progress," to George W. Bush's "Millennium Challenge," to Barack Obama's recent calls for new global development initiatives.

Under the Marshall Plan, the United States injected billions of dollars into Europe's economies to rebuild a continent ravaged by World War II. America's success in speeding European recovery informed the direction of foreign aid for a generation, as well-meaning officials struggled to apply the same template around the globe.

As the timeline at the beginning of this chapter indicates, development finance gained real momentum in the postwar years for a variety of reasons, including a wave of decolonization that led to the independence of countries once under the thumb of European imperialism. The Cold War simultaneously sparked a race between East and West to amass influence and resources in less-developed countries.

This era saw the establishment of a whole range of institutions focused on financing and promoting development as a means to promote stability in the postwar world. These included the U.S. Agency for International Development (USAID); KfW, the German development bank; the Organisation for Economic Co-operation and Development (OECD); the World Bank; the International Monetary Fund (IMF); and, of course, the United Nations itself.

The foreign aid disbursed by governments and multilateral agencies in the ensuing decades has been crucial for maintaining some level of health, education, and social services in the poorest countries. But aid alone cannot generate the kind of robust economic growth that is self-sustaining and transformative. Financial innovation is needed to step into the breach and devise new models that can supplement the role of foreign aid.

In fact, by the early 1990s, private capital flows began to outstrip bilateral and multilateral flows of government development funding.[7] This signaled a profound shift in the world economy, opening new possibilities for broad-based job growth.

A crucial change in terminology played a supporting role in attracting this new surge of investment. For many years, the "underdeveloped" label had tainted the assets of developing nations, yielding undervalued assessments and arbitrary discounts. But terms like "less developed countries (LDCs)" and "Third World" eventually gave way to "newly industrialized countries (NICs)." Then, in the early 1980s, Antoine van Agtmael, then serving as division chief for the World Bank's treasury operations and deputy director of the International Finance Corporation's Capital Markets Department, coined the term "emerging markets."[8]

This new definition proved to be a masterstroke of marketing. Now developing nations had a designation that reflected their economic potential and the investment opportunities they presented. Just two and a half decades after this nomenclature change, *The Economist* would declare, "The world is experiencing one of the biggest revolutions in history, as economic power shifts from the developed world to China and other emerging giants. Thanks to market reforms, emerging economies are growing much faster than developed ones."[9] Today emerging markets are poised to account for a majority of global GDP.[10]

It's clear that some major battle lines have shifted in the fight against global poverty. But the gains have not been shared equally, and billions of people have yet to see their standard of living improve. The challenge for today's financial innovators is to find a way to replicate the unprecedented achievements of the last three decades more widely.

A Marshall Plan for Africa, parts of Latin America, the poorest regions of Asia, and the non-oil-producing Middle East is simply not in the offing from Western nations. In 2000, the world's leaders set out an ambitious agenda for development at the United Nations. The Millennium Development Goals (MDGs) were formal pledges to eradicate extreme poverty and hunger, provide universal education, improve child and maternal health, and combat HIV/AIDS, among other worthy aspirations. It does indeed appear that the initial targets for reducing extreme poverty will be met by 2015, but the larger agenda is in doubt.

A 2002 study by the World Bank estimated that an additional $40 billion to $70 billion in additional assistance per year would be needed to meet all the MDGs.[11] In the wake of the global financial crisis, few donor nations are in a position to increase foreign aid. In 2009, a UN task force reported that donors are falling short by $34 billion per year on pledges made at the 2005 G-8 meeting in Gleneagles.[12]

Interestingly, in China, there have been calls for the country to use up to $500 billion of its $2.3 trillion foreign exchange reserves in a Chinese "Marshall Plan" to lend money to Africa, Asia, and Latin America. The idea is to help increase living standards in these parts of the world while simultaneously increasing demand for Chinese products.[13]

But is a simple increase in foreign aid the answer? After many decades and trillions of dollars in foreign aid, donors and emerging-market countries alike have understandably come to question the conventional approaches. Yes, foreign aid eases short-term macroeconomic shocks, alleviates humanitarian emergencies, and provides critical health and education services. At its best, it can build the infrastructure that makes further progress possible. But the best-case scenario isn't always how things play out.

The traditional model of foreign aid comes laden with baggage: the crushing debt burden of repayment, the frequency with which corrupt officials divert funding away from its intended purposes, the unpredictability of funding flows from donor nations, the stifling of innovation, and concerns over building a culture of dependency. There has been a growing realization that aid cannot be fully effective in the absence of strong institutions and a commitment to transparency in recipient nations.[14]

Looking beyond foreign aid, the usual economic development palliatives are not up to the task. Foreign direct investment flows are not high enough to drive aggregate demand and growth, and portfolio capital flows to many developing and frontier markets are at a trickle due to insufficient banking institutions and capital market development. Sovereign debt reduction all too often benefits the entrenched elites and does not translate into real infrastructure improvements for the poor. Microcredit, which seeks to provide small-scale entrepreneurial financing to the poorest of the poor, has been widely heralded as a fresh approach. But it is not the panacea that was once envisioned: It still has limited penetration in many neglected regions and, while alleviating poverty to some extent, can never drive economic growth to the levels required to build a global middle class. Some critics are beginning to call its effectiveness into question.[15]

This is the point at which financial innovation has to enter the game. Capital is urgently needed for vast new infrastructure projects and for funding the small and medium-size enterprises (SMEs) that are the leading engines of job growth. In addition to helping developing nations build banking systems and institutional frameworks, a major challenge is achieving "financial inclusion"—that is, expanding access to credit and financial services to previously excluded populations.

These are perhaps the most sprawling and complex challenges that have ever faced financial innovators, and creative strategies to address these issues are just beginning to emerge. Finding the right answers may involve years of trial and error, but success will unlock the kind of growth that may one day eliminate the need for interventions. With the right tools and capital structures in hand, private investors can open new markets, igniting broadly shared and sustainable prosperity by harnessing the power of entrepreneurial and infrastructure finance.

Building Financial Infrastructure, Building a Middle Class

Empirical studies using cross-country analysis have shown the strong relationship between finance and growth.[16] In comparing the financial systems and structures of both developed and developing countries, and considering their impacts on economic performance, a number of important recommendations emerge:

- It is crucial to prudently develop a diversified financial system.
- State banks should be privatized, and foreign banks should be allowed to acquire domestic banks.
- Developing countries should promote a financial system that allows for dispersed private ownership of all financial resources.
- Banks should not be prevented from adopting the latest information technology.
- Governments should provide an appropriate legal, regulatory, enforcement, and accounting environment for financial markets.[17]

In many emerging markets, systemic and institutional problems constrain growth and hinder broader participation in the economy. Financial power may be concentrated within a tiny elite circle, or a nation may lack property rights, a well-developed legal system for enforcing contracts, market transparency, and good corporate governance.[18] These obstacles make the tools of financial technology inaccessible in large parts of the world and have aborted market changes in many countries. Building market and regulatory institutions and capabilities is a critical ingredient of real economic development.

Going Mobile

The key to building a global middle class is expanding the access of ordinary people to affordable credit, savings, and equity investments. But a recent report from the Financial Access Initiative estimated that just over half the world's adult population does not use formal financial services to save or borrow. Some 2.2 billion of those unserved adults live in Africa, Asia, Latin America, and the Middle East.[19]

New mobile technology is beginning to change all that. By the end of 2007, the penetration rate for fixed telephone lines in the developing world was only 13%, but there were more than 2 billion mobile cellular subscriptions, for a penetration rate of 39%. Advances in communication technology are not only a lifeline in dangerous or remote places, but they also offer new services such as mobile banking and payment systems. Since the current generation of cellphones offers high-speed Web surfing, the gap in Internet penetration rates between the developed world and the developing world is rapidly closing as well.[20]

In regions where land lines are impossible to come by, the cellphone is already the tool of choice for small and medium-size businesses. This new platform can even allow farmers to compare commodity prices at various markets; they can now learn where to

In addition, development officials need to employ tools for screening out high-risk borrowers in advance (thus overcoming adverse selection) and protecting their repayment prospects once borrowers have the money from investment (preventing moral hazard).[24] Weak accounting standards, limited third-party credit information services, restrictions on the use of physical collateral, the high cost of managing smaller transactions and projects, and the difficulty of mobilizing a continuing supply of funds are among the issues facing the field of development finance.[25]

Advances in information technology are beginning to change this picture. Today, it is easier than ever to enable the free flow of accurate operating and financial information to provide oversight by obtain the best return for their crops before they ever leave home. (In 2009, Google launched a text service for this market, called Farmer's Friend.[21]) Harvard economist Robert Jansen has written about fishermen off the coast of India using cellphones to shop around for the best prospective buyers before bringing their catch to shore; this technology improved their profits and lowered consumer prices at the same time.[22]

Backed by $35 million in funding from the Gates Foundation, the Alliance for Financial Inclusion brought together central bank officials from 60 countries for its launch in 2009. The new alliance aims to bring financial services to 50 million previously excluded people over the next few years. Mobile banking via cellphone offers a tool for realizing that goal. One of the companies showcased at the alliance's inaugural forum was Kenya's M-PESA, which has racked up 7.4 million subscribers since its inception in 2007. The service allows customers to deposit cash for storage on their mobile phones, using the balance for transfers, bill payments, or withdrawals.[23]

Development officials once bemoaned the digital divide between the world's haves and have-nots. Just a few years ago, cellphones were status symbols for the wealthy—but today affordable models with new technology offer the world's poor an invitation to join the global economy.

investors, owners, and regulators. But financial technology has its enemies. Entrenched oligarchies in many developing countries have yet to support reforms that might decentralize political and economic power to transform state-run economies into entrepreneurial ones.

A recent study by Asli Demirguc-Kunt and Ross Levine shows how improvements in credit markets and the development of a solid financial infrastructure can translate into economic opportunity:

> [A]ccess to credit markets increases parental investment in the education of their children and reduces the substitution of children out of schooling and into labor markets when adverse shocks reduce family income. Moreover, a growing body of

evidence suggests that better functioning financial systems stimulate new firm formation and help small, promising firms expand as a wider array of firms gain access to the financial system. Besides the direct benefits of enhanced access to financial services, research also indicates that finance reduces inequality through indirect, labor market mechanisms. Specifically, cross-country studies, individual-level analyses, and firm-level investigations show that financial development accelerates economic growth, intensifies competition, and boosts the demand for labor, disproportionately benefiting those at the lower end of the income distribution.[26]

Even countries that witness an overall credit expansion due to increased multilateral foreign aid and investment flows will not experience real growth unless there is broader access to banks, formal financial institutions, and credit markets. There is considerable evidence that as the depth and breadth of financial markets increases, an accelerated level of global economic growth follows. Reduced inequality, development, and the operation of the credit markets are clearly linked.[27]

The Microfinance Revolution

In 1976, an entirely new model of development finance emerged not from Washington's halls of power, but from the forgotten back streets of Jobra, an impoverished village in Bangladesh. Abandoning his classroom, Muhammad Yunus, a professor of economics, ventured out to meet directly with the poor and learn exactly what factors kept them from earning their way out of poverty. He soon realized that their lack of access to credit left them at the mercy of unscrupulous loan sharks. Moved by their plight, he opened his own purse strings and loaned $27 to 42 women who made bamboo stools. In the process, he launched the microlending movement, taking a more grassroots approach than the traditional top-down aid model.

By 1983, Yunus had founded Grameen Bank as a formal financial institution. It offered small loans to the poor with no collateral required. The bank successfully employed a group lending model, which holds borrowers accountable to their neighbors for repayment

performance. Grameen proved that the poor were indeed creditworthy; in fact, the bank boasts that its loan recovery rate is 97.66%. It
has enjoyed phenomenal growth: It works in almost 85,000 villages,
has served almost 8 million borrowers, and has disbursed US$8.4 bil-
lion since its inception. Grameen is 95% owned by its borrowers,
most of whom are poor women, and is now completely self-sustaining
through the deposits of its customers.[28]

Appearing at the 2008 Milken Institute Global Conference,
Yunus explained the thinking behind his model. "It is amazing how
financial institutions reject such a large number of human beings on
this planet, saying they are not creditworthy. Instead of banking institutions telling people they're not creditworthy, the people should tell
the banks whether they are people-worthy," he said. "The basic principle of banking is the more you have, the more you can get. We
reversed it. The less you have, the higher priority you get."[29]

Grameen's success inspired a host of other organizations to try
microlending—and soon the model expanded beyond the provision
of small loans to become *microfinance,* which encompasses a whole
range of financial services for the underprivileged. These include savings accounts, investment products, money transfers and remittances,
bill payment services, home loans, education and consumer loans,
agricultural and leasing loans, life insurance, property and crop insurance, health insurance, and even pension products—services that
were once completely out of reach for disadvantaged populations.[30]

It is difficult to get an accurate read on the size of the industry
worldwide, but it is estimated that anywhere from 1,000 to 2,500 microfinance institutions (MFIs) serve some 67.6 million clients in over 100
different countries.[31] Of these 67 million, more than half come from the
bottom 50% of people living below the poverty line. That is, some 41.6
million of the poorest people in the world have been reached by MFIs.[32]

MFIs can take many forms, from NGOs (nongovernmental
organizations) and rural development banks to commercial banks.
Some MFIs attempt to increase their social impact by tying in additional services such as health and education. While many operate
with a purely altruistic mission, others have a for-profit model, with
service to the poor as only a secondary goal—a shift that has caused
controversy within the microfinance community.[33]

Muhammad Yunus: Creating a World Without Poverty

As the father of the microfinance movement, Muhammad Yunus is often referred to as "banker to the poor." *BusinessWeek* called him "one of the greatest entrepreneurs of all time."[34] By providing the poorest citizens of Bangladesh with previously unheard-of access to credit, his Grameen Bank has improved the quality of life for thousands of families in rural and urban areas alike. The announcement that Yunus had won the Nobel Peace Prize was a moment of international recognition that finance has the power to spark major social change and transform lives.

But having launched one revolution, Yunus is already busy fomenting the next—and this time, he is determined to change our current understanding of what it really means to turn a profit. He has turned his attention to the development of "social businesses," nonloss, nondividend companies that measure return on investment in social outcomes rather than financial gain. Such outcomes might include the number of children with improved health, the gallons of potable water delivered to regions with unsafe water supplies, or the kilowatts of energy powering a village that previously had no electricity.

One of the first social businesses was a venture formed by Grameen Bank and Dannone. The company produces an affordable yogurt enriched with nutrients that are desperately needed by impoverished children in Bangladesh. Grameen Bank and Dannone will be able to recover their investment in the enterprise, but both seek a rate of return measured in healthier children, not as a

Beyond Microfinance:
The Missing Middle of SME Finance

If there is a lesson from General Marshall's playbook, it is that the entrepreneurial growth that saved both postwar Europe and the post-Depression United States was fueled by small and medium-size enterprises (SMEs). Even today, this entrepreneurial sector contributes 57% of total employment and more than half of GDP in high-income countries. But the same growth dynamic has yet to be percentage of profits. While there is no direct profit from this endeavor, Dannone received a major public relations boost.[35]

Yunus has gone on to create social businesses with a variety of corporate partners, all aimed at improving the lives of the poor. Grameen–Veolia Water Ltd. enlisted the largest water company in France in the effort to build and operate several water production and treatment plants in some of the poorest villages in Bangladesh.[36] At the 2009 Clinton Global Initiative, Yunus announced a partnership with the Nike Foundation to launch the Grameen Nurse Institute, which will not only expand health-care services to women, but also train girls to be the health-care work force of the future.[37] Two months later, he inked a deal with Adidas to manufacture athletic shoes in Bangladesh that will sell for only 1 euro, serving millions of people who cannot afford to buy shoes.[38]

Funding a social business enterprise is not like donating to charity. While most partners are motivated by the desire to burnish their corporate social responsibility credentials, Yunus believes that social business investors can and should expect to recover their initial outlay. The return on their investment, however, will not be a financial dividend, but a tangible social benefit. The business still has the imperative to be successful in order to repay its initial investors and grow the operation, but its ultimate success will be measured by how well it achieves its stated social objective. If this concept takes off, Yunus said at a 2009 appearance at the IMF, "we can put poverty in a museum."[39]

set in motion in low-income countries, where SMEs account for only 18% of employment and 16% of GDP.[40] Ironically, development finance is available for microenterprises and large businesses, but not for this "missing middle," which would actually have the potential to solve the development conundrum if the proper momentum were put behind it.

While microcredit is at an all-time high for individual entrepreneurs and artisans, the funding to expand and thrive is scarce for growth-oriented firms of 10–300 employees in emerging markets.

SMEs typically require financing amounts between $10,000 and $1 million, with $3 million to $5 million being the upper threshold. They also need *patient* capital that gives them time to grow, but many investors are not willing to lock up their funds for extended periods. In recent World Bank Enterprise Surveys, more than 40% of entrepreneurial firms in low-income nations reported lack of capital access as their key barrier to growth.

Although they will provide retail services to these companies, commercial banks tend to avoid lending to this sector, preferring instead to allocate capital to more established companies. (Because banks in many emerging nations enjoy monopoly status, they can afford to ignore market segments such as this and still remain profitable.) Even if they will lend to SMEs, banks tend to impose such stiff requirement for posting collateral that loans are out of reach for fledgling businesses. While 30% of large firms use bank finance in developing countries, only 12% of small companies do. Less than 10% of SME demand for credit is being met by banks facing new Basel II regulations; these institutions often impose requirements of 100% collateral in liquid assets, real property, and cash deposits. In Cameroon, the minimum deposit for opening a checking account is more than $700, an amount higher than that country's per-capita GDP.[41]

External financing is also hard to come by, since few angel investors, venture capitalists, or private equity investors—the funders who specialize in startups—operate in these markets. Not only is credit and risk appraisal difficult for investors, but, above all, these markets tend to be illiquid; the difficulty of exiting investments remains perhaps the most formidable barrier to establishing a more substantial flow of foreign capital to this sector. Government and donor-directed subsidized credit programs in support of SMEs have had limited impact in the absence of wider systemic reforms and are fraught with moral hazard and adverse selection problems.

SMEs in the developing world continue to face unique and enormous challenges: barriers to market entry, expensive and time-consuming regulatory requirements, burdensome tax and legal structures, lack of management experience, labor market rigidities, and, above all, limited access to affordable capital (whether traditional bank lending or risk capital). Large firms that enjoy limited competition may influence the regulatory, legal, and financial conditions to block new entrants. Indeed, SMEs face greater financial, legal, and corruption obstacles than large firms, and these challenges constrain the growth of SMEs to a greater degree.[42]

Are there models for filling the financial service gap for SMEs? How can we identify and assess SME deal flow? What investment structures will enable credit enhancement and flexibility for SMEs on a revolving basis? What would those hybrid capital structures for development investment look like if scaled? How can multilateral and bilateral agencies manage sources of risk for such longer-term investments? What role can developing world stock exchanges play in intermediating capital for SMEs? These are all questions that can be answered with financial innovations.

There are several important barriers that impede the flow of capital to emerging-market SMEs[43]:

- **Exiting investments is difficult.** Because emerging countries typically have underdeveloped capital markets and a shortage of buyers, it can be challenging to exit equity investments. Investors are often forced to hold on to these investments longer than would be ideal as they struggle to find a buyer or wait for the entrepreneur to come up with enough cash to buy out the investors' shares. All else being equal, the longer an investment's length, the lower the overall return, so the difficulty of exiting discourages investors from putting their money in these markets.

- **SME investment returns are not fully risk-adjusted.** Due to the lack of solid information, fund managers seeking to invest in this arena are forced to spend a great deal of time and effort locating prospective investments and becoming familiar with companies' financials. Post-investment, SMEs often require a significant amount of technical assistance from fund managers to improve their businesses. As a result, these types of investments are time- and capital-intensive, leading investors to seek a higher risk-adjusted rate of return. These commercial investors tend to put their money elsewhere or move up-market to more profitable investments at the larger end of the SME continuum. Historically, the vast majority of capital in SME funds has come from multilateral and bilateral development finance institutions. Funds need to find ways to attract more private investors to small and growing businesses.

- **Information gaps exist between investors and SMEs.** Development institutions and national governments use widely varying definitions of what constitutes an SME, resulting in a lack of comprehensive and comparable data for the sector that makes it difficult for investors to accurately assess opportunities. Investors are hesitant to embrace a sector for which there are no established norms for performance, while entrepreneurs do not have an efficient way of tapping into funding sources. Clearly, there is a need to better connect the two sides to facilitate investment in these markets. Innovations in information technology—such as data reduction and storage technologies that can better index, store, and retrieve small business data sets—may present an opportunity to facilitate a more efficient flow of information in these markets.

There are a range of financial innovations that could start to address these problems. Given the difficulty of exiting investments in

Impact Investing: Doing Well by Doing Good

A new generation of financial innovators has come to believe it's possible to generate financial returns and social impact through a single investment. "Impact investing" (also known as double- or triple-bottom-line investing, or mission-related investing) has been around for some time in the form of portfolio screening. But today, recognizing that government and philanthropic dollars alone can't solve the world's social challenges, impact investors have begun to take a more active and hands-on approach.

The Acumen Fund is a case in point: This New York–based investment fund combines elements of venture capital and aid. It pools money from foundations and individual philanthropists for mission-related investing, pursuing a social return plus a profit, which is then recycled back into the fund. Although Acumen will accept below-market-rate returns, it does apply rigorous benchmarks to evaluate the effectiveness of its investments. Acumen offers "patient capital" to a variety of entrepreneurial ventures in the developing world, from manufacturers of antimalarial bed nets to the makers of clean-water systems.[44]

developing countries, creating exit finance facilities would be one possibility. In this case, a revolving loan fund could facilitate exits by providing entrepreneurs and other buyers access to capital in the absence of bank funding. Another strategy would be the creation of permanent capital vehicles, comparable to a limited-life fund, which would decrease fund costs and offer liquid shares to investors, making exits easier.

A royalty model could also ensure returns. Investors would have a claim on a percentage of an SME's sales or revenues over the life of the investment, enabling them to pull in a regular source of capital; in the case of a management buyout, it would decrease the amount that the recipient has to pay at the end of the investment.

Increasing investment through the creation of regional funds or funds of funds has the potential to broaden the investment target and decrease administrative costs relative to investment income, lifting

Another innovative organization, Root Capital, has developed a lending model to serve small rural businesses, such as coffee farmer cooperatives and artisan associations. It aims to serve businesses that are considered too small and risky for mainstream banks and too large for microfinance, offering them the capital they need to grow and sustain their operations.[45]

The Global Impact Investing Network (GIIN), launched in September 2009, aims to increase the effectiveness of impact investing by sharing best practices and advancing common performance measurements for these investments.[46] The Monitor Institute estimates that within five to ten years, the total value of impact investments could grow to $500 billion, roughly 1% of the world's total assets under management in 2008.[47]

In the wake of the economic meltdown, the time seems to be ripe for the "philanthrocapitalist" approach. As Antony Bugg-Levine and John Goldstein wrote in a recent article, "These impact investors offer a bridge between traditional philanthropy, which incubates innovation and mobilizes attention to exciting solutions, and the private-sector capital markets that ultimately hold the wealth required to advance these solutions to a level proportionate to need."[48]

net returns. Increasing the number of technical assistance funding sources and having them operate side-by-side with investment funds would separate technical assistance and boost returns for investors. The use of structured finance vehicles could broaden the investment base in SME firms, enabling different investors to use investment products that suit their risk appetite and return expectations, thus allowing more investors to participate in funding this sector. Another innovation might be first-loss credit enhancement or guarantee funds from local banks that would incentivize them to provide capital to SMEs, thereby capping downside investor risk.

Underlying all these financial innovations would be a greater use of information technology to overcome information asymmetries about these firms and increase investors' comfort level in dealing with them. This information infrastructure could be essential. It would allow the matching of investors and entrepreneurs, thus increasing the number of SMEs financed and decreasing the costs of sourcing deals. High-level financial and performance data on SMEs would enable investors to make more informed investment decisions.

The global aid architecture is evolving, with an increased role for NGOs, foundations, and private-sector entities—and some organizations are applying alternative and entrepreneurial strategies to SME development. There is an interest in creative approaches to helping SMEs gain access to forms of financing that will free up working capital for business expansion.

For-profit firms like the U.S.-based Microfinance International Corporation are mobilizing remittance flows (personal flows of money from migrants to family and friends still residing in their home country) for capital investments in small enterprises. (The importance of remittances as a source of development aid and investment has increased from $50 billion in 1995 to over $229 billion in 2007.[49]) Organizations like Small Enterprise Assistance Funds (U.S.) have defined a niche by packaging risk capital with specialized technical support for SMEs.

Others are finding ways to lower the risk premium associated with small businesses. The German bank ProCredit is training loan officers to work directly with small enterprises to manage credit risk and encourage traditional banks to enter the SME sector. The JSE Securities Exchange in South Africa has created an alternative exchange for small enterprises that provides business training for SME executives.

Public- and private-sector actors are exploring how they might underwrite an international bond for SMEs. Some are experimenting with new kinds of financial instruments (debt, equity, and quasi-equity) tailored to the credit/risk profile of SMEs.[50]

A growing number of "impact investors" (see the accompanying sidebar) are now putting their money in organizations that finance the "missing middle." For example, Small Enterprise Assistance Funds (SEAF) has found that investing in SMEs with high growth potential can deliver not only substantial financial returns, but also social impacts such as increased employment opportunities for the poor; on-the-job benefits such as training and health insurance; low-cost, high-quality goods and services for customers; greater sales opportunities for suppliers; and increased tax revenues to the government. SEAF estimates that for every dollar invested, an additional $12 is generated in the local economy, on average.[51]

SMEs are widely recognized as key contributors to employment, innovation, productivity, and economic growth. If barriers to its growth were removed, this sector would contribute to expanding the middle class. Achieving a critical mass of SMEs helps to build supply chains and forge dynamic business clusters linked to global markets through trade and investment.

Financing Infrastructure Development

Infrastructure is the lifeblood of any modern economy. No country has sustained rapid growth without also keeping up impressive rates of public investment in infrastructure, education, and health.[52] Roads, railways, airports, and seaports are vital for transporting goods, while telecommunications networks form a bridge to the ideas, markets, and technologies available in the broader global economy. Infrastructure spending also encompasses electricity, quality schools, sanitation, and clean drinking water—services that have a dramatic impact on the quality of life for residents of low-income nations.

But for decades, gaps in infrastructure have hampered growth prospects. Traditional foreign aid is too scarce to meet the developing world's immense and urgent need for investment.

After the Asian Financial Crisis of 1997–1998, infrastructure investment collapsed in the region and has never recovered. The Asian Development Bank (ADB) estimates that over the next decade, Asian governments need to spend $8 trillion at the national level and $290 billion on cross-border projects to integrate the economies of the region; it believes these outlays could generate $13 trillion in real income gains. Emphasizing that returns on telecommunications, energy, and transportation spending far exceed those of other types of spending, the ADB noted that "the inadequacies of Asia's infrastructure networks are a bottleneck to growth, a threat to competitiveness, and an obstacle to poverty reduction."[53]

Two of the world's fastest-growing economies have taken different paths to modernizing their infrastructure. China has built vast public works in recent years—and its response to the global downturn was not to scale back investment, but to consolidate recent gains. In November 2008, Chinese leaders announced a major stimulus package, with $450 billion earmarked for ports, airports, bridges, schools, hospitals, highways, and roads.[54]

But in India, where cities are similarly bursting at the seams, the infrastructure is crumbling. Not only is investment inadequate, but corruption and bureaucracy make projects difficult to execute. One adviser to India's Planning Commission estimated that the nation's economic losses from congestion and poor roads alone amount to $6 billion a year. The agricultural sector is hampered due to a lack of roads to and from the fields, while employees of multinational companies cannot commute to work due to urban congestion. The "infrastructure deficit" is so dire that it could prevent India from achieving the prosperity that finally seems to be within reach.

In one hopeful sign, India passed a new law in 2005 allowing public–private partnerships for infrastructure initiatives. The first such project was an urgently needed international airport for Bangalore. Siemens participated in building the facility, which will be managed by Switzerland's Unique Ltd; both companies are equity investors. The state contributed just 18% of the cost, and ownership will transfer to the state after 60 years. The airport opened in 2008, and it is hoped that it will be a precursor for other creative partnerships that can provide a solid foundation for India's burgeoning economy.[55]

The situation is also urgent in Africa—especially in sub-Saharan Africa, where road density, electricity, and sanitation lag far behind that of other countries. Only one in four Africans has access to electricity, and only one in three rural Africans has access to an all-season road. According to the World Bank's Africa Infrastructure Country Diagnostic (AICD), Africa's infrastructure deficit is lowering the continent's per-capita economic growth by 2 percentage points each year and reducing the productivity of firms by as much as 40%. By 2007, external financing for infrastructure (from private capital flows, development assistance, and other sources) had reached $20 billion. But the AICD report estimates that some $80 billion a year is needed.[56] (Interestingly, as trade has increased between China and Africa, Chinese investment in African infrastructure has scaled up rapidly in recent years. More than 35 African nations have engaged in infrastructure financing deals with China in recent years, including projects for hydroelectric power generation and railways.[57])

Funding for infrastructure development around the world became even more scarce in the wake of the financial crisis of 2008. In response, the World Bank and the International Finance Corporation (IFC) created an "infrastructure crisis facility" to provide rollover financing and help recapitalize existing, viable, privately funded infrastructure projects in financial distress. The IFC announced plans to invest $300 million over three years and mobilize between $1.5 billion and $10 billion from other sources.[58]

A number of financial innovations could be applied to address this daunting capital gap. Credit enhancement funds could be created to accelerate interest in capital structures, reducing the risks for private-sector investors in these projects. Developing nations could direct more domestic funds to infrastructure projects by using derivatives to free up the allocation of funds from institutional investors, such as insurance companies and provident funds. Measures could be taken to enhance the role of banks as intermediaries for local infrastructure finance projects by creating instruments and markets to shape risk, maturity, and duration.[59]

One financial innovation has recently been deployed to spur sustainable infrastructure development that fights climate change: World

Bank Green Bonds. In partnership with a consortium of investment banks, the World Bank raised $350 million via several key Scandinavian investors (first transaction) and $300 million via the State of California (second transaction) to support green development projects. These include solar and wind installations, deployment of clean technology, upgrades of existing power plants, funding for mass transit and residential energy efficiency, methane management, and forestry protection initiatives administered by the World Bank in developing countries.[60]

Engaging the capital markets more broadly for infrastructure funding is a major challenge—especially when it comes to tapping the large pools of capital managed by institutional investors such as pension funds; these entities must invest conservatively to carry out their fiduciary duties. Public-sector risk-mitigation programs that might make projects more attractive to these investors are often cumbersome and expensive because they are applied on a case-by-case basis and lack a systematic approach. The concept of "global development bonds" has been floated to overcome the historical inability to link institutional investors with developing countries. These fixed-income securities would cover a pool of diversified projects and would mobilize capital market funding, particularly from U.S. institutional investors. Institutional investors are currently unable to invest in such projects because rated securities do not exist, but this could be solved through public agency and philanthropic credit enhancement. It may be possible to utilize entities like the Overseas Private Investment Corporation (OPIC) to provide credit wraps or guaranteed credit enhancement funds to draw institutional investors into these infrastructure projects.

Financial Innovations to Enhance Food Security

Much of this chapter has discussed long-range plans to support economic growth and build a global middle class. But the reality is that famine, wars, and natural disasters will always be with us—and with the advent of global warming, we are likely to see more frequent and more severe humanitarian crises.

Global food security remains one of the paramount concerns of our time. One billion people go hungry each day.[61] In the developing

world, approximately 200 million children under the age of five suffer
from stunted growth due to malnutrition, which also plays a role in
one-third of all child deaths in this age group.[62] And the cost of hunger
from medical costs, lost productivity, and lower educational attainment
is estimated at $500 billion to $1 trillion over a generation's lifetime.[63]

Organizations providing humanitarian food assistance—including
international relief agencies, national governments, and nongovernmental organizations—provide one of the few lifelines available to
the hungry. But these aid groups face significant challenges to obtaining and quickly delivering food in a cost-effective, efficient, and
responsive manner. When commodity prices spike, as they did in
2008, critical weaknesses are revealed in the food assistance supply
chain.

Meeting these growing needs in a climate of volatile prices and
supply will require improved risk management and more predictable,
flexible funding for food assistance organizations. As the G-8 nations
discussed in July 2009, strategies for improving food security must
focus on strengthening long-term agricultural development, emergency food assistance, and safety-net and nutrition programs.

Humanitarian groups face a multitude of obstacles. Because they
rely on voluntary contributions, the timing and volume of funds available can be unpredictable. And many donors place restrictions on
how and where their funds can be used. Predictable and flexible capital is necessary to ensure that organizations can maximize their limited resources—and financial innovations can fast-track solutions that
will strengthen the food-access pipeline.[64]

The most intriguing possibility for humanitarian groups involves
raising money through the bond markets. If a group of donors made
legally binding commitments to a food assistance organization, rated
bonds could be issued. A third party could act as financial manager,
and credit enhancement could be provided by foundations.

Figure 6.1 outlines the proposed structure for a food assistance
bond. A special-purpose vehicle (SPV) would issue bonds backed by
donor commitments. The proceeds from the bonds would be transferred to a humanitarian organization. Because the money required
for humanitarian relief varies from year to year, the bond proceeds
could be based on the amount the organization regularly receives

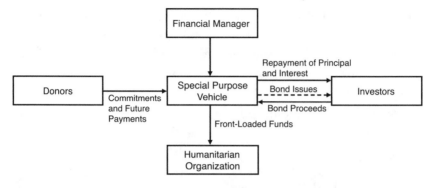

Figure 6.1   How a food assistance bond would work

Source: Milken Institute

each year. (Emergency needs could still be funded through specific appeals when a crisis occurs.) Investors in the bonds would receive their principal plus interest. A separate entity, possibly the World Bank, would act as financial manager for the transaction. Such a structure requires a credit rating, which poses a challenge if the issuing organization does not have one. In such cases, another organization would have to back the transaction.

Bonds could provide a portion of an organization's funding up front, giving it a clear budget picture and the ability to react immediately instead of waiting for donations to arrive after a crisis is announced, potentially saving more lives. In addition, up-front funding would benefit countries where the timing of delivery is important (in many nations, for example, it is extremely difficult and expensive to move food during the rainy season). The most sensible approach—particularly in Darfur and some other isolated areas—is to collect about 90% of the year's food supply by April. Proceeds from food-assistance bonds would allow this up-front purchase, and bond proceeds would likely have fewer restrictions than donations from individuals.

This model builds on an example we will examine in the next chapter on financing cures: the International Financing Facility for Immunisation (IFFIm), which secures funding for vaccines. An analysis of the IFFIm funding structure predicted it would increase the health impact of spending on vaccines by 22%, even after taking into account the costs of private-sector borrowing.[65] In the case of the IFFIm, the International Bank for Reconstruction and Development (part of the World Bank) manages the bond proceeds, tracks liquidity to meet disbursement commitments, and services the debt. The bank monitors leverage to ensure that the IFFIm meets all its long-term financial obligations. The IFFIm had a long-term rating on its bonds of AAA from Standard & Poor's as of July 2009.[66]

Food-assistance organizations could also benefit from using financial innovations to mitigate the risk of volatile food prices. Forward purchases of supplies can be made when prices dip and before food is needed. These transactions offer flexibility on price, volume, and delivery locations; allow shorter lead times; and provide predictable planning. Call options—the right, but not the obligation, to buy a commodity at a certain price for a period of time—also facilitate access to commodities at lower prices. Because they don't mandate the purchase, the buyer can back out if the commodity ultimately isn't needed, forfeiting only the premium paid for the option.

All of these mechanisms have the potential to help humanitarian groups deliver food on time and at low cost to vulnerable populations. The long-term effects of hunger on areas such as health, productivity, and national security make early and efficient crisis responses imperative.

The Success Stories: China and India

As mentioned at the start of the chapter, two developing nations stand out as powerhouses of economic growth. In China and to a lesser extent in India, hundreds of millions of people have shaken off the chains of poverty. Somehow this has been accomplished despite the fact that both countries are regarded as having corrupt legal systems and institutions that would frequently be considered inadequate by Western standards. How have they pulled it off? Innovation has played a key role. Both nations have devised financing and governance methods that fill in gaps left by the standard channels of banks and financial markets.

The Chinese and Indian financial systems are markedly different in their nature and evolution. Transitioning from a socialist system to a market-based system, China had no formal commercial legal framework or associated institutions in place when its economy entered warp speed in the 1980s. India, on the other hand, has a long history of well-developed legal institutions and financial markets.

The Chinese economy can be divided into three categories: 1) the state sector, which includes all companies ultimately controlled by the government (state-owned enterprises, or SOEs); 2) the listed sector, which includes all firms listed on an exchange and publicly traded; and 3) the private sector, which includes all other firms with various types of private and local government ownership.[67] The private sector now dominates the state and listed sectors in size, growth, and importance. Although it relies on relatively weaker legal protection and financing channels, the private sector has been racing ahead of the others and has been contributing most of the economy's growth. This indicates that the private sector has managed to develop effective, alternative financing channels and corporate governance mechanisms, such as those based on reputation and relationships, to support its momentum.

China's financial system is dominated by a large but underdeveloped banking system that is mainly controlled by the four largest state-owned banks. The Shanghai Stock Exchange and ShenZhen Stock Exchange have been growing by leaps and bounds since their inception in 1990, but their scale and importance are still not comparable to other channels of financing (especially the banking sector) for the Chinese economy as a whole.

The state sector has been shrinking as privatization proceeds apace, with greater numbers of firms going public. Equity ownership is concentrated within the state for firms converted from the state sector, and within founders' families for nonstate firms. The standard corporate governance mechanisms are weak and ineffective in the listed sector.

By contrast, the private sector is more interesting. The two most important financing channels for these firms during their start-up and subsequent periods are financial intermediaries, including state-owned banks and private credit agencies, and founders' friends and families. Firms have outstanding loans from multiple financial intermediaries, with most of the loans secured by fixed assets or third-party guarantees. During a firm's growth period, funds from "ethnic Chinese" investors (from Hong Kong, Taiwan, and other countries) and trade credits from business partners are also important sources.

Though formal governance mechanisms are practically nonexistent, alternative mechanisms have been remarkably effective in the private sector. Reputation and relationships matter above all. The most important force shaping China's social values and institutions is the widely held set of beliefs related to Confucius; these customs define family and social orders and trust, and are entirely distinct from Western reliance on the rule of law. Another important mechanism that drives good management and corporate governance is simple competition. Given the risks of failure during the early stages of a firm's development, firms have a strong incentive to gain a comparative advantage. Another important mechanism is the role of local governments. In the Chinese regions that witnessed the most successful economic growth and improvement in living standards, motivated government officials have actively supported the growth of private-sector firms.

India poses a very different set of circumstances. With its English common-law heritage, India offers one of the world's strongest sets of legal protections for investors.[68] Moreover, a British-style judicial system and a democratic government have been in place for a long time. But what exists on the books and what plays out in the day-to-day reality of the business world are two very different things. The *effective* level of investor protection and the quality of legal institutions in India both remain poor.

The reasons for the wide gap between investor protection on paper and in practice include a slow and inefficient legal system and government corruption. A firm's equity ownership is typically highly concentrated within the founder's family and/or the controlling shareholder, more so than in other Asian countries. Surveys indicate that small firms, regardless of age and industry, have little use for the legal system. Most firms prefer not to seek legal recourse in any situation, including customer defaults, breaches of contract, or commercial disputes. On the other hand, nonlegal sanctions in various forms (such as loss of reputation or future business opportunities, or even fear of personal safety) are far more effective deterrents against contract violations and nonpayment than legal recourse, and these strategies are employed widely. India's case would seem to indicate that strong legal protection is not a necessary condition for conducting business—as long as there are effective, nonlegal "institutional" substitutes.

Formal financing channels based on stock markets and banks are not essential for corporate operations and investments if alternative financing sources pick up the financing slack. In spite of poor investor protection in practice, the Indian economy has outpaced most others since the early 1990s. Further, firm-level evidence indicates that from 1996 to 2005 (a sufficiently long period for which reliable data is available), the average Indian firm grew at an impressive 10.9% compound annual rate. Moreover, in both India and China, SME firms grew even faster, although they depend little on formal legal channels and use far less formal finance than their larger counterparts.

China and India have managed to innovate around the problems that stifle growth in so many emerging economies. Developing alternate channels and mechanisms can speed the way for growth and make it possible to overcome obstacles. The main challenge facing the developing world is how to adapt these strategies to the local culture and surroundings in other nations so that the success of China and India can be emulated in other parts of the world.

Conclusions

Though recent decades have seen dramatic advances in corporate, housing, and environmental finance, this wave of progress has left the field of development finance largely untouched. But finance and information technology can converge again to unleash the potential of entrepreneurial firms in emerging markets, fund the infrastructure improvements that are needed to power growth, and even speed the flow of emergency aid in cases where lives are at stake.

Development finance, a neglected stepchild of Wall Street, Washington, and other global capitals, increasingly finds its place at the table not only for altruistic reasons, but out of self-interest. First and foremost, in this increasingly interconnected global economy, the developing world represents a huge untapped source of future demand and growth. But it's equally important to realize that development enhances security, for at the heart of most geopolitical conflicts lie persistent problems of inadequate economic growth shared unequally. Regions marked by poverty, blight, and despair are breeding grounds for terrorism and conflict.

Demographic shifts add new urgency to this imperative. While the developed world is graying, many emerging markets are characterized by very young populations. As more young people enter the labor market and seek productive opportunities, job creation, firm formation, and income and wealth generation become imperative. Fostering higher rates of economic growth may always have been the right way to approach development, but over the next half-century, there is really no choice but to finally accomplish it to avoid geopolitical instability.

The examples of China and India show what it is possible. Now the challenge is replicating their success on a worldwide scale.

Endnotes

[1]Shaohua Chen and Martin Ravallion, "The Developing World Is Poorer Than We Thought, but No Less Successful in the Fight Against Poverty," World Bank Development Research Group (August 2008).

[2]International Monetary Fund, World Economic Outlook database.

[3]World Bank press release, "World Bank Updates Poverty Estimates for the Developing World" (28 August 2008). Available at http://web.worldbank.org/WBSITE/EXTERNAL/NEWS/0,,contentMDK:21882162~menuPK:51062075~pagePK:34370~piPK:34424~theSitePK:4607,00.html.

[4]United Nations, press release, "Sub-Saharan Africa's Progress Towards Anti-Poverty Goals Is Encouraging, But Needs to Be Accelerated to Meet 2015 Targets," September 12, 2008.

[5]Gary S. Becker, *Human Capital: A Theoretical and Empirical Analysis, with Special Reference to Education* (Chicago: University of Chicago Press, 1994).

[6]"The Growth Report: Strategies for Sustained Growth and Inclusive Development," Commission on Growth and Development (2008): 1.

[7]OECD, quoted in "Foreign Aid in the National Interest: Promoting Freedom, Security, and Opportunity," USAID (2002): 133. Available at www.usaid.gov/fani/index.htm.

[8]Antoine van Agtmael, *The Emerging Markets Century: How a New Breed of World-Class Companies Is Overtaking the World* (New York: Free Press, 2007).

[9]"Dizzy in Boomtown," *The Economist* (15 November 2007).

[10]Victoria Papandrea, "Emerging Markets Set to Dominate Global GDP," *Investor Daily* (22 October 2009).

[11]Shantayanan Devarajan, Margaret J. Miller, and Eric V. Swanson, "Goals for Development: History, Prospects, and Costs," (working paper no. WPS 2819, World Bank, 2002).

[12]United Nations, MDG Gap Task Force Report 2009, "Strengthening the Global Partnership for Development in a Time of Crisis": ix.

[13]Geoff Dyer, "Global Insight: Springing China's Forex Trap," *Financial Times* (19 October 2009).

[14]Dambisa Moyo, *Dead Aid: Why Aid Is Not Working and How There Is a Better Way for Africa* (New York: Farrar, Straus, and Giroux, 2009). See also Chris Lane and Amanda Glassman, "Smooth and Predictable Aid for Health: A Role for Innovative Financing?" (working paper no. 1, Brookings Global Health Financing Initiative, 2008). For an overview of the debate surrounding the effectiveness of the traditional aid model, see Nicholas Kristof, "How Can We Help the World's Poor?" *New York Times* (22 November 2009).

[15]Steve Beck and Tim Ogden, "Beware of Bad Microcredit," *Harvard Business Review* online (September 2007). Available at http://hbr.harvardbusiness.org/2007/09/beware-of-bad-microcredit/ar/1.

[16]Robert G. King and Ross Levine, "Finance and Growth: Schumpeter Might Be Right," *Quarterly Journal of Economics* 108, no. 3 (1993): 717–737.

[17]James R. Barth, D. E. Nolle, Hilton L. Root, and Glenn Yago, "Choosing the Right Financial System for Growth," *Journal of Applied Corporate Finance*, 13, no. 4 (2001): 116–123. See also James R. Barth, Gerard Caprio Jr., and Ross Levine, *Rethinking Bank Regulation: Till Angels Govern* (Cambridge, MA: Cambridge University Press, 2005).

[18]Hernando de Soto, *The Mystery of Capital: Why Capitalism Succeeds in the West and Fails Everywhere Else* (New York: Basic Books, 2000); and D. C. North, *Institutions, Institutional Change, and Economic Performance* (Cambridge, MA: Cambridge University Press, 1990).

[19]Financial Access Initiative, "Half the World Is Unbanked" (October 2009). Available at http://financialaccess.org.

[20]United Nations, "The Millennium Development Goals Report 2009": 51–52.

[21]Nancy Gohring, IDG News Service, "Google and Grameen Launch Mobile Services for the Poor," *PC World* (29 June 2009).

[22]Sara Corbett, "Can the Cellphone Help End Global Poverty?" *New York Times* (13 April 2008).

[23]Sarah McGregor, "Alliance on Banking Services for the Poor Starts First Meeting," Bloomberg (14 September 2009).

[24]Torsten Wezel, "Does Co-Financing by Multilateral Development Banks Increase 'Risky' Direct Investment in Emerging Markets?" Discussion Paper Series I: Economic Studies, Deutsche Bundesbank Research Centre (2004).

[25]David de Ferranti and Anthony J. Ody, "Beyond Microfinance: Getting Capital to Small and Medium Enterprises to Fuel Faster Development," Policy Brief no. 159, Brookings Institution (2007).

[26]Asli Demirguc-Kunt and Ross Levine, "Finance and Inequality: Theory and Evidence," *Annual Review of Financial Economics* 1 (2009): 15.

[27]Timothy Besley and Robin Burgess, "Halving Global Poverty," *Journal of Economic Perspectives*, American Economic Association 17, no. 3 (2003): 15.

[28]Grameen Bank website, "At a Glance," www.grameen-info.org/index.php?option= com_content&task=view&id=26&Itemid=175.

[29]Milken Institute Global Conference 2008 panel summary, "Business Innovations That Are Changing the World." Available at www.milkeninstitute.org/events/ gcprogram.taf?function=detail&eventid=GC08&EvID=1395.

[30]Elisabeth Rhyne and Maria Otero, "Microfinance Through the Next Decade: Visioning the Who, What, Where, When and How," Global Microcredit Summit (2006).

[31]Estimates from Microfinance Information Exchange and the Microcredit Summit Campaign.

[32]Rajdeep Sungupta and Craig P. Aubuchon, "The Microfinance Revolution: An Overview," *Federal Reserve Bank of St. Louis Review* 90, no. 1 (January/February 2008): 9–30.

[33]"Yunus Blasts Compartamos," *BusinessWeek* Online Extra (13 December 2007). Available at www.businessweek.com/magazine/content/07_52/b4064045920958.htm.

[34]"The Greatest Entrepreneurs of All Time," *BusinessWeek* (27 June 2007).

[35]Milken Institute Forum, Creating a World Without Poverty (January 16, 2008). Available at www.milkeninstitute.org/events/events.taf?function=detail&ID=219& cat=Forums.

[36]Veolia press release. Available at www.veoliawater.com/press/press-releases/ press-2008/20080331,grameen.htm.

[37]Clinton Global Initiative press release (23 September 2009).

[38]"Adidas to Make 1€ Trainers," *Daily Telegraph* (16 November 2009).

[39]International Monetary Fund, www.imf.org/external/np/exr/cs/news/2009/ 021009.htm.

[40]Meghana Ayyagari, Thorsten Beck, and Asli Demirguch-Kunt, "Small and Medium Enterprises Across the Globe: A New Database" (working paper no. 3217, World Bank, August 2003).

[41]"Finance for All? Policies and Pitfalls in Expanding Access," World Bank Policy Research Report (2008).

[42]Thorsten Beck, Asli Demirguc-Kunt, and Vojislav Maksimovic, "Financial and Legal Constraints to Growth: Does Firm Size Matter?" *Journal of Finance* (2005): 133–177.

[43]This discussion draws on Jill Scherer, Betsy Zeidman, and Glenn Yago, "Structuring Scalable Risk Capital for Small and Medium-Sized Enterprises in Emerging Markets," Financial Innovations Lab Report, Milken Institute (August 2009).

[44]Acumen Fund, "About Us," www.acumenfund.org/about-us.html. See also Nicholas Kristof, "How Can We Help the World's Poor? *New York Times* (22 November 2009).

[45]Root Capital, "What We Do," www.rootcapital.org/what_we_do.php.

[46]"A Place in Society," *The Economist* (25 September 2009).

[47]Monitor Institute, "Investing for Social & Environmental Impact: A Design for Catalyzing an Emerging Industry" (2009).

[48]Antony Bugg-Levine and John Goldstein, "Impact Investing: Harnessing Capital Markets to Solve Problems at Scale," Federal Reserve Bank of San Francisco, *Community Development Investment Review* 5, no. 2 (2009): 30–41.

[49]Krishnan Sharma and Manuel Montes, "Strengthening the Business Sector in Developing Countries: The Potential of Diasporas" (United Nations working paper, 2008); Krishnan Sharma, "The Impact of Remittances on Economic Security" (working paper no. 78, Department of Economic and Social Affairs, July 2009).

[50]Glenn Yago, Daniela Roveda, and Jonathan White, "Transatlantic Innovations in Affordable Capital for Small- and Medium-Sized Enterprises: Prospect for Market-Based Development Finance," German Marshall Fund/Milken Institute (2007).

[51]Small Enterprise Assistance Funds, "From Poverty to Prosperity: Understanding the Impact of Investing in Small and Medium Enterprises" (2007).

[52]Commission on Growth and Development, "The Growth Report" (2008): 5.

[53]Alan Wheatley, "Asia Could Benefit from Cooperating on Infrastructure," *New York Times* (24 November 2009). See also "Study on Intraregional Trade and Investment in South Asia," Asian Development Bank (2009).

[54]Simon Elegant and Austin Ramzy, "China's New Deal: Modernizing the Middle Kingdom," *Time* (1 June 2009)..

[55]Steve Hamm and Nandini Lakshman, "The Trouble with India: Crumbling Roads, Jammed Airports, and Power Blackouts Could Hobble Growth," *BusinessWeek* (19 March 2007).

[56]"Africa's Infrastructure: A Time for Transformation," Africa Infrastructure Country Diagnostic (AICD), World Bank (2009).

[57]Vivien Foster, William Butterfield, Chuan Chen, and Nataliya Pushak, "Building Bridges: China's Growing Role as Infrastructure Financier for Sub-Saharan Africa," World Bank/Public-Private Infrastructure Advisory Facility (July 2008).

[58]World Bank press release, "World Bank Group Boosts Support for Developing Countries" (11 November 2008). Available at http://web.worldbank.org/WBSITE/EXTERNAL/NEWS/0,,contentMDK:21973077~pagePK:64257043~piPK:437376~theSitePK:4607,00.html.

[59]Nachiket Mor and Sanjeev Sehrawat, "Sources of Infrastructure Finance," Centre for Development Finance, working paper series, Institute for Financial Management and Research, India (October 2006).

[60]World Bank press release, "First World Bank Green Bonds Launched" (5 January 2009). Available at http://web.worldbank.org/WBSITE/EXTERNAL/NEWS/0,,contentMDK:22024264~pagePK:64257043~piPK:437376~theSitePK:4607,00.html.

[61]Food and Agriculture Organization of the United Nations, "More People Than Ever Are Victims of Hunger" (June 2009).

[62]UNICEF, "Tracking Progress on Child and Maternal Nutrition" (2009).

[63]Food and Agriculture Organization of the United Nations, "The State of Food Insecurity in the World 2004."

[64]This discussion is drawn from Jill Scherer, Betsy Zeidman, and Glenn Yago, "Feeding the World's Hungry: Fostering an Efficient and Responsive Food Access Pipeline," Financial Innovations Lab Report, Milken Institute (October 2009).

[65]Owen Barder and Ethan Yeh, "The Costs and Benefits of Front-Loading and Predictability of Immunization," Center for Global Development (January 2006).

[66]Larry Hays, Standard & Poor's Ratings Direct report, "International Finance Facility for Immunisation" (9 July 2009).

[67]See Franklin Allen, Jun Qian, and Meijun Qian, "Law, Finance, and Economic Growth in China," *Journal of Financial Economics* 77, (2003): 57–116; and Franklin Allen, Jun Qian, Meijun Qian, and Mengxin Zhao, "A Review of China's Financial System and Initiatives for the Future," in James R. Barth, John A. Tatom, and Glenn Yago (eds.), *China's Emerging Financial Markets: Challenges and Opportunities* (New York: Springer, 2009).

[68]Franklin Allen, Rajesh Chakrabarti, Sankar De, Jun Qian, and Meijun Qian, "Financing Firms in India" (working paper, Wharton Financial Institutions Center, 2008).

7

Financing Cures

Science has entered a thrilling new era. Study of the human genome has brought us tantalizingly close to discoveries that can reduce suffering and save lives. But translating research into real treatments is a tortuous process that requires major long-term investment and no small risk of failure.

At the very moment when profound new breakthroughs seem to be within our grasp, there has been a precipitous decline in financing for early-stage biomedical research. This constraint is first and foremost a tragedy for those individuals who are waiting desperately for cures. It is also a factor that limits productivity gains in the global economy and keeps developing nations mired in poverty.

Large pharmaceutical companies, with their powerful research arms and great depth of resources, have traditionally driven most research and development of new treatments. Today, however, that engine of innovation is stalling. Major pharmaceutical firms have seen their business models stagnate, and most have withdrawn from risky early-stage drug discovery and development, instead directing more resources into late-stage developments, line extensions, and "me too" drugs (slight variations on existing medications).[1]

Research and development (R&D) productivity—as measured by applications to the FDA, both to initiate clinical trials and to market new drugs—has lost momentum.[2] Despite increased overall R&D spending and technological advances, the introduction of new priority drugs (treatments that the FDA defines as constituting "a significant therapeutic or public health advance") has declined, from more than 13 per year in the 1990s to approximately 10 per year in this decade.[3]

A 2007 report on the industry's outlook from *The Economist* summed up the problem of the dwindling drug pipeline, quoting a study from CMR International, a consulting firm. In a typical year during the 1990s, CMR found that the industry typically spent $35 billion to $40 billion a year on R&D and came out with 35–40 new drugs. By 2004, annual spending exceeded $50 billion, but fewer than 30 new drugs were introduced. In 2006, those numbers deteriorated even further: Spending had swelled past $60 billion, with no increase in the number of new drugs brought to market.[4]

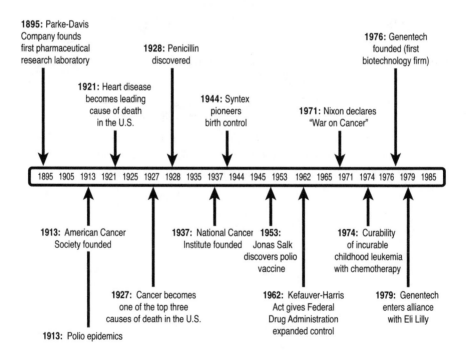

The old business model, in which vertically integrated pharma-ceutical giants banked on developing the next blockbuster drug, was once extremely profitable but is becoming unsustainable. In addition to coping with pricing pressures and the prospect of an unprece-dented wave of blockbuster patent expirations in the next decade,[5] the industry must find ways to respond to the smaller niche markets that are likely to be created as we enter an era of personalized medicine.[6]

A fresh approach to innovation is needed. The industry is experi-menting with new research models, including the outsourcing of R&D operations. But in the meantime, financial innovators have a role to play in supporting the scientific discovery process by bridging the funding gap, which is most acute from very early-stage drug dis-covery R&D through Phase II clinical trials. This is the point of scien-tific risk in which capital is critically needed to see that projects make it to the marketplace.

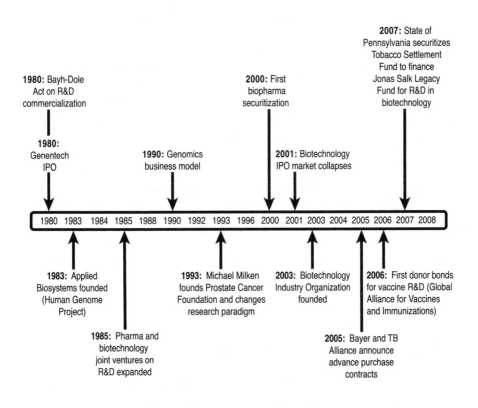

2007: State of Pennsylvania securitizes Tobacco Settlement Fund to finance Jonas Salk Legacy Fund for R&D in biotechnology

1980: Bayh-Dole Act on R&D commercialization

2000: First biopharma securitization

1980: Genentech IPO

1990: Genomics business model

2001: Biotechnology IPO market collapses

1980 1983 1984 1985 1988 1990 1992 1993 1996 2000 2001 2003 2004 2005 2006 2007 2008

1983: Applied Biosystems founded (Human Genome Project)

1993: Michael Milken founds Prostate Cancer Foundation and changes research paradigm

2003: Biotechnology Industry Organization founded

2006: First donor bonds for vaccine R&D (Global Alliance for Vaccines and Immunizations)

1985: Pharma and biotechnology joint ventures on R&D expanded

2005: Bayer and TB Alliance announce advance purchase contracts

TABLE 7.1   Types of Financial Innovations for Accelerating Cures

Products and Services	Processes and Operations	Organizational Forms
First biopharma securitization (2000)	Venture capital biotech investments (1970s)	Rise of large integrated pharmaceutical corporations (IG Farben, Bayer, Smith–Kline; 1930s)
First donor bonds for vaccine R&D (2006)	Black–Scholes formula for option pricing (1973)	First pharmaceutical R&D lab (Parke–Davis Co., 1895)
European Union and European Investment Bank (EIB) launch a risk-sharing finance facility to support research and innovation in Europe (2007)	Bayh–Dole Act (1980) allows universities, small businesses, and nonprofits control over intellectual property resulting from government-funded research	National Cancer Institute (1937)
	State of Pennsylvania securitizes Tobacco Settlement Fund to finance Jonas Salk Legacy Fund for biotechnology (2007)	Kefauver–Harris Amendment to the Federal Food, Drug and Cosmetic Act (1962) requires drug manufacturers to prove the safety and effectiveness of their products before obtaining government approval
		The U.S. government launches the Human Genome Project (1990), which eventually became an international consortium of researchers working to sequence the thousands of genes in human DNA
		Genentech IPO brings biotech to Wall Street (1980)
		Pharma/biotech alliances (1990s)

The Structural Demand for Capital

Though the first efforts to finance cures date back to the rise of large integrated pharmaceutical corporations in the 1930s, the business of directing capital to achieve greater results in the life sciences has intensified most rapidly over the past few decades.[7] Applying the tools of venture capital, public equity markets, securitization, and public–private partnerships greatly increased the accessibility of capital for drug and medical device development. Valuation methodologies (including Black–Scholes and Monte Carlo estimations) made it possible to monetize intellectual property in new ways, while policy and organizational changes enabled commercialization from government and university labs (via the Bayh–Dole Act of 1980) and other knowledge-sharing organizations (from the National Cancer Institute to the Human Genome Project). A complex ecosystem has formed over the years to support medical innovation, with private-sector R&D complemented by publicly funded health-related research, much of which falls under the auspices of the National Institutes of Health (NIH).

The decline in R&D productivity, which first emerged in the 1990s, is captured by the following contradiction: From 1993 to 2004, the pharmaceutical industry reported that annual R&D spending increased by 147%, but the number of new drug applications submitted annually grew by only 38% (and generally declined over the past several years). In 2004, only 102 applications were submitted to the FDA, representing a 21% drop from 1999 levels. While applications for "new molecular entities"—truly novel drugs—increased from 1993 to 1995, they fell by 40% in the following decade.[8]

From 1998 to 2003, steady annual increases doubled the NIH budget, increasing federal support for biomedical R&D. But from 2004 through 2008, NIH research funding remained static (and its purchasing power actually decreased due to inflation).[9] Hopefully, the infusion of $10 billion into the NIH under the American Reinvestment and Recovery Act of 2009 may start to change these dynamics, but future funding levels will, of course, be subject to the prevailing political and economic winds.

The decline in R&D productivity has painful real-world consequences, as promising discoveries in the fight against cancer and other diseases languish for lack of capital resources and development expertise. But current trends do not point to easy solutions. According to the pharmaceutical industry's trade group, we have entered the era of the billion-dollar drug; the average cost of bringing a new therapy through development, clinical trials, and market launch has risen sharply, from $138 million in 1975 to $1.318 billion in 2006.[10] And market launch is no guarantee of success: Only two out of ten drugs generate enough revenue to recover R&D costs.[11]

Generic drugs, a major source of competition, currently capture almost two-thirds of U.S. prescription drug volume (but only 16% of total pharmaceutical sales dollars).[12] Although generics obviously lower costs for consumers and many health insurers now insist on them, this competition does create another pressure that discourages big companies from deploying their extensive research capacity in risky and expensive drug development.

The major drugs launched in 1965 could expect to thrive in the marketplace for 10–12 years without competition. By 1985, this window had shrunk to 5 years, and the high-profile therapies launched after 1995 have faced immediate competition, sometimes within the same year.[13] When one blockbuster drug debuts against another, large pharmaceutical companies cannot recoup their investments.[14] Over time, the industry has become more risk averse as a result. The estimated average out-of-pocket cost per new drug has increased at an annual rate of 7.4% above inflation.[15]

For pharmaceutical and biotech firms, increasingly unfavorable cost–benefit considerations can stifle experimentation, especially for high-risk or niche products. Because of the huge commitment of time and resources it takes to obtain FDA approval for a new drug, many pharmaceutical companies prefer to invest in a safer bet: promoting existing drugs by extending labels, changing doses, or changing drug combinations for existing treatments.[16] This diversion of resources to "me too" drugs exacerbates the deficiency in the pipelines. The numbers reveal an extreme picture. In 2006, 123 new drug applications were submitted to the FDA, but only 22 were for truly novel drugs (new molecular entities). The rest were variations on existing therapies.[17] Biologically based drugs (new biologic license applications) are even scarcer. Only four such treatments were approved by the FDA in 2006.[18]

Faced with tough market conditions, pharmaceutical companies often take a shortcut to innovation by purchasing the rights to drugs under development from biotech firms. Yet candidates are scarce on the horizon these days. Emerging biotech companies face a tough slog to commercialize their discoveries and keep going through the arduous process of proving their potential in the early phases of clinical development. Their funding limitations are about to affect the industry at large.[19]

Biotech firms work on the frontier of medical science, applying the latest technologies in the quest to develop breakthrough therapies. But operating on the cutting edge has its risks, and young biotech firms face many practical business hurdles to fulfilling their scientific promise. The process of developing cures requires a long-term capital commitment that cannot be cut short by premature investor exits.

The old model of venture-based biotech development (often referred to as the "California model") that dominated in the 1980s and 1990s went like this: You take great research work from the University of California or Stanford, form a company, land venture capital, issue an IPO, and grow up to be Genentech or Amgen. But that model is dead (see Figure 7.1). In today's environment, few investors are willing to take a chance on premature IPOs with excessive valuations and unproven cash flows. The current recession has seen the market for biotech IPOs grind to a virtual standstill. With the closing of the IPO window, many firms fail to secure the funding they need for development needs.

Number of IPOs

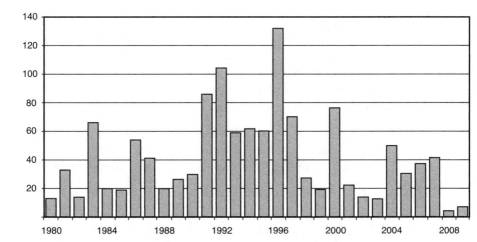

Figure 7.1   Biotech IPOs over the past three decades

Sources: SDC (Thomson Reuters), Milken Institute.

Note: date for 2009 up until 11/3/09.

A Tough Journey through Two "Death Valleys"

The process of commercializing a new cure in the United States is a long and winding road. This initial phase of scientific discovery, when promising targets are discovered and linked to disease, can take many years of work in both university and industry labs. Going from discovery and validation to assay development can be equally as painstaking, followed by stages that include high-throughput screening and identification of compounds that safely alter the activity of a particular target cell or disease before its efficacy can be tested in clinical trials. Then it's on to the steps described below[20]:

- **Phase I.** This is the first time the drug is tested on humans. Usually 20–80 normal, healthy volunteers take the drug to test it for toxicity (negative side effects) and demonstrate its effect on people of different races.

- **Phase II.** This is still a pilot stage. But this time the volunteers suffer from the disease the drug aims to help. About 100–300 patients are involved, and the trial can last up to two years. Phase IIA typically focuses on refining dosage requirements, while IIB analyzes efficacy. This phase provides the preliminary data needed to prepare for the larger, Phase III trials.

- **Phase III.** This is the main clinical trial, usually involving 1,000–3,000 patients. The trial tests for both therapeutic effects and adverse reactions. If there are established drugs for the disease, the new drug is tested against the best on the market. If there is no existing drug, the new drug is tested against a placebo. One group of patients will be given the new drug; another will get either a placebo or an established drug.

- **Phase IV.** Phase IV is carried out after the drug has been registered with the FDA. The trial is conducted to allow local doctors to become familiar with the drug and to gain their trust.

Many fledgling biotech companies start to undertake this process before their viability has been proven, and they may lack an experienced management team. The financial bottleneck created in the preclinical phase dooms many projects that show high potential for medical success. Due to its harsh nature, this roadblock has been termed the first "death valley."

A second death valley occurs a few years later, starting at Phase IIB and continuing throughout the approval and marketing phases. In other words, funds are lacking during most clinical trial stages and also after FDA approval. A lucky few biotech firms resolve the funding problem through collaborations with pharmaceutical companies that can provide appropriate marketing resources after FDA approval.

In their long sojourn for FDA approval, drugs face complex regulatory barriers. Even the successful launch of a drug does not guarantee financial success. In some cases, safety issues become apparent only after a drug has been widely used, leading regulators to issue "black box" warnings or even ban certain products that had already made it through the FDA approval process.

From the small start-up in a funding squeeze to the behemoth under pressure from shareholders, generic competition, and regulators, the biopharmaceutical industry is undergoing a painful shakeup that could impede, if not derail, the advancement of next-generation treatments and cures—unless new financial innovations and public policies are applied to help the industry better deal with risk.

Sources for Biomedical Funding

Predominant Methods

The avenues available for emerging biotech firms to finance the development of new therapies include the following:

- **Venture capital (VC).** Pooling investment dollars from pension funds, universities, and wealthy individuals, venture capitalists have been drawn to the potential of biotech ever since the success of Genentech. But many of the long-shot bets made on early-stage discoveries in the 1990s failed to pan out, causing more risk aversion in this arena. From 2002 through 2007, more than $29 billion in VC funding went to the life sciences, with most of that money concentrated in biotech.[21] Biotech also claimed the largest share of VC in the second quarter of 2009, with $888 million going into 85 deals.[22] But current levels of VC funding in all industries is a fraction of the levels seen in 2000; and in the aftermath of the financial meltdown, there is a shortage of capital in the sector. Stepping into the void are the large pharmaceutical firms themselves.[23] The venture-capital arm of Johnson & Johnson, for example, provided some 30% of the funding to Novocell, a privately owned company focused on producing insulin from human embryonic stem cells for use in diabetes treatment.[24] Pfizer, Eli Lilly & Co., Roche, and Merck, among others, have likewise established venture capital operations specifically to invest in promising biotech startups.

- **The financial markets.** Especially in the 1990s, many biotech companies banked on the prospect of eventually going public. Even after the initial IPO, publicly traded companies can issue secondary offerings of shares, and this strategy has been used frequently by U.S. biotech and pharmaceutical firms. But the demand for shares in public offerings has weakened worldwide, and particularly in the United States, significantly affecting biotech. Yet even when it is applicable, this funding method holds clear disadvantages, as new offerings dilute existing shareholders' stake in the company. At the same time, the value of the company's shares does not usually reflect its intrinsic value or the potential value of the company it were to be acquired. Moreover, in recent years, demand from investors has mainly been directed toward companies at advanced phases of development.

- **Private investments in public equity (PIPEs).** Small to medium-size companies that are already publicly traded but continue to experience funding constraints are increasingly turning to private sources, a.k.a. private investments in public equity (PIPEs), for capital injections. PIPE deals offer much greater speed and efficiency than issuing a secondary offering of shares and fulfilling the related regulatory requirements. In a traditional PIPE, the investor gets to purchase common or preferred stock at a discounted price, while a structured PIPE deal involves purchasing convertible debt. In November 2009, for example, StemCells Inc., a Palo Alto–based biotech company focused on developing treatments for neurological disorders, announced its ninth PIPE offering; the company has raised $133.8 million through these financings. San Diego–based Cardium Therapeutics, which develops novel biologic therapeutics and medical devices for cardiovascular and ischemic disease, has similarly conducted multiple rounds of PIPE financing to raise almost $83 million.[25]

- **Mergers and acquisitions (M&A).** The large pharmaceutical companies are increasingly innovating by acquisition, and selling out to one of these giants is considered a profitable endgame for many biotech entrepreneurs. A thriving M&A market has yielded numerous purchases of promising drugs, some at relatively early phases. In one of the most recent deals, European pharmaceutical giant Sanofi-Aventis in 2009 paid $500 million to acquire BiPar Sciences, a small California-based biotech firm that is developing cancer therapies.[26]

- **Sales of promising drug pipelines, still in development, to large pharmaceutical companies.** Pharmaceutical firms can also bolster their pipelines by acquiring specific drugs or drug portfolios rather than acquiring an entire biotech firm. In November 2009, Japan's Takeda Pharmaceutical Co. announced plans to pay up to $1 billion for obesity treatments being developed by Amylin Pharmaceuticals, a San Diego–based biotech. Takeda also agreed to pay 80% of the cost of obtaining FDA approval for the drugs.[27]

Innovative Business and Financial Models to Bridge the Capital Gap

Opening New Avenues

While most capital is raised through the channels described previously, several new and innovative financing techniques have emerged to see drugs through the difficult journey shown in Figure 7.2:

- **Financing by projected royalty streams.** Future royalty streams from expected product sales can be sold in exchange for immediate capital by means of debt or investment. One of the earliest examples of this type of deal took place in 2000, when Yale University, in conjunction with Royalty Pharma AG and BancBoston Capital, agreed to pay royalties on an HIV/AIDS drug discovered at Yale to Bristol-Myers Squibb in exchange for $79 million in funding. A few years later came a

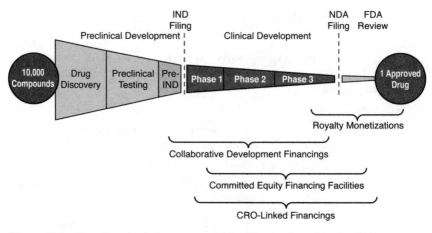

Figure 7.2   Funding techniques prominently employed in the U.S.

Source: Mark Kessel and Frederick Frank, *Nature Biotechnology,* 2007

deal that built in greater diversification: the Royalty Securitization Trust I, which securitized royalties from 23 biopharmaceutical products, medical devices, and diagnostics from 19 companies for $228 million. In that deal, the Paul Royalty Fund had invested in the young companies and then exchanged a portion of its royalty rights for an upfront payment. In 2005, the royalties from eight drugs owned by a subsidiary of Drug Royalty LLC that had been in the market an average of seven years were collateralized for $68.5 million. And in 2007, Northwestern University sold an undisclosed portion of its royalty interests to Royalty Pharma for $700 million. Each transaction required a rating by Standard & Poor's and/or Moody's; the ratings ranged from AAA to BB. Two of the deals also had credit insurance.[28] This model and its potential variations will be discussed in greater detail in the following section.

- **Collaborative development financing.** In this model, biotech company A grants license and access to its promising drug pipeline to pharmaceutical firm B, which has the resources to bring these projects to their final phases of development and secure FDA approval. In return, company A receives right of first refusal to repurchase the drugs from firm B at a pre-established price. Firm B assumes the risk of development costs in case of failure.

- **Contract research organization (CRO)–linked financings.** A CRO provides R&D services to biotech companies, supplying required funding and resources (such as skilled manpower or infrastructure for clinical trials, as well as other services required for FDA approval) at a relatively inexpensive price in return for future royalties of drug sales or ownership in the companies it serves. A recent study estimated that demand for CRO services will grow by 16% annually over the next three years.[29] In addition to lowering expenses, this strategy may allow biotech firms to write off overhead as a variable cost rather than a fixed cost, rendering the services even cheaper.
- **Committed-equity financing facilities (CEFF).** This model involves a financing commitment for a limited timeframe, during which publicly traded companies may sell a predefined amount of stock at a price lower than market price, thus securing funds over longer periods of times.
- **Designated funds.** Funds designated to promote treatment for specific diseases occasionally finance R&D up to Phase II. Often disease-specific philanthropic foundations will become involved in this form of mission-related investment.
- **Incubators promoted by large pharmaceutical companies.** Large pharmaceutical firms can team up with venture capital funds to finance promising drug development and create incubators to support emerging biotechnology companies. Approximately 40% of funds invested in emerging U.S. biotech companies are raised this way.[30]

University Partnerships, Private Equity, and Public-Sector/Foundation Investing

More than 30 years ago, researchers from Stanford and the University of California, San Francisco, achieved new breakthroughs in recombinant DNA. This cutting-edge science seemed to present an astounding array of possibilities for commercial applications—and thus the biotech industry was born. This resulted in a flourishing ecosystem of spin-offs, start-ups, and collaborations among biotech firms, investors, and academia. The 1980 Bayh–Dole Act shored up these collaborations by opening up the ivory tower to commerce—allowing universities to own, license, and market the results of their faculty research. The United States led the way in this regard, and nations around the globe quickly followed.

Corporate labs once generated the bulk of research and innovation, but those processes are increasingly shifting back to where they began: the university campus. A number of private/university collaborations have emerged to fund preclinical and Phase I trials. These partnerships were formed to help projects progress out of the university lab and begin early commercialization.

As the global economy increasingly becomes a knowledge economy, universities are natural partners for both business and government. They contribute not only talent and facilities, but an average of approximately $2 million in equity for each venture they fund. But the catch with this business model is that universities need to attract outside investors or partners for the more expensive Phase II funding.[31]

Private equity has produced additional financing and partnership models. Symphony Capital, a hands-on private equity firm based in New York City, not only funds biotech research, but also, through partnership with RRD International, manages the development process, from preclinical and regulatory phases through manufacturing.

The public sector can also play a role in investing. In 2007, the European Union and the European Investment Bank (EIB) created a risk-sharing finance facility (RSFF). Under the RSFF, the EIB will match up to $1.29 billion from the EU with $1 billion of its own resources to support riskier R&D programs by lending to new entities.[32] The EIB will financially sponsor up to 50% of loans, based upon due diligence, thus encouraging other lenders to participate. No external rating is imposed upon the debt, thus enabling companies with low credit ratings but exciting potential to obtain funding.

Another intriguing template mitigates risk and speeds scientific innovation by utilizing disease-specific foundations to establish a "science commons" that designs and defines funding agreements to create a body of shared research and clinical data for a single disease. For example, a foundation may fund projects at a number of universities but find that it must negotiate with each university's technology transfer office if professors from different universities want to work on the same stem cell lines and reagents. The commons is a mechanism for streamlining contracts, definitions, and funding agreements, allowing funded researchers direct access to the research materials of other researchers also funded by the foundation.[33] A further possibility would be to structure a funding and research company that would out-license intellectual property funded by the foundation. The holding company, a specialized special-purpose vehicle (SPV), could then create a royalty stream used to entice university technology transfer offices into the commons. There has been ongoing interest in the scientific community in adopting these ideas, particularly as they relate to sharing of data and resources.[34]

Overcoming the Limits of Public Equity and Venture Capital Funding

Venture capital and the public equity markets are currently the major sources of funding for medical research, but these two channels alone are proving unable to finance faster cures.

The typical venture capital cycle spans three to six years prior to exit. That timeline, too, presents a fundamental mismatch with the 20-year development cycle that some science requires. The resulting misallocation of capital can prevent medical advances.

Going public does not magically solve the problem for most biotech firms. The difficulties of running a publicly traded company with ten-year or longer investment cycles but short-term earnings pressure is considerable. Most of the typical company's funding is generated through a single IPO. But due to the volatility of the equity market—particularly for the biotech sector—such offerings may generate less capital than expected or may have to be delayed. The value of a company's specific technology may be overshadowed by the market's prevailing sentiment on biotech in general. Potentially life-saving breakthroughs may fall victim to the market's whim in a given week regarding the sector as a whole.

Since the prevailing channels of financing are problematic, it makes sense to consider a paradigm shift. If there is a way to estimate the value of royalties over time from a portfolio of patents relevant to a particular disease group or medical problem, then the portfolio could be turned into a marketable security that would provide capital for accelerating research. By securitizing or "monetizing" preexisting technology licenses, a company can achieve short-term financing with no negative financial statement or tax consequences and without having to issue additional equity (in other words, with little or no negative impact on the ability to complete an IPO at a later date when market conditions might be more favorable). This structure also has the advantage of enabling investors to bypass the volatility of the equity market and invest more directly in a company's technology, ultimately sharing in the profitability of that technology.

Potential securitizations for drug development should be considered in the context of intellectual property (IP) protection and commercialization. In general, only about 5% of the innovations in a given intellectual property portfolio has commercialization value.[35] Many types of intellectual property (such as copyright royalties, the value of patents, and the value of drug compounds) display a similar distribution of risk and returns (with only a small number of units accounting for large payoff). This pattern of discovery, development, and concentration of financial returns is common to all industries (including entertainment, media, and publishing) in which value overwhelmingly rests upon intangible assets such as ideas. The pooling of multiple patents provides crucial risk diversification, since not all scientific avenues will come to full fruition. The larger the pool of early-stage projects, the greater the odds that one will succeed.

The challenge is to devise a capital structure with credit enhancement, advance sales, and other financial, marketing, or business strategies that align the interests of foundations, investors, patients, governments, and businesses. It should be able to tap liquid capital markets and diversify risks; lower the costs of capital to biotech, pharmaceutical, and medical device companies; and attract scientific and management talent with equity-based compensation. The rules of fundamental analysis and capital structure necessary for financing these vehicles remain constant.

The role of insurance and risk management in meeting this challenge can be crucial. Undertaking this (by providing loan-loss guarantees or credit enhancement through program-related investing at a below-market rate) would require a fundamental shift in the thinking of foundations that focus on disease cures. It would mean using their balance sheets to leverage further private investment in cures rather than following a model of handing out scientific grants.

The most natural analogy with past innovations in the financial markets comes from the corporate bond market. At one time, no one would invest in below-investment-grade debt. But given a transparent valuation model (which clarified the attributes of value and risk to all) and market liquidity, investors were willing to take on the risk and flocked to the new market segment. The odds hadn't suddenly changed, but transparency made those odds understandable. Similarly, the options markets soared after the introduction of the Black–Scholes option-pricing model. Once investors could identify risks and returns, they could calibrate option prices against other traded securities.

In both of these examples, a market gap was closed by the combination of transparent valuation models and market liquidity. In the pharmaceutical industry, transparent valuation models should be able to play an important role in closing the Phase II funding gap for drug discovery, attracting new sources of funding.

To ensure full transparency, a securitization related to the drug discovery process would have to involve patent attorneys with expertise in the life sciences; medical experts who can assess scientific methods, risks, and implications; pharmaceutical industry experts who can quantify the prospects for commercialization and expected royalties; and foundations with an interest in providing funding and/or credit guarantees.

Strategies for Credit Enhancement in Medical Financing

Credit risk in biomedical securitizations could be reduced by utilizing collateral, insurance, or risk-sharing agreements that would basically subsidize the risk of other investors independent of the balance sheet or performance of the target biomedical companies or projects. Credit enhancement has been used in corporate bonds, securitized debt, derivatives, and other financial instruments. It can be accomplished internally (by providing excess spread over the interest rate received on the underlying collateral, overcollateralization, or a reserve account that could reimburse losses) or externally (through surety bonds, a wrapped security insured or guaranteed by a third party, a letter of credit, a cash collateral account, or another method by an external party in case of default).

Let's consider two examples of how this could accelerate medical development and commercialization.

Credit Enhancement by Disease-Specific Foundations

When it comes to credit enhancement, it is insufficient for medical IP holders and capital providers to simply join forces. They need a legal structure to capture the governance, obligations, and payouts of their collaboration. Figure 7.3 illustrates the requisite elements of a transaction.

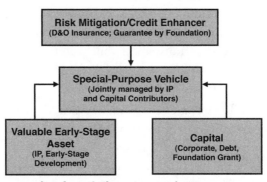

Figure 7.3   Leveraging foundations to accelerate cures

Source: Technology Option Capital, LLC

The capital provider could be an experienced pharmaceutical industry player with the know-how to reduce development and commercialization risk and create a productive environment for the working scientists. Or it might be a foundation wishing to contribute funding (for a share of the returns) or a guarantee to other capital providers.

The assets could consist of a diversified patent pool (with IP rights obtained from universities or pharmaceutical/biotech firms) and the human capital involved in early-stage development. In this case, a special-purpose vehicle (SPV), a private company, would be comprised of the assets (the intellectual property and talent) provided in exchange for equity, and would be jointly managed by the IP holder and the investors. The goal of the SPV would be to develop the technology or science, increase its value, and reduce the commercial risk to large pharmaceutical firms. (Under this scenario, the IP suppliers would become minority investors with certain protections that ensure them a reasonable return on their equity.)

The SPV could be adapted to the interests of a foundation focused on specific disease research. A foundation focused on Alzheimer's, for example, might assemble a diversified pool of drugs under development for the disease. While this would reduce the risk of scientific failure, significant commercialization risks would remain, preventing the SPV from issuing investment-grade debt. The foundation could provide the financial guarantee—a credit enhancement that raises the credit quality of the pool—thus opening up the SPV to a larger market of investors. If the guarantee is actually used, it could become a grant, although the diversification of scientific approaches should help to mitigate this risk.

Disease-specific medical foundations, however, require predictable spending on projects, since their budgets typically consist of returns on endowments and can't support intermittent calls on their capital from a guarantee. To accommodate this process, a disease-specific foundation could provide credit enhancement through the following scenarios:

1. After a ratings agency reviews the deal structure to help raise it to investment grade, the foundation could invest 10%–15% of the funding and place a smaller guarantee to raise the credit quality.

2. The foundation could work with insurance companies to structure a credit enhancement that better fits its budgetary needs.

3. A disease-focused foundation could collaborate with larger foundations, again providing just enough capital and guarantee to bring the transaction structure to investment grade.

The SPV's equity capital, which could be structured as the purchase price of a call option on control of the SPV, could come from a major pharmaceutical player (much as large pharmaceuticals invest in later-stage biotech firms today). To reduce investor risk, the equity capital could be leveraged 3:1 with debt capital, which, in turn, would be supported by credit enhancements to mitigate risk (such as directors and officers liability insurance, R&D tax credits, or foundation credit enhancements).

Risk mitigation using a market-based analysis allows risk apportionment to different parts of the capital markets and capital providers (including foundations) based on their unique risk appetites. The venture would be successful once the large pharmaceutical firm exercised its call option (and, with that payment, retired the debt). Other scenarios exist for the exercise of the option through a sales/license-back transaction of the IP rights with a private equity investor. Alternatively, the principal on the bonds could be settled with cash raised through the patent investment entity's exercise of a put option to the insurer.

Using Directors and Officers (D&O) Liability Insurance to Enhance Credit Quality

Directors and officers (D&O) insurance covers the actions of senior corporate management and board members, and includes actions pertaining to intellectual property and product development. For a premium increase, this coverage could be expanded to the scientific and commercial risks of biotech product development.

As a commercial entity, the SPV in Figure 7.3 could carry D&O insurance, which would serve as an additional credit enhancement. The policy would insure against actions the board may take that could harm the value of the firm, including technology management, in general, and drug development failure, in particular. Insurers are already exposed to technology risk, and because the SPV governance structure increases transparency, they should be willing to provide extra coverage for an extra premium.

Financial Innovations to Improve Global Health

In addition to the industry-wide phenomenon of faltering R&D productivity, there is a larger and more pressing problem at work: glaring imbalances in the allocation of health-care investment worldwide. Less than 10% of global investment in pharmaceutical R&D targets diseases such as malaria, AIDS, and tuberculosis that cause untold suffering in developing nations and may affect up to 90% of the world's population.[36]

The elimination of widespread ailments such as malaria would have a significant impact on economic growth in emerging nations, reducing inequality around the globe.[37] But profit pressures lead pharmaceutical companies to focus on "lifestyle" drugs and treatments for "Western" diseases that are concentrated in more affluent nations, leaving other drug development issues unaddressed. In the current financial environment, good ideas with the potential to cure diseases of poverty are nearly impossible to fulfill. Creative strategies are needed to channel capital to where it is most urgently needed.

The fight against tuberculosis (TB) is a case in point. The World Health Organization (WHO) estimates that one-third of the world's population is vulnerable to TB, which claims 1.7 million lives each year.[38] The nonprofit Global Alliance for TB Drug Development (the TB Alliance) formed a public–private partnership between Bayer Healthcare AG to jumpstart the fight against this deadly disease. It has been estimated that the global market for a tuberculosis drug is $261 million to $418 million.[39] The relatively small profit potential in this market (especially when weighed against drug development costs), plus the fact that TB disproportionately affects emerging nations, has made this effort unattractive for any single drug company. As a consequence, doctors treating TB patients are forced to rely on drugs that were developed decades ago; these outdated therapies must be taken for six months at a time.[40]

The Alliance has taken steps to catalyze medical solutions and save lives. It pursues intellectual property rights in the area of TB research, as well as coordinating drug trials and research efforts. It is funded through country donations (primarily from Europe and the United States), as well as the Bill & Melinda Gates Foundation and the Rockefeller Foundation.[41]

The Bayer/TB Alliance partnership, announced in 2005, is illustrated in Figure 7.4. Its goal is to coordinate global clinical trials to study the potential of an existing antibiotic, moxifloxacin, in the treatment of TB. In an animal study, moxifloxacin shortened the standard six-month clinical treatment of TB by two months.

The TB Alliance has been coordinating and helping to cover the cost of the trials, leveraging substantial support from several U.S. and European government agencies. As Figure 7.4 shows, the partnership's goal is to make an anti-TB drug available at a not-for-profit price. With its costs covered, Bayer could sustain the supply. Further-more, if the drug development process is successful, Bayer will receive approval from the FDA for an additional prescriptive use for moxifloxacin (under the brand name Avelox); approval may come as soon as 2011.[42] As of January 2009, moxifloxacin is in Phase III trials in several locations in Africa.[43] After decades with no progress being made on this deadly affliction, this innovative partnership model has revived the drug pipeline for TB.

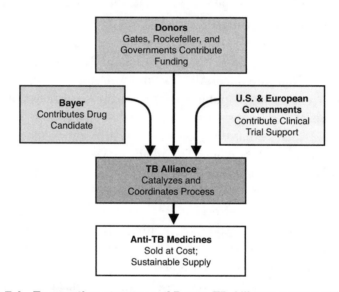

Figure 7.4   Transaction structure of Bayer–TB Alliance partnership

Source: Milken Institute

Another interesting public–private partnership was forged between GlaxoSmithKline Biologicals (GSK) and the International Aids Vaccine Initiative (IAVI). Similar to the TB partnership dis-cussed previously, GSK and IAVI are collaborating to stop the spread of HIV/AIDS. Their goal is to make a sustained supply of an AIDS vaccine available at a not-for-profit price by GSK.[44] In the first years of the alliance, new neutralizing antibodies have been discovered that give promise for further drug development for a vaccine drug target.

In late 2004, Britain announced major support to shore up the fight against HIV/AIDS. A key element of the British proposal was a major advance purchase agreement (also known as an advance market agreement)—a pledge to purchase millions of doses of an AIDS vaccine, if and when it is developed.[45] Under advance market commitments, donors commit money to vaccine makers, guaranteeing the price of vaccines once they have been developed; this gives vaccine makers the incentive to invest the sums required to conduct research, pay staff, and utilize or build manufacturing facilities. Participating companies make binding commitments to supply the vaccines at lower, sustainable prices after donor funds are used up.

Also in 2004, Britain joined with other nations to make a similar commitment to ensure delivery of a breakthrough malaria vaccine developed by GSK. In an interview with the BBC, Gordon Brown, then Britain's chancellor of the exchequer, summed up why these advance purchases work, stating, "The challenge is in an area where there are insufficient purchasers with funds. We need to ensure that the vaccine does go into commercial production and is available at affordable prices. And therefore I can announce that the British government, working with other governments, is ready to enter into agreements to purchase these vaccines in advance, to ensure a secure market and that these vaccines are available more cheaply."[46]

The idea continues to gain traction: In early 2007, a new $1.5 billion multilateral program called the Advance Market Commitment was launched to finance the development of vaccines for children in the world's poorest countries, using funding donated by international governments. The first phase has focused on producing the pneumococcal vaccine, which prevents deadly pneumonia in children. The plan calls for developed nations to make advance purchases of the vaccine on behalf of poor countries that request them, giving them purchasing power they did not have before. The program "creates market incentives where the private market fails," noted Tommaso Padoa-Schioppa, the Italian finance minister, at the program's official launch.[47]

Advance purchase agreements, illustrated in Figure 7.5, change the economics of the public–private partnership by creating a stable market that will pay fair market price for the therapy. They create a privatization effect, eliminating the need for complex coordination between multiple government agencies, foundations, and the non-profit catalyst. Where drug makers were once reluctant to enter markets for treating diseases of poverty, this innovation reduces their uncertainty about future returns. By creating a stable market, governments and nongovernmental organizations (NGOs) can redirect the industry's research capacity to where it is most desperately needed.

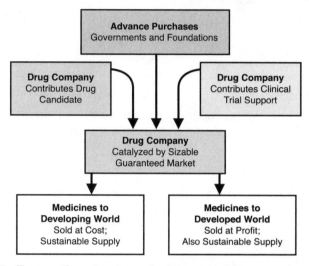

Figure 7.5   Transaction structure of advance purchase agreements

Source: Milken Institute

Health economics experts have argued that advance purchases can create a market for treatments in the developing world that is just as robust as that for pharmaceutical products in developed countries. This "pull mechanism," whereby products are delivered on a demand basis, is likely to be a cost-effective use of public funds.

In a recent study, economists at the National Bureau of Economic Research (NBER) calibrated the potential of advance purchase agreements. Estimates show that biotech and pharmaceutical companies are motivated to pursue drug prospects for markets of $3 billion in revenue or larger. At $15 per dose for the first 200 million vaccines purchased, and $1 per dose thereafter, a $3 billion market could be created by advance purchases. The economists found that the $15-per-dose cost of this financial mechanism is several orders of magnitude more cost effective than current treatments in underfunded countries.[48]

A critic of the advanced purchase commitment, Andrew Farlow of Oxford University, has argued that the program design will not lead to the most effective cure because it rewards the *first* pharmaceutical solution to market.[49] What if the second vaccine to market is the better cure? Program supporters say that not all funds will be spent at once, so there will be purchasing power left if newer alternatives emerge. Farlow also argues that the program design is rife with potential corruption, as the host government is asked to contribute $1 per vaccine, while the foundations pay $14. An unscrupulous firm could potentially bribe government officials to allocate millions of dollars in revenue.

While these are substantive criticisms, they must be weighed against the apparent preference of foundations and country donors for advance purchase commitments as the best avenue currently available for accelerating treatments to save lives now rather than at some future date.

Using Donor Bonds to Underwrite Medical Research and Drug Delivery

In March 2005, six European governments announced application of a new financial innovation, donor bonds, to accelerate the delivery of medicines to Africa. The bond offerings, expected to total $4 billion over several years, will increase the available funding for immunization in Africa.

Donor bonds, like credit card companies, use future customer repayments as the collateral for borrowing. (In this case, future gifts are the collateral.) Donors guarantee binding commitments that can be advanced under borrowing facility arrangements through bank consortia or capital market securitizations. The future stream of payments is transformed into an immediate lump sum.

Say the pharmaceutical company has already developed a drug and is now marketing it in the developed world at a profit and selling it in the developing world at cost. The donor bonds infuse the developing market with greater demand in the near-term. As the drug is already in production, the mechanics of meeting challenge are now simple ones of production and supply-chain expansion.

The first donor bonds were issued in November 2006, backed by a stream of future donations from the United Kingdom, France, Italy, Norway, Sweden, South Africa, and Spain. (The U.S. government has declined to participate, saying that the federal budget process does

not allow for the long-term commitments required by this securitization structure.) The bonds were issued by an SPV known as the International Finance Facility for Immunisation (IFFIm), with the World
Bank acting as its financial advisor and treasury manager.[50] The programs financed by the bonds will be managed by the Global Alliance
for Vaccines and Immunization (GAVI), which has received a pledge
of $750 million over ten years from the Bill & Melinda Gates Foun-
dation. GAVI expects that the acceleration of immunizations through
donor bonds will save the lives of 5 million children and protect
another 5 million as adults. In 2007 alone, some $633 million in
IFFIm funding went to efforts such as immunization safety programs, strengthening of health services in developing nations, and
efforts to eradicate polio, measles, maternal and neonatal tetanus,
and yellow fever.[51] Multiple vaccine bonds have been issued, including one launched in June 2009 for $1.5 billion in commitments to
guarantee prices to drug makers to produce vaccines for developing
countries.

Another organizational model has emerged to address infectious
diseases of poverty: the nonprofit pharmaceutical company. Industry
veteran Dr. Victoria Hale founded OneWorld Health in 2000 to
develop effective and affordable new medicines for neglected diseases
that disproportionately affect emerging nations. She has assembled a
scientific team that identifies promising drug candidates for diseases
that are not profitable for the pharmaceutical giants to pursue.

As a nonprofit, OneWorld Health receives funding from foundations and governments, and provides a tax deduction based on the
projected future value of donated intellectual property. It frequently
enters into research collaboration with major drug makers and provides a viable path for off-patent drugs that otherwise would not be
pursued for new uses. Therapies are being developed for parasitic
diseases like kala azar in India, and special focus is given to creating
new treatments for common killers like diarrhea and malaria.[52]

Conclusions

Tangible capital (such as stock, factories, and bank accounts),
important as it may be, is not the driver of the twenty-first-century

economy. That distinction belongs to human capital. Ideas, research, and new technologies are the new currency—and nowhere are the possibilities more exciting than in the field of medical research.

But it is a sad irony of our time that while immense scientific and technological potential exists to cure disease, customize treatment, and improve global health standards, a funding gap hampers the journey from early-stage research to marketplace. The process of commercializing basic research into new therapies has become fraught with pitfalls.

Although the current state of R&D productivity looks discouraging, we cannot afford to allow stagnation. Today's challenge is to rethink the financial underpinnings of the research model, finding a way to infuse the system with momentum. If financial innovators apply their best ideas to this arena, we can free scientists to pursue *their* most promising ideas, hopefully bringing us closer to the long-sought goals of saving lives and reducing suffering in the developing and developed worlds alike.

Whether the solution is diversification and pooling, enhanced D&O insurance, an increased role for foundations and public–private partnerships, advance purchases, donor bonds, or a combination of strategies, one thing remains clear: The capital gaps in the development of drug, medical devices, and health-care technology can be surmounted. Financial technologies, innovative securitization, and structured finance can overcome these barriers, allowing science to fulfill its promise.

Endnotes

[1]Jeffrey S. Handen, *Industrialization of Drug Discovery* (Boca Raton, FL: CDC Press, 2005).

[2]Patrick O'Hagan and Charles Farkas, "Bringing Pharma R&D Back to Health," Bain & Company research report (2009): 1–2.

[3]Congressional Budget Office, "Pharmaceutical R&D and the Evolving Market for Prescription Drugs," Economic and Budget Issue Brief (26 October 2009).

[4]"Billion Dollar Pills," *The Economist* 27 January 2007.

[5]Standard & Poor's, "Industry Surveys: Healthcare: Pharmaceuticals" (June 2009): 15.

[6]Deloitte Consulting LLP, "Reinventing Innovation in Large Pharma" (December

2008); 2. Available at www.deloitte.com/view/en_US/us/Services/consulting/article/fbec1ec6f6001210VgnVCM100000ba42f00aRCRD.

[7]This chapter draws on research and presentations from multiple Milken Institute Financial Innovations Labs on accelerating medical solutions. Reports detailing the research, presentations, and findings of these workshops are available for download at www.milkeninstitute.org. We are also indebted to the work of our sister organization, *Fastercures* (www.fastercures.org).

[8]U.S. Government Accountability Office, "New Drug Development: Science, Business, Regulatory, and Intellectual Property Issues Cited as Hampering Drug Development Efforts," Report to Congress (November 2006).

[9]American Association for the Advancement of Science Budget and Policy Programs, www.scienceprogress.org/2009.02/nih-funding-to-states.

[10]Pharmaceutical   Research   and   Manufacturers   of   America   (PhRMA), *Pharmaceutical Industry Profile 2009*. Available at www.phrma.org/publications/.

[11]J. Vernon, J. Golec, and J. DiMasi, "Drug Development Costs When Financial Risk Is Measured Using the Fama-French Three Factor Model," unpublished working paper (January 2008), cited in PhRMA's *Pharmaceutical Industry Profile 2009*.

[12]Standard & Poor's, "Industry Surveys: Healthcare: Pharmaceuticals" (June 2009): 21.

[13]A. Jena, J. Calfee, D. Goldman, E. Mansley, and T. Philipson, "Me-Too Innovation in Pharmaceutical Markets," forthcoming, Forums for Health Economics and Policy. See also Tomas Philipson, "The Regulation of Medical Innovation and Pharmaceutical Markets," *Journal of Law and Economics* 45, no. S2 (October 2002): 583–586.

[14]Joseph A. DiMasi, Ronald W. Hansen, and Henry G. Grabowski, "The Price of Innovation: New Estimates of Drug Development Costs," *Journal of Health Economics* 22 (2003): 151–185.

[15]Gary P. Pisano, *Science Business: The Promise, the Reality, and the Future of Biotech* (Cambridge, MA: Harvard Business School Press, 2006).

[16]Thomas H. Lee, "Me-Too Products: Friend or Foe?" *New England Journal of Medicine* 350, no. 3 (2004): 211–212.

[17]FDA, Summary of NDA Approvals & Receipts, 1938 to the Present, www.fda.gov/AboutFDA/WhatWeDo/History/ProductRegulation/SummaryofNDAApprovals Receipts1938tothepresent/default.htm.

[18]FDA, NME Drug and Biologic Approvals in 2006, www.fda.gov/Drugs/DevelopmentApprovalProcess/HowDrugsareDevelopedandApproved/DrugandBiologic ApprovalReports/NMEDrugandNewBiologicApprovals/ucm081673.htm.

[19]IMS Annual U.S. Pharmaceutical Market Performance Review(12 March 2008).

[20]Mark C. Fishman and Jeffrey A. Porter, "Pharmaceuticals: A New Grammar for Drug Discovery," *Nature* (22 September 2005): 491–493.

[21]Patrick Mullen, "Where VC Fears to Tread," *Biotechnology Healthcare* (29 October 2007): 29–35.

[22]PricewaterhouseCoopers and National Venture Capital Association, MoneyTree Report (Q2 2009 U.S. Results): 2–3.

[23]"Big Pharma Invests Where VC Fears to Tread," *Boston Business Journal* (14 August 2009).

[24]Heidi Ledford, "In Search of a Viable Business Model," Nature Reports: Stem Cells, published by *Nature* online (30 October 2008). Available at www.nature.com/stemcells/2008/0810/081030/full/stemcells.2008.138.html.

[25]The PIPES Report, DealFlow Media, *PipeWire* (19 October 2009 and 2 November 2009).

[26]Adam Feuerstein, "Sanofi-Aventis to Buy Cancer Drug Firm BiPar," TheStreet.com (15 April 2009). Available at www.thestreet.com/story/10486199/sanofi-aventis-to-buy-cancer-drug-firm-bipar.html.

[27]Elizabeth Lopatto and Kanoko Matsuyama, "Takeda Agrees to Buy Rights to Amylin's Obesity Drugs," Bloomberg (2 November 2009).

[28]Glenn Yago, Martha Amram, and Teresa Magula, "Financial Innovations Lab Report: Accelerating Medical Solutions," Milken Institute (October 2006).

[29]Tufts Center for the Study of Drug Development, Outlook 2008: 6.

[30]G. Steven Burrill, *Biotech 2009: Life Sciences. Navigating the Sea Changes* (San Francisco: Burrill & Company LLC, 2009).

[31]Bioaccelarate Holdings changed its name to Gardant Pharmaceuticals in 2006 and was later acquired by Switch Pharma. Principals from the company participated in a Milken Institute Financial Innovations Lab.

[32]"Life Support for Life Science Innovation," *Nature Biotechnology* 25, no. 2 (2007): 144.

[33]Marty Tenenbaum and John Wilbanks, "Health Commons: Therapy Development in a Networked World," MIT (May 2008).

[34]Paul Schofeld, et al., "Post-Publication Sharing of Data and Tools," *Nature* 461 (10 September 2009): 171–73.

[35]Glenn Yago, Martha Amram, and Teresa Magula, "Financial Innovations for Accelerating Medical Solutions," Financial Innovations Lab Report, Milken Institute (October 2006).

[36]Frank Lichtenberg, "Pharmaceutical Innovation, Mortality Reduction, and Economic Growth," in *Measuring the Gains from Medical Research: An Economic Approach*, Kevin M. Murphy and Robert H. Topel, eds. (Chicago: University of Chicago Press, 2003).

[37]J. L. Gallup and J. D. Sachs, "Cause, Consequence, and Correlation: Assessing the Relationship between Malaria and Poverty," Commission on Macroeconomics and Health, World Health Organization (2001). See also Gary S. Becker, T. J. Philipson, and R. R. Soares, "The Quantity and Quality of Life and the Evolution of World Inequality," *American Economic Review* 95, no. 1 (2005): 277–291; David N.

Weil, "Accounting for the Effect of Health on Economic Growth," *Quarterly Journal of Economics* 122, no. 3 (August 2007): 1,265–1,306; and Daron Acemoglu and Simon Johnson, "Disease and Development: The Effect of Life Expectancy on Economic Growth," *Journal of Political Economy* 115, no. 6 (December 2007): 925–985.

[38]World Health Organization, Initiative for Vaccine Research, Selection of Diseases in IVR Portfolio. Available at www.who.int/vaccine_research/diseases/ari/en/index4.html.

[39]N. R. Schwalbe, et al., "Estimating the Market for Tuberculosis Drugs in Industrialized and Developing Nations," *International Journal of Tuberculosis and Lung Disease* 12, no10 (2008): 1173–1181.

[40]TB Alliance, Mission & History, www.tballiance.org/about/mission.php.

[41]TB Alliance, Donors, www.tballiance.org/about/donors.php.

[42]John Lauerman, "Bayer Drug May Cut Tuberculosis Cure Time by Months," Bloomberg (17 September 2007).

[43]Economist Intelligence Unit, "World Pharma: TB Initiatives Bearing Fruit," Industry Brief (January 2009). Available at www.tballiance.org/newscenter/view-innews.php?id=830.

[44]"GSK Biologicals and IAVI Partner to Develop AIDS Vaccine," IAVI press release (21 June 2005). Available at www.iavi.org/news-center/Pages/PressRelease.aspx?pubID=3044.

[45]Ben Russell, "Brown to Earmark £200 M a Year to Fund AIDS Vaccine," *The Independent* (1 December 2004).

[46]"Britain Backs Anti-Malaria Fight," BBC Online (24 November 2004). Available at http://news.bbc.co.uk/2/hi/uk_news/politics/4038377.stm.

[47]Elizabeth Rosenthal, "Wealthy Nations Announce Plans to Develop and Pay for Vaccines," *New York Times* (10 February 2007).

[48]Ernst Berndt, Rachel Glennerster, Michael Kremer, Jean Lee, Ruth Levine, Georg Weizsäcker, and Heidi Williams, "Advanced Purchase Commitments for a Malaria Vaccine: Estimating Costs and Effectiveness," (working paper no. 11288, NBER, May 2005).

[49]"Push and .Pull: Should the G8 Promise to Buy Vaccines That Have Yet to Be Invented?" *The Economist* (23 March 2006). More of Professor Farlow's critiques can be found at www.economics.ox.ac.uk/members/andrew.farlow.

[50]IFFIm, Offering Memorandum (9 November 2006).

[51]IFFIm, "Results," www.iff-immunisation.org/immunisation_results.html.

[52]One World Health: A New Model for the Pharmaceutical Industry, Case Western Reserve, Weatherhead School of Management (19 January 2006).

8

Six Cardinal Rules of Financial Innovation

Ever since the seismic jolts that shook world markets in 2008, a full-throated debate has raged about whether financial innovation got us into this mess in the first place. Critics have been all too eager to break out the torches and pitchforks.

But it's our contention that dreaming up intentionally opaque financial instruments for the sole purpose of speculating or deceiving has nothing whatsoever to do with *real* innovation. The genuine article is all about increasing transparency, measuring and reducing risk, and finding new ways to direct capital to where it's vitally needed. At this perilous moment in history—burdened with a deep recession and facing unprecedented challenges in health, housing, the environment, business, and global development—we need *more* financial innovation, not less. Even staunch critics of financial innovation are forced to recognize that we need "good" innovations to deliver financial services to the poor, fund medical solutions, and achieve other social objectives.[1] We need to find a better way to evaluate and introduce new financial products so that we can separate the wheat from the chaff.

The ultimate test for financial innovations is their ability to function successfully in capital markets, attracting investment that is sustainable. If either the investor or the promoter of the investment knows that he will not be accountable and will not bear the costs of failure, the whole basis of the underlying social and financial contract dissolves.

Debate continues about the government's role in reining in financial excesses, but it is important to proceed here with caution.

Measures that undermine incentives to innovate or create moral hazard could have dramatic unintended consequences that ultimately harm the resiliency of financial markets and the real economy. Financial innovation—in the true sense of the term—is needed to help us move beyond the crisis by taming volatility, unlocking frozen credit markets, and enabling better corporate decision making.

If recent events have taught us anything, it is that we need new and better tools for confronting asset bubbles and mitigating risks in real estate markets (which are the source of most financial crises).[2] During the giddy days of the bubble, investors discarded historical pricing data, happy to ride the wave of easy money. Even though it was apparent that returns were unsustainable, a kind of optimistic tunnel vision took hold. Going by expectations alone (as indicated by narrowing interest rate spreads among various assets before the crisis), it appears that investors assumed very high rates of return everywhere for the foreseeable future. In this environment, consumers and financial institutions alike became dangerously overleveraged—and both seemed oblivious to the risks buried in the complex products on their balance sheets.

It turns out that the "irrational exuberance" and market failures that preceded the tech bubble of 2000 never really dissipated. They were simply transferred to real estate assets, where they assumed an even more toxic form. Clearly, we have to find a better way to prevent the recurrence of boom-and-bust cycles.

Blame for the crisis was wrongly placed at the feet of financial innovation, which soon became everyone's favorite punching bag. But the excesses were fueled by artificially low interest rates and the easy availability of credit. In this hyperliquid environment, the introduction of convoluted, opaque financial products that created incentives to default through nonrecourse contracts and negative amortization mortgages was like adding a flame to dry tinder.

Though the crisis originated in the United States, countries with little or no financial innovation (such as Ireland, Spain, and Greece) also experienced asset bubbles and real estate–driven financial crises.[3] It is spurious to suggest that financial innovation was the chief culprit.

Real financial innovation requires going back to the basics of valuation and risk assessment, tasks that were neglected in the heady days prior to 2007. When all the arrows were pointing up, few people asked the hard questions: What about the lack of transparency in the $1 trillion market for collateralized debt obligations? Was it possible for financial firms to extend their leverage ratios from 5:1 to 30:1 over just five years without consequences? What cash flows and corporate strategies supported that leverage? Were any asset valuations—on homes, securities, or commodities—based in reality? At the end of the day, who paid and who benefited from the massive socialization of credit risks by the government?

Newly gun-shy after the crisis, many officials and pundits have suggested curbing the entire field of financial innovation. But this stance ignores the reality that monetary policy and government actions that encourage moral hazard lie at the root of the story. Financial innovation is a process of trial and error—and you don't advance science by blowing up laboratories. We are facing unresolved questions on how to price and manage risk, and we can waste no time in finding the answers. The resiliency and vitality of the financial sector—plus its future ability to generate growth and solve social problems—depends on our ability to develop better applications.

Financial innovators always look ahead. But as the old saying goes, those who cannot learn from history are doomed to repeat it. Before we can finance the future, we have to understand and correct the excesses of the past.

Lesson 1: Complexity Is Not Innovation

At some point in the last decade, new securities became so complex that even the CEOs of investment houses couldn't understand them. But *intricate* and *innovative* aren't synonyms, and they never were.

Financial innovations don't have to be laboriously contrived and complicated Rube Goldberg contraptions (see Figure 8.1). Yes, some valuable financial technologies involve daunting equations and specialized jargon, but the level of complexity alone doesn't qualify something as a breakthrough. Even the best of financial models will fail with bad or unexamined data. Sometimes the best solutions are elegant in their simplicity. Many of the byzantine financial products that failed in the recent crisis obscured rather than disclosed data, concentrated rather than distributed risks, raised rather than reduced costs of capital, and created rather than resolved capital gaps. In that sense, many of these products pushed back financial innovation rather than advancing it.

Figure 8.1 Dodging bill collectors

Used with permission by Rube Goldberg. Rube Goldberg is the ® and © of Rube Goldberg, Inc.

Product differentiation is not, in itself, an innovation in any field. It's a marketing strategy. A me-too drug that simply mimics an existing drug offers no therapeutic advance. Another sugar-coated breakfast cereal created to capture additional shelf space in the supermarket offers no new nutritional value. A credit card, mobile calling plan, or insurance policy that includes more hidden fees fails to solve the problems of standardization and transparency required of a real financial innovation, and leaves the underlying product unchanged. Hiding charges and risks is not innovative—it's just opaque. The ultimate objective of real innovation is not to trick or cheat consumers or investors in any market.

Financial markets and innovations create benefits for businesses, households, and governments when they provide value by overcoming, rather than creating, information asymmetries. By obscuring information about risk and failing to examine data fundamental to credit analysis, which is key to any investment decision, the products that proved toxic in the most recent crisis distorted the whole purpose of financial innovation.

Lesson 2: Leverage Is Not Credit

Ever since Modigliani and Miller first got us thinking about capital structure in creative ways, we've known that nothing inherent in leverage creates value. Credit is a vital tool for enabling healthy growth, but when monetary policy is too loose, market participants at every level have a temptation to use excessive amounts of borrowed money in pursuit of greater profits. When investors are highly leveraged, it takes only a small decline in the value of underlying assets to leave them underwater.

The dangers of misaligned incentives (such as mortgage brokers passing along all the risks involved in making questionable loans, or rating agencies accepting fees from the issuers of securities they were rating) became magnified during an era of freewheeling credit and easy money. Homeowners who put no money down—and there were many at the height of the housing boom—were likewise given increased incentives to default.

The same story played out with Fannie Mae and Freddie Mac, which were encouraged to expand and buy various complex securitizations, thereby creating a "too big to fail" problem for both the government and the private financial institutions that held their obligations.[4] Ultimately, this pyramiding of risk suggests that some government actions might have transformed the problem into institutions that are now "too big to save." Too many financial institutions were caught with too little capital to support their growing leverage ratios. The issue was compounded among those firms that used short-term borrowing to fund their assets. Unfortunately, when the house of cards collapsed, we careened abruptly from an era of easy credit to an era of frozen credit.

The ability to excessively leverage caused market players to skip vital steps: the fundamental analysis of financial statements, financial products, management, and market conditions. No matter how sophisticated a new financial product may be, its ultimate value rests on data-driven, back-to-basics scrutiny. Restoring the fundamentals of due diligence and prudence will be key to ensuring that credit can once again flow appropriately.

Lesson 3: Transparency Enables Innovation

Financial innovation works best when it incorporates the accurate, fundamental data necessary to assess risks. This holds true whether the issue is evaluating the risk associated with a bond or credit-scoring a mortgage applicant. Consumers, businesses, investors, and the overall economy all benefit from adequate disclosure and transparent information. Better credit data enables broader capital access.

The need to get solid information and carefully evaluate risk was tossed aside during the bubble years. Borrowers signed on the bottom line whether or not they understood the fine print on the complex mortgages they were taking out. Investors speculating with borrowed money relied too heavily on rubber-stamp ratings from agencies rather than doing their own homework on credit quality. The risks of overly complex securities (the CDO-squared and the CDO-cubed spring to mind) were underestimated by rating agencies and investment banks alike. The opacity of special-purpose vehicles and the shadowy market for credit default swaps enabled the situation to metastasize.

Problems mushroom in the dark; but, as Supreme Court Justice Louis Brandeis once said, "Sunlight is the best disinfectant." Real innovation quantifies and mitigates risk rather than obscures it. This tenet will need to guide our reshaping of the market's oversight and enforcement structures, as well as future financial products.

Lesson 4: Capital Structure Matters

Designing the right capital structure to allow a firm's expansion or fund an ambitious infrastructure project is equal parts art and science. The optimal capital structure may take different forms at different times to account for industry dynamics, the state of the economy, government regulations, or growing demand. The ratio of debt to equity that works in one business cycle may be dangerous in the next—as we've seen with companies that found themselves with too much debt when the recent liquidity freeze descended. The means and methods to manage capital structure flexibly enable managers to deleverage when needed. Finding that sweet spot is especially important for start-ups and growth-oriented firms, as well as traditional industries seeking to reinvent themselves for the future.

Finance is a continuum, and a successful financial innovator must select just the right combination of technologies and securities when designing a firm or project's capital structure. The art of improvisation, which has grown so sophisticated in corporate finance, will enable the development of instruments with new applications in fields such as environmental finance and economic development.

Lesson 5: Democratizing Access to Capital Spurs Growth

The largest firms in America held an iron grip on employment, profits, and market share during the first seven decades of the twentieth century. This concentration of power created oligopolies in many industries, stifling competition. But the wave of financial innovation that emerged from the credit crunch and market collapses of 1974 incorporated many of the practices and principles outlined in this book. By opening new channels of capital to entrepreneurs, it paved the way for new businesses, technologies, and industries to thrive. A high-tech, knowledge-based economy was the ultimate result.

Broadening access to capital has this kind of transformative effect. When start-ups gained the financing they needed to grow and challenge the existing monopolies, the competition and innovation that followed made the U.S. economy more vibrant and diversified.

American democracy became stronger when lenders ceased to marginalize minorities and redline urban centers. Participation in the global economy is beginning to erase poverty in the developing world.

Markets are healthier when there are fewer barriers to entry, greater economic participation, and increased competition that generates further product and process innovations. But to get a level playing field in product markets, you sometimes need financial bulldozers—and capital market solutions provide them.

The ultimate test of financial innovation is its ability to drive growth. Making credit, financial services, and physical and social infrastructure accessible to wider segments of society around the globe can power that growth and generate broad-based prosperity.

Lesson 6: Financial Innovation Can Be a Force for Positive Social Change

Financial innovation isn't just an exercise in rearranging numbers on a balance sheet or income statement. It's about creating tangible, real-world impact. This book has chronicled dozens of instances in which financial innovation has paved the way for progress—and laid out a series of urgent challenges that are still to be met.

Business and corporate finance has always been a fertile laboratory for financial innovators. Here in the United States, we have seen capital market solutions finance a young nation's expansion across a vast continent. Trailblazers opened commercial banking and investment products to the middle class, while venture capitalists bankrolled the ambitions and ideas of entrepreneurs. Today small businesses are struggling and jobs are evaporating. We urgently need to bridge the capital gap and find new ways to get credit and equity investments flowing to the entrepreneurial companies that generate most of America's jobs.

Where homeownership was once exclusively for the wealthy, innovations changed the face of the housing market. The advent of the 30-year self-amortizing mortgage made it possible for millions of middle- and working-class families to realize their dreams of owning a home. While a number of products have recently failed with serious consequences, we cannot afford to cease innovating altogether in this field.

We need fresh solutions that will stabilize the housing market and attract private capital back into the system. Innovators will have to find new ways to more responsibly promote homeownership and address the shortage of affordable housing.

Environmental finance has seen a major burst of momentum in recent decades. State revolving funds have been used to finance clean drinking water systems and preserve wetlands. The cap-and-trade market for sulfur dioxide emissions permits has virtually eliminated the problem of acid rain. Debt-for-nature swaps have preserved some of the planet's most endangered landscapes and species, while individual transferable quotas have restored depleted fisheries. Despite this remarkable progress, the biggest challenges of all still lie ahead: implementing a market-based solution for curbing carbon emissions and financing a new green economy.

Development finance was once left to government officials and NGOs, but today there is a growing awareness that foreign aid alone is not enough to permanently eradicate poverty. We need to direct private capital to stimulate growth in emerging markets. Microfinance has found creative ways to help the poorest of the poor start small businesses to support their families, while mobile banking via cellphone is beginning to bring financial services to millions who were once excluded from the global economy. Impact investors are forging new models that combine elements of venture capital and aid. World Bank Green Bonds are financing the introduction of clean technology and sustainability projects in low-income nations. The next great task is financing the "missing middle"—the small and medium-size businesses that are too big for microcredit but too small to be served by commercial banks in the developing world. This sector has an enormous capacity to generate jobs, and with adequate capital, it could unleash the kind of broad-based and sustainable growth that lifts large populations out of poverty.

In medicine, financial innovation can smooth the translation of basic research into cures. Because development and clinical trials can be a long, risky process, financing solutions are urgently needed to make sure that breakthrough ideas don't wither and die in the lab. New structures such as PIPEs, royalty-based models, contract research organization (CRO)–linked financings, and public-sector risk-sharing facilities have been devised to try to bridge this capital gap. In global health, public–private partnerships are providing new funding for once-neglected diseases of the developing world. Advance purchase agreements and donor bonds are making it possible to pursue new cures for diseases of poverty.

Despite the recent crisis, finance remains a powerful catalyst for expanding opportunity. By analyzing economic, social, environmental, and public policy challenges through the lens of finance, and then deploying the right tools in a responsible way, we can conquer problems that were once considered insurmountable.

Endnotes

[1]Simon Johnson and James Kwak, "Finance: Before the Next Meltdown," *Democracy: A Journal of Ideas*, no. 13 (2009): 23–24.

[2]Richard J. Herring and Susan Wachter, "Real Estate Booms and Banking Busts: An International Perspective," Wharton School Center for Financial Institutions, working paper no. 99-27 (July 1999).

[3]Rudiger Ahrend, Boris Courned, and Robert Price, "Monetary Policy, Market Excesses and Financial Turmoil," OECD Economic Department working papers, no. 597 (March 2008).

[4]John B. Taylor, "The Financial Crisis and the Policy Responses: An Empirical Analysis of What Went Wrong," NBER working paper no. 14631 (January 2009).

Appendix:
The Black–Scholes Formula

There are a number of assumptions underlying the formula:

1. There are no transaction costs and no taxes.
2. The risk-free rate is constant for the life of the option.
3. The market operates continuously (day and night).
4. The stock price moves continuously, with no sudden jumps.
5. The stock pays no cash dividends.
6. The option can be exercised only at the expiration date.
7. The underlying stock can be sold short without penalty.
8. The distribution of returns on the underlying security (the common stock) is lognormal.

Based on these assumptions, it is possible to derive their

$$C = P \times N(d_1) - EX \times e^{-rt} \times N(d_2),$$

where

$$d_1 = \frac{\log_e(\frac{P}{EX}) + rt + \frac{\sigma^2 t}{2}}{\sigma\sqrt{t}},$$

$$d_2 = d_1 - \sigma\sqrt{t},$$

C = the value of the call option

N(d) = the cumulative normal probability density function

EX = the exercise price of the option

σ^2 = the variance per period of continuously compounded rate of return on stock

t = the time to the maturity date

r = the continuously compounded risk-free rate of interest

P = the price of the stock now

INDEX

Ginnie Mae, 92-93
GlaxoSmithKline Biologicals
  (GSK), 206
Global Alliance for TB Drug
  Development, 205
Global Alliance for Vaccines and
  Immunization (GAVI), 210
Global Impact Investing Network
  (GIIN), 167
global warming. *See* climate
  change; environmental finance
Goldstein, John, 167
Grameen Bank, 160
  Dannone and, 162
green finance. *See* environmental
  finance
greenhouse gases cap-and-trade
  system, 135-137
growth. *See* economic growth
GSK (GlaxoSmithKline
  Biologicals), 206
Guaranty Trust, 62

H

Hale, Victoria, 210
Hamilton, Alexander, 57-59
Hardin, Garrett, 121
healthcare finance. *See*
  biomedical development finance
HEFI (home equity franctional
  interest security), 109
Hickman, W. Braddock, 70
high-yield corporate bonds
  history of, 15
  in history of corporate finance,
    70-71

history
  of corporate finance
    Alexander Hamilton, role of,
      57-59
    capital structure
      innovations, 69-74
    CDS (credit default swaps),
      77-79
    creative destruction (finance
      and technology), 63-64
    credit scoring, 77
    democratization of capital,
      65-66
    investment banking, 61-62
    LBOs (leveraged buyouts),
      75-77
    nineteenth century
      innovations, 59-61
    private equity, 74-75
    venture capital, 66-69
  of development finance, 153-157
  of finance, 5-7
  of financial innovation, 2-3
    in age of discovery, 12-13
    in ancient world, 10-12
    capitalism, 13-16
  of housing finance, 86-95
    increased demand for, 89-92
    savings and loan crisis,
      92-93
    securitization, 93-95
  of microfinance, 160-161
HIV/AIDS vaccine
  development, 206
home equity fractional interest
  security (HEFI), 109
Home Owner's Loan
  Corporation, 91

U–V

W–Z

⊔⊔ Wharton School Publishing

In the face of accelerating turbulence and change, business leaders and policy makers need new ways of thinking to sustain performance and growth.

Wharton School Publishing offers a trusted source for stimulating ideas from thought leaders who provide new mental models to address changes in strategy, management, and finance. We seek out authors from diverse disciplines with a profound understanding of change and its implications. We offer books and tools that help executives respond to the challenge of change.

Every book and management tool we publish meets quality standards set by The Wharton School of the University of Pennsylvania. Each title is reviewed by the Wharton School Publishing Editorial Board before being given Wharton's seal of approval. This ensures that Wharton publications are timely, relevant, important, conceptually sound or empirically based, and implementable.

To fit our readers' learning preferences, Wharton publications are available in multiple formats, including books, audio, and electronic.

To find out more about our books and management tools, visit us at whartonsp.com and Wharton's executive education site, exceed.wharton.upenn.edu.

1970s

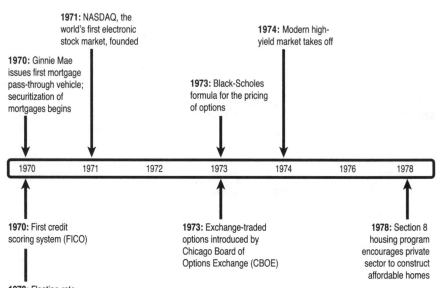

1971: NASDAQ, the world's first electronic stock market, founded

1974: Modern high-yield market takes off

1970: Ginnie Mae issues first mortgage pass-through vehicle; securitization of mortgages begins

1973: Black-Scholes formula for the pricing of options

| 1970 | 1971 | 1972 | 1973 | 1974 | 1976 | 1978 |

1970: First credit scoring system (FICO)

1973: Exchange-traded options introduced by Chicago Board of Options Exchange (CBOE)

1978: Section 8 housing program encourages private sector to construct affordable homes

1970: Floating-rate notes introduced

1980s

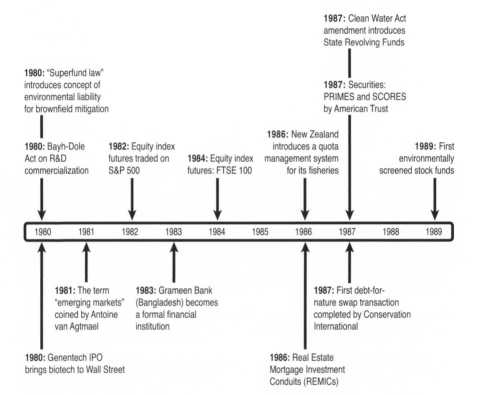

1987: Clean Water Act amendment introduces State Revolving Funds

1980: "Superfund law" introduces concept of environmental liability for brownfield mitigation

1987: Securities: PRIMES and SCORES by American Trust

1980: Bayh-Dole Act on R&D commercialization

1982: Equity index futures traded on S&P 500

1984: Equity index futures: FTSE 100

1986: New Zealand introduces a quota management system for its fisheries

1989: First environmentally screened stock funds

| 1980 | 1981 | 1982 | 1983 | 1984 | 1985 | 1986 | 1987 | 1988 | 1989 |

1981: The term "emerging markets" coined by Antoine van Agtmael

1983: Grameen Bank (Bangladesh) becomes a formal financial institution

1987: First debt-for-nature swap transaction completed by Conservation International

1980: Genentech IPO brings biotech to Wall Street

1986: Real Estate Mortgage Investment Conduits (REMICs)

1990s

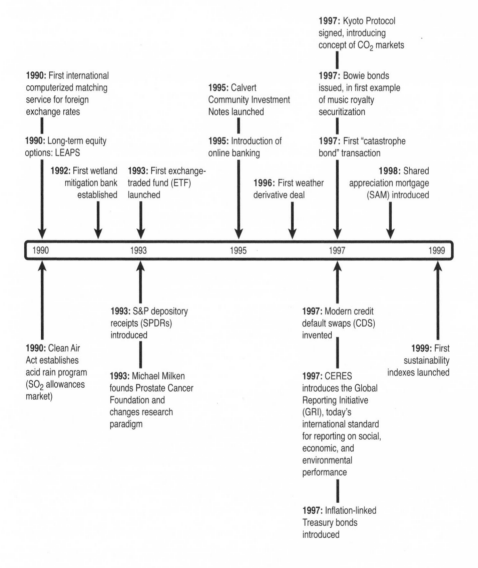

1997: Kyoto Protocol signed, introducing concept of CO_2 markets

1990: First international computerized matching service for foreign exchange rates

1995: Calvert Community Investment Notes launched

1997: Bowie bonds issued, in first example of music royalty securitization

1990: Long-term equity options: LEAPS

1995: Introduction of online banking

1997: First "catastrophe bond" transaction

1992: First wetland mitigation bank established

1993: First exchange-traded fund (ETF) launched

1996: First weather derivative deal

1998: Shared appreciation mortgage (SAM) introduced

| 1990 | 1993 | 1995 | 1997 | 1999 |

1993: S&P depository receipts (SPDRs) introduced

1997: Modern credit default swaps (CDS) invented

1999: First sustainability indexes launched

1990: Clean Air Act establishes acid rain program (SO_2 allowances market)

1993: Michael Milken founds Prostate Cancer Foundation and changes research paradigm

1997: CERES introduces the Global Reporting Initiative (GRI), today's international standard for reporting on social, economic, and environmental performance

1997: Inflation-linked Treasury bonds introduced